In Our Own Tongues

In Our Own Tongues

Perspectives from Asia on Mission and Inculturation

Peter C. Phan

ORBIS BOOKS

Maryknoll, New York 10545

Copyright © 2003 by Peter C. Phan
Published by Orbis Books, Maryknoll, New York, U.S.A. All rights reserved.
No part of this publication may be reproduced or transmitted in any form or by any means, electronic or mechanical, including photocopying, recording, or any information storage or retrieval system, without prior permission in writing from the publishers. For permissions, write to Orbis Books, P. O. Box 308, Maryknoll NY 10545-0308, U.S.A.
Manufactured in the United States of America.
Manuscript editing and typesetting by Joan Weber Laflamme.

Library of Congress Cataloging in Publication Data

Phan, Peter C., 1943-
  In our own tongues : perspectives from Asia on mission and inculturation / Peter C. Phan.
      p. cm.
Includes index.
  ISBN 1-57075-502-7 (pbk.)
  1. Missions—Asia. 2. Missions—Theory. 3. Christianity and culture—Asia. 4. Catholic Church—Missions—Asia. I. Title.
  BV3151.3 .P5 2003
  266'.0095—dc21
                                        2003010321

To
Gerard Austin, OP
John Ford, CSC
Patrick Granfield, OSB
doctissimis theologis amicisque dilectissimis
in profunda gratitudine

Contents

Preface

For the last three decades the Federation of Asian Bishops' Conferences (FABC) and Asian theologians have been promoting a new way of being church in Asia, so that the church will be not only *in* Asia but also *of* Asia. This new way of being church consists in being-in-dialogue. Dialogue must be the modality in which everything is done, *within* as well as *by* the church. Of course, the church must continue its evangelizing mission by proclaiming Jesus as God's gift of salvation to all, Asians included. But the way to do this is through dialogue, that is, by first listening to and learning from Asians and by recognizing the already active and saving presence of God's Spirit among them before sharing, humbly and gratefully, the good news with them.

To achieve its goal, this kind of dialogue cannot be just talk. Indeed, following the Pontifical Council for Interreligious Dialogue and the Congregation for the Evangelization of Peoples, the FABC speaks of a fourfold dialogue: life, action, theological exchange, and religious experience. Furthermore, in Asia this fourfold dialogue must be carried out with three partners: the Asian peoples, especially the poor (liberation and integral development); their cultures (inculturation); and their religions (interreligious dialogue).

This book, which is part of a trilogy dealing with this dialogue, focuses on inculturation. Though a neologism, inculturation is as old as Christianity. As the Christian faith moved out of its Jewish matrix, it came to be embodied in the various cultures it encountered, assimilating, transforming, and rejecting their different elements depending on their suitability for expressing the Christian faith. Other terms have been used to describe such a process, such as *adaptation, accommodation, indigenization, contextualization, incarnation,* and *interculturation,* though they do not connote this process in the same way.

While an ancient enterprise, inculturation assumes a special urgency in our times, in both the Roman Catholic and Protestant churches, especially in missionary circles, as we gain a sharper consciousness of the historicity and cultural conditions of Christian doctrines and practices as well as of church structures. If liberation was a hotly debated topic in the last three decades of the twentieth century, inculturation, along with interreligious dialogue, promises to be a bone of theological contention for many years to come. The recent controversial Declaration of the Congregation for the Doctrine of the Faith *Dominus Jesus* (6 August 2000) is rumored to have been directed at Asian theologians whose writings on the triple dialogue—liberation, interreligious dialogue, and inculturation—are alleged to have moved beyond the realm of Roman orthodoxy.

This book, composed of essays written on various occasions, is undergirded by five convictions. First, the most urgent and controversial issue in mission for decades to come will be inculturation as the Catholic church is increasingly becoming a world church. Second, the current Catholic theology and practices of inculturation are being severely challenged as the notions of culture and inculturation themselves are undergoing radical revision. Third, popular religion will assume a greater role in inculturation as a more adequate understanding of this religious phenomenon is gained. Fourth, mission history, particularly mission in Asia, offers the church universal useful lessons on the process of inculturation and the role of popular religion within it, as the multicultural, multireligious, multi-ethnic, and multilingual context of Asia makes inculturation a far more complex and challenging enterprise than in Europe and North America. Finally, the future of the church, especially of Asian Christianity, depends greatly on whether the work of inculturation is taken seriously and carried out thoroughly and consistently.

Inculturation is admittedly a highly complex process for which different theological models have been developed. Stephen Bevans, a noted theologian of contextual theology, has proposed six nonexclusive models: translation, anthropological, praxis, synthetic, transcendental, and counter-cultural. All six models are present in varying degrees in the following pages, and should this modest book make some small contribution to the mission of the church in its manifold aspects, its author will be more than satisfied.

In broaching this controversial issue of inculturation I have been encouraged and sustained by the account in the Book of Acts of the apostles' preaching on the day of Pentecost. It is reported that people coming from various parts of the world heard the apostles speak and asked, amazed and perplexed: "Are not all these who are speaking Galileans? And how is it that we hear, each of us, in our own native language?" (Acts 2: 8). Inculturation, in a nutshell, is an attempt to help people hear the word of God today, each in his or her native tongue.

It is my great pleasure to express my profound gratitude to Dr. William Burrows, managing editor of Orbis Books and a missiologist of international reputation in his own right, whose wise advice and constant support I shall always treasure. If there is an Academy Award for gentle editorial guidance and gracious encouragement, Bill is certainly a strong contender. My thanks are also given to Catherine Costello and Joan Laflamme, who have worked expertly on the manuscript. This book is dedicated to three of my colleagues at The Catholic University of America whose friendship, humor, and magnanimity have made my years at this institution a cherished memory.

The majority of the chapters in this book saw the light of day previously in other venues. They have all been edited, some of them quite substantially, for this volume. I express profound gratitude to those who responded to the earlier versions. Their remarks have been helpful for me to clarify ambiguities, to avoid mistakes, and to gain new insights into things I only thought I understood before getting feedback from my audiences.

Chapter 3 appeared first in *SEDOS* 33/11 (2001), 300-307; Chapter 4 in *SEDOS* 34/1 (2002), 19-28. Chapter 5 was published in *Proceedings of the North*

American Academy of Liturgy: Annual Meeting, 23-58; this conference was held in Reston, Virginia, 3-6 January 2002. Chapter 6 appeared first in *Ephemerides Mariologicae* 51 (2002), 457-71. Chapter 7 may be found in *Worship* 76/5 (2002), 403-30. Chapter 9 was published in *Gregorianum* 81 (2000), 723-49, and Chapter 11 in *Gregorianum* 83 (2002), 269-85. To the editors and publishers of the earlier versions, I am grateful for permission to publish these revised versions.

Abbreviations

ACHTUS	Academy of Catholic Hispanic Theologians of the United States
AG	*Ad gentes (Decree on the Church's Missionary Activity)*
AMCU	Asian Movement for Christian Unity
ARSI JS	*Archivium Romanum Societatis Jesus, Jap.-Sin.*
ASIPA	Asian Integral Pastoral Approach
CCA	Christian Conference of Asia
CELAM	Latin American Episcopal Conference
CM	*Clergy Monthly*
DI	*Dominus Iesus*
DP	*Dialogue and Proclamation*
EA	*Ecclesia in Asia*
EAPR	*East Asian Pastoral Review*
EATWOT	Ecumenical Association of Third World Theologians
EN	*Evangelii nuntiandi*
FABC	Federation of Asian Bishops' Conferences
IMR	*Indian Missiological Review*
ISPCK	The Indian Society for Promoting Christian Knowledge
LG	*Lumen gentium (Dogmatic Constitution on the Church)*
LWF	Lutheran World Federation
MD	*Mediator Dei*
MEP	Société des Missions-Étrangères de Paris (the Paris Foreign Mission Society)
NA	*Nostra aetate*
RM	*Redemptoris missio*
SC	*Sacrosanctum concilium (Constitution on the Sacred Liturgy)*
TAN	*Teaching All Nations*
VJTR	*Vidyayjoti: Journal of Theological Reflection*
WCC	World Council of Churches
WCC-WCME	WCC Commission on World Mission and Evangelism
WW	*Word and Worship*

PART ONE

Mission and Inculturation

1

Introduction

THE GOSPEL IN CULTURES

It is a truism in contemporary ecclesiology that the nature of the church is defined by its mission.[1] The church is what it does. But what it does, designated by the umbrella term *mission,* is complex and multiple: witness, proclamation, catechesis, worship, inculturation, interreligious dialogue, liberation, to name only the most obvious activities the church performs.[2] These activities are carried out not in the abstract, above space and time, but in concrete situations, at a specific time, in a particular place, with and for determinate groups of people in their own socio-political, economic, cultural, and religious settings.

Though the term *inculturation* is a neologism to describe this way of performing the church's mission, it has been the church's modus operandi, with varying degrees of success, since its very beginning, as it moved out of its Jewish matrix into the Greco-Roman, then Franco-Germanic worlds. With the Second Vatican Council (1962-65), as Karl Rahner has pointed out, there occurred an epochal shift in outlook: The church was moving away from a predominantly Hellenistic-Latin (Eurocentric) world view and transforming itself into a world church characterized by cultural and religious pluralism and consequently facing a host of new theological and pastoral issues unprecedented in Christian history.[3]

That the theme of mission and inculturation is highly complex is not in doubt. In spite of an avalanche of publications on the subject, what is meant by *inculturation* is by no means clear. Indeed, there is no consensus among church

---

[1] See Francis A. Sullivan, "The Evangelizing Mission of the Church," in *The Gift of the Church: A Textbook on Ecclesiology*, ed. Peter C. Phan (Collegeville, Minn.: Liturgical Press, 2000), 231-48.

[2] John Paul II's *Redemptoris missio (RM)* names as "paths of mission" the following activities (though by no means an exhaustive list): witness, proclamation of Christ the Savior, conversion and baptism, forming local churches, forming "ecclesial basic communities," incarnating the gospel in peoples' cultures, dialogue with other religions, promoting development by forming consciences, and charity (see nos. 41-60). For an English text of *RM*, see William Burrows, ed., *Redemption and Dialogue: Reading* Redemptoris Missio *and* Proclamation (Maryknoll, N.Y.: Orbis Books, 1993), 5-55.

[3] Karl Rahner, "Toward a Fundamental Interpretation of Vatican II," *Theological Studies* 40 (1979), 716-27.

official documents, theologians, and missiologists on what the process of inculturating the Christian faith and worship into local cultures involves and demands. There is first of all a matter of terminology. Different terms, of varying degrees of appropriateness, have been used to describe the process of introducing the Christian faith into a local culture: *translation, accommodation, adaptation, localization, indigenization, contextualization, incarnation, acculturation, inculturation, interculturation,* and so on.[4] In addition to terminological confusion, there is the more important fact of the widely divergent understandings in contemporary theologies of the relation between the gospel and culture. Such discrepancies are all the more bewildering when the same term is used to mean different things.

INCULTURATION:
THE ENCOUNTER BETWEEN THE GOSPEL AND CULTURES

Within the Roman Catholic circle, inculturation has been the subject of prolonged and intense debates in the decades following the Second Vatican Council. It has been treated, repeatedly and in various ways, by papal documents, from Paul VI's *Africae terrarum* (1967) and *Evangelii nuntiandi* (1975) to John Paul II's *Catechesi Tradendae* (1979), *Slavorum apostoli* (1985),[5] *Redemptoris missio* (1993),[6] and *Fides et ratio* (1998);[7] by official church declarations, such as the Latin American Episcopal Conference's (CELAM) Final Documents at Medellín (1968), Puebla (1979), and Santo Domingo (1992), the International Theological Commission's *Faith and Inculturation* (1988), the Congregation for the Clergy's *General Directory for Catechesis* (1997), the post-synodal apostolic exhortations following the special assemblies of the Synod of Bishops for Africa (1994),[8] Asia (1998),[9] and Oceania (1999), and especially the numer-

---

[4] See Anscar Chupungco, *Cultural Adaptation of the Liturgy* (New York: Paulist Press, 1982), 81-86; idem, *Liturgies of the Future: The Process and Methods of Inculturation* (New York: Paulist Press, 1989), 23-35; idem, *Liturgical Inculturation: Sacramentals, Religiosity, and Catechesis* (Collegeville, Minn.: Liturgical Press, 1992), 13-27; Peter C. Phan, "Contemporary Theology and Inculturation in the United States," in *The Multicultural Church: A New Landscape in U.S. Theologies*, ed. William Cenkner (New York: Paulist Press, 1995), 109-30; 176-92; Aylward Shorter, *Toward a Theology of Inculturation* (Maryknoll, N.Y.: Orbis Books, 1988), 3-16.

[5] On the teaching of these documents on inculturation, see Shorter, *Toward a Theology of Inculturation*, 206-38.

[6] On inculturation according to *Redemptoris missio*, see Marcello Zago, "Commentary on *Redemptoris Missio*," in Burrows, *Redemption and Dialogue*, 56-90. *RM* speaks of inculturation especially in nos. 52-57.

[7] On inculturation in *Fides et ratio*, see Peter C. Phan, "*Fides et ratio* and Asian Philosophies: Sharing the Banquet of Truth," *Science et Esprit* 51/3 (1999), 333-49.

[8] For the African Synod, see *African Synod: Documents, Reflections, Perspectives*, ed. Maura Browne (Maryknoll, N.Y.: Orbis Books, 1996). Pope John Paul II's post-synodal apostolic exhortation *Ecclesia in Africa* devotes a chapter to inculturation (Chapter III: "Evangelization and Inculturation").

[9] On inculturation in *Ecclesia in Asia*, see Peter C. Phan, "*Ecclesia in Asia*: Challenges for Asian Christianity," *East Asian Pastoral Review* 37/3 (2000), 215-32. See also *The Asian Synod: Texts and Commentaries*, ed. Peter C. Phan (Maryknoll, N.Y.: Orbis Books, 2002).

ous statements of the Federation of Asian Bishops' Conferences (FABC).[10] In liturgical matters, there is the Congregation for Divine Worship and the Disciplines of the Sacraments' *Inculturation of the Roman Liturgy within the Roman Rite* (1994) and *Liturgiam Authenticam: Fifth Instruction on Vernacular Translation of the Roman Liturgy* (2001).

Among Protestants, too, the concern for inculturation, even though the term is not frequently used, has been paramount in recent years, especially in the context of evangelization and mission. Of special interest are the Lutheran World Federation's Nairobi Statement on Worship and Culture (1996), the World Council of Churches' Jerusalem Statement on Intercultural Hermeneutics (1995), and the Report from the World Council of Churches Commission on World Mission and Evangelism (WCC-WCME) Ecumenical Conference in Salvador, de Bahia, Brazil (1996).[11]

Given the wide divergences in the understanding of inculturation, it may be helpful to list in summary form the current points of agreement, albeit not a general consensus, on inculturation, as these can be culled from the official documents, both Catholic and Protestant:

1. *Inculturation is an integral and constitutive dimension of the church's evangelizing mission.*

John Paul II declares in *Redemptoris missio:* "As she carries out missionary activity among the nations, the Church encounters different cultures and becomes involved in the process of inculturation. The need for such involvement has marked the Church's pilgrimage throughout her history, but today it is particularly urgent" (no. 52). The Nairobi Statement affirms: "Contextualization is a necessary task for the Church's mission in the world, so that the Gospel can be ever more deeply rooted in diverse local cultures."[12] The WCC-WCME Ecumenical Conference in Salvador, de Bahia, Brazil, says that "the churches need to be empowered for culture-sensitive evangelism which takes seriously people's history and cultures. Thus will the gospel be proclaimed through people's own cultural symbols, myths and rituals, stories and festivals."[13]

---

[10] For a collection of the final statements of FABC's plenary assemblies as well as assorted documents of FABC's various institutes, see Gaudencio Rosales and C. G. Arévalo, eds., *For All Peoples of Asia: Federation of Asian Bishops' Conferences. Documents from 1970 to 1991*, vol. 1 (Maryknoll, N.Y.: Orbis Books, 1991); Franz-Josef Eilers, ed., *For All the Peoples of Asia: Federation of Asian Bishops' Conferences. Documents from 1992 to 1996*, vol. 2 (Quezon City, Philippines: Claretian Publications, 1997); and idem, ed., *For All the Peoples of Asia: Federation of Asian Bishops' Conferences. Documents from 1997-2001*, vol. 3 (Quezon City, Philippines: Claretian Publications, 2002).

[11] These three texts are available in *New Directions in Mission and Evangelization,* vol. 3, *Faith and Culture,* ed. James A. Scherer and Stephen B. Bevans (Maryknoll, N.Y.: Orbis Books, 1999), 177-234. For a presentation of the Ecumenical Conference in Salvador, de Bahia, Brazil, see Michael Paul Gallagher, *Clashing Symbols: An Introduction to Faith and Culture* (New York: Paulist Press, 1998), 56-66.

[12] Scherer and Bevans, *New Directions in Mission and Evangelization,* 3:182.

[13] Ibid., 3:217.

2. *Inculturation is a double process comprising (a) insertion of the gospel into a particular culture, and (b) introduction of the culture into the gospel.*

John Paul II, quoting the 1985 Extraordinary Assembly of the Synod of Bishops, says: "Inculturation 'means the intimate transformation of authentic cultural values through their integration in Christianity and the insertion of Christianity in the various human cultures'" (no. 52).

3. *The result of inculturation is both the transformation of the culture from within by the gospel and the enrichment of the gospel by the culture with its new ways of understanding and living it. Hence, the end result of inculturation is something new, a* tertium quid, *going beyond the current culture and the previous ways of understanding and living the gospel.*

The transformation of cultures by the gospel is well explained by the WCC-WCME Ecumenical Conference in Salvador, de Bahia, Brazil:

> The gospel gives culture an orientation towards the glory of God. . . . Transformation means being freed from the oppression of particular aspects of culture. . . . Transformation means purification of certain elements of cultures. . . . Transformation implies the empowerment of people to gain deeper insights into both the gospel and their own culture. Transformation further implies that a missionary entering a different culture to proclaim the gospel must begin a journey of conversion in knowing, living, and loving that culture.[14]

On the other hand, cultures also offer a fresh understanding of and new ways of living the gospel. The same conference says: "The gospel may be made more accessible and given a deeper expression through cultural activities. To affirm that cultures illuminate the gospel is to hold that culture, manifested in art and other forms of human creativity, enlightens and enhances our understanding of the gospel."[15] The conference expresses the mutual transformation of the gospel and the culture in inculturation in a terse sentence: "The gospel of Jesus Christ encountering any given culture becomes incarnate in and illumined by that culture, but also transforms and transcends that culture."[16]

4. *The gospel, though not to be identified with any culture, is never independent of culture. It always comes already enfleshed in a particular culture. Consequently, inculturation is necessarily interculturation and must abide by the laws and dynamics of intercultural dialogue. Hence, one of the fundamental tasks in inculturation is to discern the gospel apart from the cultural forms in which it is clothed and to re-express it in new cultural forms.*

The transcendence of Christ and the gospel over cultures is asserted by all the official texts, Catholic and Protestant. The International Theological Commission's *Faith and Inculturation* affirms: "We cannot however forget the transcendence of the gospel in relation to all human cultures in which the

---

[14] Ibid., 3:203.
[15] Ibid., 3:204.
[16] Ibid., 3:226.

Christian faith has the vocation to enroot itself and come to fruition according to all its potentialities" (no. 14; see also nos. 8-11). The Nairobi Statement affirms categorically: "The resurrected Christ whom we worship, and through whom by the power of the Holy Spirit we know the grace of the Triune God, transcends and indeed is beyond all cultures."[17] Similarly, the WCC-WCME Ecumenical Conference in Salvador, de Bahia, states: "The gospel cannot be identified with particular cultures. Culture is not to be regarded as divine. No culture can claim to have grasped the fullness of God."[18]

Concerning the necessarily inculturated character of the gospel, the WCC text "On Intercultural Hermeneutics" affirms: "There is no 'pure' gospel that can be understood apart from the various forms in which it is embodied in culture and language."[19]

Inculturation as interculturation is strongly affirmed by the WCC text "On Intercultural Hermeneutics":

> Intercultural communication is essentially a conversation in which both parties try to communicate to each other what is important to them. Thus it requires that both try to speak and both try to listen. Each of these is an active role: speaking requires deciding how to communicate so that the other might better understand; listening requires patient and attentive engagement both to the speaker and to our own memory and knowledge.[20]

The task of distinguishing the gospel from its cultural forms is emphasized by the WCC. "On Intercultural Hermeneutics" sees the challenges of inculturation as follows: "How can we recognize that we share the same story when it can be *told* in so many different ways? How can we recognize that we share the same story when it can be *appropriated* in so many different ways? How can we distinguish between *authentic* and *inauthentic* ways of telling and living out the gospel?"[21]

5. *Since religion—a system of beliefs, values and practices—is a constitutive dimension of culture, inculturation is of necessity an interreligious dialogue. Hence, it cannot be carried out effectively without dealing with extremely difficult theological issues in the theology of religion such as the universality and uniqueness of Christ as the savior, the status of non-Christian religions as ways*

---

[17] Ibid., 3:181.

[18] Ibid., 3:201.

[19] Ibid., 3:187. This point has been strongly emphasized by Michael Amaladoss, who argues that the image of incarnation as the model for inculturation, may misleadingly suggest that the gospel is somehow culture free and needs only to be "incarnated" in each culture. He rightly points out that inculturation is really an intercultural dialogue between two cultures, that of a particular type of Christianity that is being introduced and the local culture that is being evangelized. Hence, he suggests that "dialogue" rather than "embodiment" serve as the model for the encounter between the gospel and cultures (See Michael Amaladoss, *Beyond Inculturation: Can the Many Be One?* [Delhi: The Indian Society for Promoting Christian Knowledge, 1998], 14-17).

[20] Scherer and Bevans, *New Directions in Mission and Evangelization,* 3:191.

[21] Ibid., 3:188.

of salvation, the inspired character of their sacred scriptures, and the salvific values of their rituals and religious practices.

Interreligious dialogue has been a prominent concern of John Paul II.[22] The WCC-WCME Ecumenical Conference in Salvador, de Bahia, is well aware that mission involves dialogue with peoples of other faiths and devotes several pages to this theme.[23]

6. *In addition to interreligious dialogue, inculturation must also go hand in hand with liberation, not least because often it is the culture of the poor, colonized, and marginalized people that has been suppressed and therefore requires retrieval and promotion.*

The WCC-WCME conference points out that racism and sexism have been obstacles to the inculturation of the gospel.[24] After invoking the oppressive features of globalization, it states: "The churches need to reaffirm that God's purpose includes liberating all people from all forms of exploitation and exclusion so that they can live and share their lives in freedom and justice"[25] John Paul II stresses the link between evangelization and liberation: "Through the Gospel message, the Church offers a force for liberation which promotes development precisely because it leads to conversion of heart and of ways of thinking, fosters the recognition of each person's dignity, encourages solidarity, commitment and service of one's neighbor, and gives everyone a place in God's plan, which is the building of his Kingdom of peace and justice, beginning already in this life" (*RM*, no. 59).

7. *Inculturation as a theological process is governed by the mysteries of the incarnation, death, resurrection of Jesus, and the descent and active presence of the Holy Spirit (Pentecost).*

The Nairobi Statement skillfully correlates the transcultural aspect of Christian worship to Christ's resurrection, its contextuality to his incarnation, its counter-culturality to his passion and death, and its cross-culturality to his universal lordship and saving role.[26]

---

[22] On John Paul II and interreligious dialogue, see Byron L. Sherwin and Harold Kasimow, eds., *John Paul II and Interreligious Dialogue* (Maryknoll, N.Y.: Orbis Books, 1999). On the relationship between evangelization and interreligious dialogue, see *RM*, nos. 55-57, and the 1991 document issued by the Pontifical Council for Inter-Religious Dialogue and the Congregation for the Evangelization of Peoples, *Dialogue and Proclamation [DP]: Reflections and Orientations on Interreligious Dialogue and the Proclamation of the Gospel of Jesus Christ* (the English translation is available in Burrows, *Redemption and Dialogue*, 94-118).

[23] See Scherer and Bevans, *New Directions in Mission and Evangelization,* 3:222-25.

[24] See ibid., 3:193-95.

[25] Ibid., 3:216.

[26] See Scherer and Bevans, *New Directions in Mission and Evangelization,* 3:181-83. Shorter puts it concisely: "One cannot use only one aspect of the Christ-event to illuminate the dialogue between Gospel and culture. The whole mystery of Christ, passion, death and resurrection, has to be applied analogically to the process of inculturation. It is only when this is done that a Christological understanding of inculturation becomes possible. The emphasis must be shifted from Incarnation to Paschal Mystery" (*Toward a Theology of Inculturation*, 82-83).

8. *The principal agent of inculturation is the local church, not the experts and the central authorities.*

John Paul II says:

Inculturation must involve the whole people of God, and not just a few experts, since the people reflect the authentic *sensus fidei* which must never be lost sight of. Inculturation needs to be guided and encouraged, but not forced, lest it give rise to negative reactions among Christians. It must be an expression of the community's life, one which must mature within the community itself, and not be exclusively the result of erudite research (*RM*, no. 54).

9. *Inculturation is comprehensive in scope: It must be carried out in all areas of church life.*

In his discourse to the bishops of Zaire on 12 April 1983, John Paul II asked: "How is it that a faith which has truly matured, is deep and firm, does not succeed in expressing itself in a language, in a catechesis, in theological reflection, in prayer, in the liturgy, in art, in the institutions which are truly related to the African soul of your compatriots?" (no. 5).

10. *Inculturation must bring about diversity in unity and unity in diversity. It must therefore develop criteria by which pluralism can be judged as not detrimental to the unity of the church and by which unity is prevented from being reduced to uniformity.*

John Paul II lists two criteria: "Properly applied, inculturation must be guided by two principles: 'compatibility with the Gospel and communion with the universal Church'" (*RM*, no. 54). The WCC's "On Intercultural Hermeneutics" proposes three:

The first criterion is that whatever is proposed must be *according to the Scriptures*, that is, in harmony with the confession of the triune God, salvation through Christ and the final destiny of humanity and creation as witnessed to in the Scriptures and the testimony of the undivided church of the first centuries. The second is that of *praxis*: how that which is proposed resonates with the praise of God in the liturgy and in the action by which Christians commit themselves to the furtherance of God's reign and its justice. The third criterion is that of commitment to seek the truth within the communion of the church and the upbuilding of the church in a peaceable, non-dominating way: accepting prophetic critique from others and in turn exercising a prophetic critique of other communities of faith for the sake of the truth.[27]

The WCC-WCME conference lists four criteria for the appropriateness of contextualization: "faithfulness to God's self-disclosure in the totality of the scriptures; commitment to a life-style and action in harmony with the reign of

---

[27] Scherer and Bevans, *New Directions in Mission and Evangelization,* 3:193.

God; openness to the wisdom of the communion of saints across space and time; relevance to the context."[28]

11. *It must be guided by a robust theology of the local church.*

The WCC speaks of the necessity of both contextuality and catholicity. The contextuality of the church's faith "is reflected in the diverse ways in which the gospel story is told and lived out in various contexts"; whereas its catholicity is "the quality by which the church expresses the fullness, the integrity, and the totality of life in Christ."[29] The mutual relationship between contextuality and catholicity is well expressed: "At the root of genuine catholicity is the participation of the local in the global and of the global in the local. Catholicity is not the destruction or overwhelming of the local; it is the local in communion."[30]

The WCC-WCME conference also affirms that "any authentic understanding of the gospel is both contextual and catholic. The gospel is contextual in that it is inevitably embodied in a particular culture; it is catholic in that it expresses the apostolic faith handed down from generation to generation within the communion of churches in all places and all ages."[31]

MISSION AND INCULTURATION FROM THE ASIAN PERSPECTIVE

The essays here presented all deal, in one way or another, with the theme of inculturating the gospel into various countries and cultures. The perspective from which it is treated is that provided by the FABC and Asian theologians. The church's mission, in this perspective, must be carried out in the form of dialogue: dialogue of life lived together, of common action, of shared religious experience, and of theological exchange. In Asia this fourfold dialogue is performed in at least three areas: dialogue with Asian peoples, especially the poor (liberation); with Asian religions (interreligious dialogue); and with Asian cultures (inculturation).

In this volume focus will be on the third area of dialogue. Part 1 relates the church's mission to inculturation, with this chapter providing introductory concepts of the process of inculturation as culled from some official documents, both Catholic and Protestant. Chapter 2 examines a new way of being church in Asia in terms of the three tasks of the church's mission—liberation, inculturation, and interreligious dialogue—with attention to the Asian context of crushing and widespread poverty, multiplicity of ancient cultures, and diversity of religious traditions.

The third chapter discusses the relationship among the four central realities of the Christian faith—reign of God, mission, proclamation, and church—in order to find correct answers to the five questions regarding the church's evangelizing mission: for what? to whom? by whom? with whom? and how? What

---

[28] Ibid., 3:226.
[29] Ibid., 3:189.
[30] Ibid., 3:190.
[31] Ibid., 3:226.

emerges from this discussion is nothing less than a revolution in the theology of mission.

The fourth chapter focuses on one aspect of the church's mission that was undisputed in past missiologies but has now been challenged: Should mission aim at "converting" non-Christians? Reviewing the concept of conversion in the New Testament and the history of mission, the essay argues for an understanding of conversion not primarily as abandoning a religious tradition and joining another but as "turning to" Jesus in a radical way, in a personal and absolute commitment to him and his way of life, and "taking over" and continuing his mission for the reign of God.

Part 2 examines the issue of inculturation of worship and prayer. One of the most thorny issues in mission and in liturgical inculturation, at least in Asia, is the presence of what has been called popular religion. Chapter 5 shows that the official positions so far taken by the Roman Catholic and Lutheran churches are inadequate. It argues that inculturation in matters of popular religion cannot be satisfactorily accomplished unless inculturation is undertaken as part of the process of becoming a local church in Asia through the triple dialogue with the Asian people, especially the poor, their cultures, and their religions. Furthermore, other theological issues, such as the role of power and the nature of the liturgy as "culmen et fons" of the church's life, are reexamined.

Asian Christians are often praised for their devotion to Mary. The Filipinos are said to be a "pueblo amante de Maria." Vietnamese Catholics, too, are famous for their Marian piety. The sixth chapter surveys the history of Marian devotion in Vietnam, its various layers, and the two alleged Marian apparitions at La Vang and Tra Kieu. It proposes to see Mary as the embodiment of divine compassion, as the Mother of Mercy, in the Buddhist tradition of Kwan-Yin; as a powerful protectress of the poor and the persecuted in the tradition of Vietnamese heroines; and as an interreligious figure uniting Vietnamese Catholics and Buddhists.

One of the most painful and tragic episodes of Christian mission in China and other parts of Asia is the so-called Chinese Rites Controversy. The seventh chapter revisits this history, highlights the theological issues underlying this controversy, and shows how the veneration of ancestors has been incorporated, at least in some forms, into the liturgy of the church. Chapter 8 rounds up considerations on prayer and worship with reflections on missionary spirituality as "border crossing." It argues that new arenas and situations of mission require new forms of spirituality of presence, kenotic spirituality, spirituality of reconciliation and harmony, and holistic spirituality. It proposes Jesus as the "border-crosser" par excellence, serving as the model for border-crossing spirituality.

Part 3 examines theology as a form of inculturation. Inculturation must be extended to theology, beyond official worship and popular devotions. Chapter 9 delineates the contours of an intercultural theology, first from the experiments of the seventeenth-century Jesuit missionary to Vietnam, Alexandre de Rhodes (1593-1660), and then from contemporary attempts such as those of Francis Clooney, another Jesuit. It argues for the need of a comparative theology based on an accurate translation of religious texts, complemented by an examination of how these texts have affected people's lives, and concerned with the question of truth and the proper ordering of doctrines.

Chapter 10 outlines an Asian style of doing theology characterized by a deep concern to serve the church's evangelizing mission. In contrast to theologies that have held hegemony in the West, such a theology is shown to be a prayerful and participatory scholarly activity, employing a distinct set of sources and re-sources and deploying a hermeneutics that is postcolonialist, interfaith, multicultural, and people-based.

Finally, Asian theology, as embodied in the official documents of the FABC and as developed by individual Asian theologians, could not have emerged and reached maturity without the reforms spawned by Vatican II. The last chapter documents the reception of the council by the Asian churches in all the areas of their lives. The fruits of Vatican II were in magnificent display during the spe-cial assembly of the Synod of Bishops for Asia, one of the five assemblies con-voked by John Paul II to celebrate the third millennium of Christianity, and arguably the best of them all. With the Asian Synod in Rome the Asian churches have made a full circle. It was from the Second Vatican Council held in Rome that they had learned how to be church, "receiving" and appropriating the council's ecclesiology and the various reforms coming out of it. At the Asian Synod, the Asian churches returned to Rome and showed how well they have "received" Vatican II and, as a result, have something to teach the Church of Rome and the church universal.

2

Christian Mission in Asia

A NEW WAY OF BEING CHURCH

No doubt Christian mission in Asia should count as one of the splendid achievements of the church.[1] Born in Asia, Christianity soon moved to the West, but its early presence in Asia should not be forgotten.[2] Contrary to many Western historical accounts, Christianity did not first arrive in Asia with Vasco de Gama in 1498. Even before Saint Paul arrived on the scene, the Christian movement had already expanded into Syria. Moreover, we cannot discount the historical possibility that Saint Thomas reached India. Christian presence was also significant in Persia, even after Zoroastrianism was made the state religion under the Sassanid dynasty (224-425) and despite frequent and violent persecutions. From the Persian capital the church expanded east along the Silk Road that led from Northern Iran to China. From the first solid evidence of a Christian presence in China, namely, the famous monument erected near Xian in 781, we know that a Syrian-speaking, Nestorian mission, led by Alopen, was active in the Chinese imperial capital in 635.[3] We also know of the translation or composition of the first Christian sutra in Chinese and the establishment of the first Christian monastery in the imperial city with the permission of the T'ang emperor T'ai-tsung (627-49). In the thirteenth century the good news was announced to the Mongols, the Turks, and the Chinese once more.

---

[1] For helpful histories of Christian mission in Asia, see Samuel H. Moffett, *A History of Christianity in Asia,* vol. 1, *Beginnings to 1500* (Maryknoll, N.Y.: Orbis Books, 1998); Ian Gillman and Hans-Joachim Klimkeit, *Christians in Asia before 1500* (Ann Arbor, Mich.: University of Michigan Press, 1999); and Nicolas Standaert, ed., *Handbook of Christianity in Asia,* vol. 1, *635-1800* (Leiden: Brill, 2001).

[2] For a brief overview of Christian mission in Asia, see John Paul II's apostolic exhortation *Ecclesia in Asia* [*EA*] (1999), no. 9. For an English translation of *EA*, see *Origin* 29/23 (18 November 1999), 358-84.

[3] For an English translation of this Nestorian monument, discovered in 1623, see Moffett, *A History of Christianity in Asia*, 1:291. This monument, erected in 781, has the title: "A Monument Commemorating the Propagation of the Ta-ch'in [Syrian] Luminous Religion in China." The inscription was composed by Bishop Adam (his Chinese name is Ching-Ching) and introduced by a brief presentation of the Christian doctrines. For an English text of this introduction, see 514-16.

While these facts should not be forgotten, it is still true that by historical circumstances Christianity was and continues to be regarded as a foreign religion by Asians. Even Pope John Paul II points out the paradoxical fact that "most Asians tend to regard Jesus—born on Asian soil—as a Western rather than an Asian figure" (*EA,* no. 20). One of the reasons for this persistent impression of Christianity's foreignness is the Asian churches' past connections with colonial powers. Despite the enormous positive contributions of Western missionaries to not only the religious but also the educational, medical, and social advancement in mission lands, the fact that the missionary movement in Asia was financially underwritten by colonialist countries such as Spain and Portugal in the seventeenth century through the *padroado* system and that at times missionaries colluded with their governments in subjugating the indigenous peoples severely compromised the church's spiritual mission and made Christianity appear to be the handmaid of colonial powers. Indeed, in seventeenth-century Vietnam, Christianity was known in Vietnamese as the "religion of the Portuguese."[4] Consequently, the most urgent task for the Asian churches is to become churches not only *in* but also *of* Asia, in other words, to become local churches.

A NEW WAY OF BEING CHURCH

This new way of being church in Asia requires a different ecclesiology, one that decenters the church in the sense that it makes the center of the Christian life and worship not the church but the reign of God.[5] This sort of Copernican revolution in ecclesiology sees the goal and purpose of the mission of the church to be not the geographical and institutional expansion of the church (the *plantatio ecclesiae*). Rather, it is to be a transparent sign of and effective instrument for the saving presence of the reign of God, the reign of justice, peace, and love, of which the church is a seed.[6]

This theme has been repeatedly emphasized by the FABC,[7] especially in its first and fifth plenary assemblies (Taipei, Taiwan, 1974, and Bandung, Indonesia,

---

[4] See Peter C. Phan, *Mission and Catechesis: Alexandre de Rhodes and Inculturation in Seventeenth-Century Vietnam* (Maryknoll, N.Y.: Orbis Books, 1998), xv. De Rhodes felt it necessary to protest that even though Christianity might have come from countries in Europe, it belongs to all countries. Comparing it to the sun, he says: "For example, when the suns sends its rays on a kingdom, it illuminates it, though the other kingdoms on which it has not sent its rays still remain in darkness. Nevertheless, no one would say that the sun belongs to that kingdom upon which it sends its rays first, because the sun is common to the whole world and exists before the kingdom it illuminates" (223).

[5] For a reflection on the concept of reign of God for Asia, see Peter C. Phan, "Kingdom of God: A Theological Symbol for Asia?" *Gregorianum* 79/2 (1998), 295-322.

[6] For reflections on the mission of the church in this new context, see Chapters 3 and 4 herein.

[7] The FABC was founded in 1970, on the occasion of Pope Paul VI's visit to Manila, Philippines. Its statutes, approved by the Holy See *ad experimentum* in 1972, were amended several times and were also approved again each time by the Holy See. For the

1990, respectively).[8] In Taipei, the FABC affirmed categorically: "To preach the Gospel in Asia today we must make the message and life of Christ truly incarnate in the minds and lives of our peoples. The primary focus of our task of evangelization then, at this time in our history, is the building up of a truly local church."[9] In Bandung, the FABC spoke of alternative ways of being church in Asia in the 1990s and envisioned four specific ways. The church in Asia, it said, must be (1) a *"communion of communities*, where laity, Religious and clergy recognize and accept each other as sisters and brothers," (2) "a *participatory* Church where the gifts that the Holy Spirit gives to all the faithful—lay, Religious, and clerics alike—are recognized and activated," (3) "a Church that faithfully and lovingly *witnesses* to the Risen Lord Jesus and reaches out to the people of other faiths and persuasions in a dialogue of life towards the integral liberation of all," and (4) a church that "serves as a *prophetic sign* daring to point beyond this world to the ineffable Kingdom that is yet fully to come."[10]

This necessity to be local churches was reiterated by the FABC's seventh plenary assembly (Samphran, Thailand, 3-12 January 2000). Coming right after the Asian Synod (19 April—May 9, 1998) and the promulgation of the apostolic exhortation *Ecclesia in Asia* (6 November 1999) and celebrating the Great Jubilee, with the general theme "A Renewed Church in Asia: A Mission of Love and Service," this assembly is of particular significance for the future of the mission of the Asian churches. In the first place, the FABC takes a retrospective glance over a quarter of a century of its life and activities and summarizes its "Asian vision of a renewed Church." It sees it as composed of eight movements that constitute a sort of Asian ecclesiology. Given its central importance, the text deserves to be quoted in full:

> 1. A movement toward a Church of the Poor and a Church of the Young. "If we are to place ourselves at the side of the multitudes in our continent, we must in our way of life share something of their poverty,"

---

documents of the FABC and its various institutes, see Gaudencio Rosales and C. G. Arévalo, eds., *For All the Peoples of Asia: Federation of Asian Bishops' Conferences. Documents from 1970 to 1991*, vol. 1 (Maryknoll, N.Y.: Orbis Books; Quezon City: Claretian Publications, 1992); Franz-Josef Eilers, ed., *For All the Peoples of Asia: Federation of Asian Bishops' Conferences. Documents from 1992 to 1996*, vol. 2 (Quezon City: Claretian Publications, 1997); and Franz-Josef Eilers, ed., *For All the Peoples of Asia: Federation of Asian Bishops' Conferences. Documents from 1997 to 2002*, vol. 3 (Quezon City: Claretian Publications, 2002).

[8] See *For All the Peoples of Asia,* 1:12-25, 53-61, 274-89.

[9] Ibid., 1:14. It continues: "The local church is a church incarnate in a people, a church indigenous and inculturated. And this means concretely a church in continuous, humble and loving dialogue with the living traditions, the cultures, the religions—in brief, with all the life-realities of the people in whose midst it has sunk its roots deeply and whose history and life it gladly makes its own."

[10] Ibid., 1:287-88. For a development of this ecclesiology, see Peter C. Phan, "*Ecclesia in Asia*: Challenges for Asian Christianity," *East Asian Pastoral Review* [*EAPR*] 37/3 (2000), 220-26. See also S. J. Emmanuel, "Asian Churches for a New Evangelization: Chances and Challenges," *EAPR* 36/3 (1999), 252-75.

"speak out for the rights of the disadvantaged and powerless, against all forms of injustice." In this continent of the young, we must become "in them and for them, the Church of the young" (Meeting of Asian Bishops, Manila, Philippines, 1970).

2. A movement toward a "truly local Church," toward a Church "incarnate in a people, a Church indigenous and inculturated" (2 FABC Plenary Assembly, Calcutta, 1978).

3. A movement toward deep interiority so that the Church becomes a "deeply praying community whose contemplation is inserted in the context of our time and the cultures of our peoples today. Integrated into everyday life, "authentic prayer has to engender in Christians a clear witness of service and love" (2 FABC Plenary Assembly, Calcutta, 1978).

4. A movement toward an authentic community of faith. Fully rooted in the life of the Trinity, the Church in Asia has to be a communion of communities of authentic participation and co-responsibility, one with its pastors, and linked "to other communities of faith and to the one and universal communion" of the holy Church of the Lord. The movement in Asia toward Basic Ecclesial Communities expresses the deep desire to be such a community of faith, love and service and to be truly a "community of communities" and open to building up Basic Human Communities (3 FABC Plenary Assembly, Bangkok, 1982).

5. A movement toward active integral evangelization, toward a new sense of mission (5 FABC Plenary Assembly, Bandung, Indonesia, 1990). We evangelize because we believe Jesus is the Lord and Savior, "the goal of human history, . . . the joy of all hearts, and the fulfillment of all aspirations" (GS, 45). In this mission, the Church has to be a compassionate companion and partner of all Asians, a servant of the Lord and of all Asian peoples in the journey toward full life in God's Kingdom.

6. A movement toward empowerment of men and women. We must evolve participative church structures in order to use the personal talents and skills of lay women and men. Empowered by the Spirit and through the sacraments, lay men and women should be involved in the life and mission of the Church by bringing the Good News of Jesus to bear upon the fields of business and politics, of education and health, of mass media and the world of work. This requires a spirituality of discipleship enabling both the clergy and laity to work together in their own specific roles in the common mission of the Church (4 FABC Plenary Assembly, Tokyo, 1986). The Church cannot be a sign of the Kingdom and of the eschatological community if the fruits of the Spirit to women are not given due recognition, and if women do not share in the "freedom of the children of God" (4 FABC Plenary Assembly, Tokyo, 1986).

7. A movement toward active involvement in generating and serving life. The Church has to respond to the death-dealing forces in Asia. By authentic discipleship, it has to share its vision of full life as promised by Jesus. It is a vision of life with integrity and dignity, with compassion and

sensitive care of the earth; a vision of participation and mutuality, with a reverential sense of the sacred, of peace, harmony, and solidarity (6 FABC Plenary Assembly, Manila, Philippines, 1995).

8. A movement toward the triple dialogue with other faiths, with the poor and with the cultures, a Church "in dialogue with the great religious traditions of our peoples," in fact, a dialogue with all people, especially the poor.[11]

This eightfold movement describes in a nutshell a new way of being church in Asia. Essentially, it aims at transforming the churches *in* Asia into the churches *of* Asia. Inculturation, understood in its widest sense, is the way to achieve this goal of becoming local churches. This need for inculturation in the church's mission of "love and service," according to the FABC's seventh plenary assembly, has grown even more insistent in light of the challenges facing Christianity in Asia in the new millennium, such as the increasing marginalization and exclusion of many people by globalization, widespread fundamentalism, dictatorship and corruption in governments, ecological destruction, and growing militarization. The FABC sees these challenges affecting special groups of people in a particular way, namely, youth, women, the family, indigenous people, and sea-based and land-based migrants and refugees.[12] To meet these challenges fully, the FABC believes that it is urgent to promote the "Asianness" of the church, which it sees as "a special gift the world is waiting for": "This means that the Church has to be an embodiment of the Asian vision and values of life, especially interiority, harmony, a holistic and inclusive approach to every area of life."[13]

In terms of ecclesiology, the church is defined primarily as a communion of communities. Hence, this Asian way of being church places the highest priority on communion and collegiality at all the levels of church life and activities. At the vertical level, communion is realized with the trinitarian God whose *perichoresis* the church is commissioned to reflect in history. On the horizontal level, communion is achieved with other local churches, and within each local church, communion is realized through collegiality, by which all members, especially lay women and men, are truly and effectively empowered to use their gifts to make the church an authentically local church.

DIALOGUE AS THE MODALITY OF MISSION

The modality in which this process of becoming the local church takes place is dialogue. It is important to note that dialogue is understood here not as a separate activity—for example, ecumenical and interreligious dialogue—but as

---

[11] *A Renewed Church in Asia: A Mission of Love and Service: The Final Statement of the Seventh Plenary Assembly of the Federation of Asian Bishops' Conferences. Samphran, Thailand, January 3-12, 2000*, 3-4. The document is available from the FABC, 16 Caine Road, Hong Kong. E-mail: hkdavc@hk.super.net.

[12] See ibid., 6-12.

[13] Ibid., 9.

the *modality* in which everything is to be done by and in the church in Asia, including liberation, inculturation, and interreligious dialogue. It is through this triple dialogue—with the Asian people, especially the poor, their cultures, and their religions—that the church in Asia carries out its evangelizing mission and thus becomes the local church. Hence, dialogue is not a substitute for proclamation or evangelization, as Asian theologians have sometimes been accused of promoting; rather, it is the way, and indeed the most effective way, in which the proclamation of the good news is done in Asia.

The reason for this dialogical modality is the presence in Asia of the many living religions and rich cultures, among whom Christians are but a tiny minority and therefore must, even on the purely human level, enter into dialogue with other believers in an attitude of respect and friendship for survival. But, more than pragmatic considerations, there is the theological doctrine today, at least in the Roman Catholic Church, that, as John Paul II says, "the Spirit's presence and activity affect not only individuals but also society and history, peoples, cultures and religions. Indeed, the Spirit is at the origin of the noble ideals and undertakings which benefit humanity on its journey through history" (*RM*, no. 28). In light of this divine presence in people's cultures and religions, and not just in individuals, and in view of the socio-historical nature of human existence, it is possible to say, as some Asian theologians have done, that the followers of other religions are saved not in spite of them but in and through them, though it is always God who saves, and Christians will add, in and through Jesus.[14] At least in this restricted sense, then, religions are "ways of salvation."[15]

Given this religious pluralism, it is only natural that dialogue is the preferred mode of proclamation. As Michael Amaladoss puts it:

---

[14] The Catholic Bishops' Conference of India, in its response to the *Lineamenta* in preparation for the Special Synod of Bishops for Asia (1998), writes: "Salvation is seen as being channeled to them [followers of non-Christian religions] not in spite of but through and in their socio-cultural and religious traditions. We cannot, then, deny a priori a salvific role for these non-Christian religions" (see Peter C. Phan, ed., *The Asian Synod: Texts and Commentaries* [Maryknoll, N.Y.: Orbis Books, 2002], 22).

[15] The Congregation for the Doctrine of the Faith in *Dominus Iesus* (6 August 2000) warns: "It would be contrary to the faith to consider the Church as *one way* of salvation alongside those constituted by the other religions, seen as complementary to the Church or substantially equivalent to her, even if these are said to be converging with the Church toward the eschatological Kingdom of God" (no. 22). The operative words here are "complementary" and "substantially equivalent." Obviously, it is theologically possible to hold that non-Christian religions are "ways of salvation" without holding the view implied in those two expressions. Furthermore, it does not seem necessary to affirm, as the declaration does, that "if it is true that the followers of other religions can receive divine grace, it is also certain that *objectively speaking* they are in a gravely deficient situation in comparison with those who, in the Church, have the fullness of the means of salvation" (no. 22) since (1) what is ultimately important, from the point of view of salvation, is that the person receives divine grace, no matter where and how; and (2) it does not do the Christians much good to have "the fullness of the means of salvation" and not in fact make effective use of them. As Augustine has observed, there are those who are in the church but do not belong to the church, and those who are outside of the church but do belong to it. At any rate, such expressions as those used in the declaration are nowhere found in Vatican II.

As soon as one no longer sees the relationship of Christianity to other religions as presence/absence or superior/inferior or full/partial, dialogue becomes the context in which proclamation has to take place. For even when proclaiming the Good News with assurance, one should do it with great respect for the freedom of God who is acting, the freedom of the other who is responding and the Church's own limitations as a witness. It is quite proper then that the Asian Bishops characterized evangelization itself as a dialogue with various Asian realities—cultures, religions and the poor.[16]

It is important to note also that dialogue as a mode of being church in Asia does not refer primarily to the intellectual exchange among experts of various religions, as it often does in the West. Rather, it involves a fourfold presence:

a. The *dialogue of life*, where people strive to live in an open and neighborly spirit, sharing their joys and sorrows, their human problems and preoccupations. b. The *dialogue of action*, in which Christians and others collaborate for the integral development and liberation of people. c. The *dialogue of theological exchange*, where specialists seek to deepen their understanding of their respective religious heritages, and to appreciate each other's spiritual values. d. The *dialogue of religious experience*, where persons, rooted in their own religious traditions, share their spiritual riches, for instance, with regard to prayer and contemplation, faith and ways of searching for God or the Absolute (*DP*, no. 42).[17]

As noted above, the FABC suggests that this dialogue take place in three areas: dialogue with the Asian poor, with their cultures, and with their religions.[18] In other words, the three essential tasks of the Asian churches are liberation, inculturation, and interreligious dialogue.[19] It is vital to note that for the FABC these are not three distinct and separate activities of the church; rather, they are three intertwined dimensions of the church's one mission of evangelization.[20] As the FABC's seventh plenary assembly puts it concisely:

---

[16] Michael Amaladoss, *Making All Things New: Dialogue, Pluralism, and Evangelization in Asia* (Maryknoll, N.Y.: Orbis Books, 1990), 59.

[17] See also *For All the Peoples of Asia*, 2:21-26.

[18] See *For All the Peoples of Asia,* 1:14-16, 22-23, 34-35, 107, 135, 141-43, 281-82, 307-12, 328-34, 344; *For All the Peoples of Asia,* 2:196-203.

[19] As Archbishop Oscar V. Cruz, secretary general of the FABC, said at the seventh plenary assembly: "The triple dialogue with the poor, with cultures, and with peoples of other religions, envisioned by FABC as a mode of evangelization, viz., human liberation, inculturation, interreligious dialogue." See *A Renewed Church in Asia: Pastoral Directions for a New Decade*, FABC Papers, no. 95 (Hong Kong: FABC, 2000), 17.

[20] For reflections on the connection between evangelization and liberation according to the FABC, see Peter C. Phan, "Human Development and Evangelization: The First to the Sixth Plenary Assembly of the Federation of Asian Bishops' Conferences," *Studia Missionalia* 47 (1998), 205-27.

These issues are not separate topics to be discussed, but aspects of an integrated approach to our Mission of Love and Service. We need to feel and act "integrally." As we face the needs of the 21st century, we do so with Asian hearts, in solidarity with the poor and the marginalized, in union with all our Christian brothers and sisters and by joining hands with all men and women of Asia of many different faiths. Inculturation, dialogue, justice and option for the poor are aspects of whatever we do.[21]

MISSION AND THE TRIPLE DIALOGUE IN ASIA

Dialogue with the Poor and Mission

David Bosch, in his monumental study on the theology of mission, has pointed out that "the relationship between the evangelistic and the societal dimensions of the Christian mission constitutes one of the thorniest areas in the theology and practice of mission."[22] It is common knowledge that the medieval paradigm of mission tends to privatize and spiritualize the concept of salvation so that the purpose of mission is understood as saving individual souls from the ravages of sin. A clear distinction was drawn between God's "providential" care and his "saving" acts, between the "horizontal" dimensions of mission (for example, education, health care, and charity works) and its "vertical" dimensions (such as preaching, sacramental celebrations, and pastoral *cura animae*), the former ancillary to and preparatory for the latter but not to be considered as missionary activities as such.

In contrast, the modern paradigm of mission understands salvation to include, beside forgiveness of sin and reconciliation with God, liberation from all forms of socio-political oppression and promotion of economic well-being. Included as an essential part of the church's mission are activities that bring about socio-political and economic transformation. The Commission for World Mission and Evangelism of the World Council of Churches, which met in Bangkok in 1973, depicts mission in terms of a fourfold struggle for (1) economic justice against exploitation, (2) human dignity against oppression, (3) solidarity against alienation, and (4) hope against despair in personal life.[23] On the Roman Catholic side, this view of mission is espoused with vigor by liberation theologians.[24] This is not the place to rehearse the history, methodology, and basic themes of liberation theology, whose growth has been nothing short of phenomenal since its origins in the late sixties.[25] The two points at issue are

[21] FABC, *A Renewed Church in Asia,* 8.

[22] David Bosch, *Transforming Mission: Paradigm Shifts in Theology of Mission* (Maryknoll, N.Y.: Orbis Books, 1991).

[23] See World Council of Churches, *Bangkok Assembly 1973: Minutes and Reports of the Assembly of the Commission on World Mission and Evangelism of the World Council of Churches* (Geneva: World Council of Churches, 1973), 98.

[24] For a representative discussion of mission from the perspective of liberation theology, see Leonardo Boff, *New Evangelization: Good News to the Poor*, trans. Robert Barr (Maryknoll, N.Y.: Orbis Books, 1991).

[25] For an evaluation of recent liberation theology, see Peter C. Phan, "The Future of Liberation Theology," *The Living Light* 28/3 (1992), 259-71.

whether social transformation belongs to the evangelizing mission of the church and, if so, how to understand the relationship between the former and the latter.

With regard to the first point, in light of the official teaching of the church, from the general conferences of Latin American Bishops at Medellín and Puebla to John Paul II's social encyclical *Centesimus annus*, there is little doubt that the proclamation of the gospel includes a denunciation of injustice and an active working for the promotion of peace, justice, and progress. The Synod of Bishops in 1971 declared: "Action on behalf of justice and participation in the transformation of the world fully appear to us as a constitutive dimension of the preaching of the Gospel, or, in other words, of the Church's mission for the redemption of the human race and its liberation from every oppressive situation."[26] In his apostolic exhortation on evangelization, *Evangelii nuntiandi,* Paul VI declares:

> But evangelization will not be complete unless it constantly relates the gospel to men's actual lives, personal and social. Accordingly, evangelization must include an explicit message, adapted to the various conditions of life and constantly updated, concerning the rights and duties of the individual person and concerning family life, without which progress in the life of the individual is hardly possible. It must deal with community life in society, with the life of all nations, with peace, with justice and progress. It must deliver a message, especially relevant and important in our age, about liberation (*EN,* no. 29).

The pope goes on to provide three reasons for the close links between evangelization and human development and liberation. First, there is a connection in the anthropological order: Humans are not abstract beings but persons subject to economic and social factors. Second, there is a connection in the theological order: God's plan of creation cannot be isolated from God's plan of redemption, which requires the eradication of injustice and the establishment of justice. And finally, there is a connection in the order of charity: The good news cannot be proclaimed effectively unless it promotes justice and peace (see *EN,* no. 31).

That liberation from all forms of oppression, both individual and societal, is now accepted as an integral part of the evangelizing mission of the church is illustrated by the fact that the phrase "the church's preferential option for the poor," at first controversial and suspect, is now regularly used by magisterial documents to describe one of the essential dimensions of the church's task of evangelization.[27] The same thing should be said about the expressions "social sin" or "sinful structures," which have now become the standard ways of describing

---

[26] *Convenientes ex universo (Justice in the World)*, in *Vatican Council II: More Postconciliar Documents*, ed. Austin Flannery (Collegeville, Minn.: Liturgical Press, 1982), 696.

[27] See in particular the final document of the third general conference of Latin American bishops at Puebla (1979) entitled "Puebla: La evangelización en el presente y en el futuro de America Latina," especially part II, chap. 2, section 4. For the English translation, see John Eagleson and Philip Sharper, eds., *Puebla and Beyond* (Maryknoll, N.Y.: Orbis Books, 1979). See also *RM,* esp. nos. 20, 58, 59, 60.

the oppressive social situations, structures, and systems that must be transformed in the quest for justice.[28]

Of course, magisterial documents contain important caveats and qualifications with regard to liberation theology and its emphasis on solidarity with the poor in evangelization. In particular, objections are voiced against the adoption of the Marxist method of social analysis and theory of class struggle, the fostering of violence and revolution, the one-sidedly political interpretation of the Bible, the use of praxis as a criterion of truth, the anthropocentric reduction of faith, and the politicization of sacramental celebrations.[29] Nevertheless, John Paul II acknowledges, in his letter to the Brazilian Episcopal Conference (9 April 1986), that with due corrections "the theology of liberation is not only timely but useful and necessary."[30]

This acknowledgment of the intimate connection between action on behalf of justice and evangelization still leaves unanswered the question of how to view their mutual relationship. As mentioned above, the 1971 Synod of Bishops speaks of the former as a "constitutive dimension" of the latter, and Pope Paul VI delineates in some detail the three connections between the two. More specifically, however, how should the relationship be understood in terms of priority?

In papal teachings from Paul VI to John Paul II there is, first of all, an emphatic affirmation that the two activities, though intimately united, are distinct. Paul VI says: "While recognizing the connection between them, the church never identifies human liberation with salvation in Jesus Christ. . . . She knows that the achievement of liberation, the development of prosperity and progress are not of themselves sufficient to assure the coming of the Kingdom of God" (*EN*, no. 35). John Paul II affirms no less clearly this distinction and goes on to deplore the anthropocentric reduction of the kingdom of God to socio-economic, political, and cultural liberation that is "one more ideology of purely earthly progress" (*RM*, no. 17). Indeed, for him, this temporal dimension of the kingdom of God "remains incomplete unless it is related to the kingdom of Christ present in the church and straining toward eschatological fullness" (*RM*, no. 20).

This distinction between human development and Christian salvation is also forcefully underscored by the International Theological Commission in

---

[28] See The Congregation for the Doctrine of the Faith, *Instruction on Christian Freedom and Liberation* (22 March 1986), nos. 74-75; English translation in *Liberation Theology: A Documentary History*, ed. Alfred T. Hennelly (Maryknoll, N.Y.: Orbis Books, 1990), 461-97; see also Mark O'Keefe, *What Are They Saying about Social Sin?* (New York: Paulist Press, 1990).

[29] See The Congregation for the Doctrine of the Faith, *Instruction on Certain Aspects of the "Theology of Liberation"* (6 August 6 1984); English translation in Hennelly, *Liberation Theology*, 393-414. A more balanced view of liberation theology by the same Congregation is found in its later document *Instruction on Christian Freedom and Liberation*. For a detailed and balanced evaluation of these criticisms, see Arthur F. McGovern, *Liberation and Its Critics: Toward an Assessment* (Maryknoll, N.Y.: Orbis Books, 1989).

[30] In Hennelly, *Liberation Theology*, 503.

its interpretation of the 1971 Synod of Bishops' description of action in favor of justice as a constitutive element of the preaching of the gospel:

> The words "constitutive element" *(ratio constitutiva)* are still the subject of controversy. If we look at their strict meaning, it seems more accurate to interpret them as meaning an integral part, not an essential part. . . . It is useful, therefore, while maintaining unyieldingly the unity that links the two, to spell out again, with even sharper clarity, the distinction between them.[31]

Similarly, the *Instruction on Christian Freedom and Liberation* affirms:

> Therefore, when the church speaks about the promotion of justice in human societies or when it urges the faithful to work in this sphere according to their own vocations, it is not going beyond its mission. It is, however, concerned that this mission should not be absorbed by preoccupations concerning the temporal order or reduced to such preoccupations. Hence it takes great care to maintain clearly and firmly both the unity and the distinction between evangelization and human promotion: unity, because it sees the good of the whole person; distinction, because these two tasks enter in different ways into its mission (no. 64).

Besides the maintenance of the distinction between social transformation and evangelization, magisterial documents also affirm the primacy or priority of the latter over the former. Paul VI writes:

> The church proclaims liberation and cooperates with all those who are working and suffering on its behalf. She does not assert that her function is strictly confined to the religious sphere without regard for the temporal problems of men. But she reaffirms the primacy of her spiritual function and refuses to substitute for the preaching of the kingdom of God a proclamation of liberation of the merely human order. She declares that her advocacy of liberation would not be complete or perfect if she failed to preach salvation in Jesus Christ (*EN*, no. 34).[32]

This priority or primacy of evangelization over action in favor of justice is also affirmed by many evangelical churches. The Lausanne Covenant (1974) declared

---

[31] International Theological Commission, *Declaration on Human Development and Christian Salvation*; English text in Hennelly, *Liberation Theology*, 214.

[32] See also John Paul II's *RM*, no. 20: "The church contributes to mankind's pilgrimage of conversion to God's plan through her witness and through such activities as dialogue, human promotion, commitment to justice and peace, education and the care of the sick, and aid to the poor and to children. In carrying on these activities, however, she never loses sight of the priority of the transcendent and spiritual realities which are premises of eschatological salvation."

that "in the Church's mission of sacrificial service evangelism is primary."[33] The Lausanne Committee on World Evangelization and World Evangelical Fellowship (1982) clarified further the relationship between evangelization and social action and the primacy of the former over the latter. There are, in its view, at least three possible ways of viewing the relationship between evangelization and social action. First, social activity is a *consequence* or even one of the principal *goals* of evangelism. The weakness of this view is that in practice social activity does not always follow evangelism, as the history of mission abundantly shows. Second, social activity can be a *bridge* to evangelism; that is, missionaries can move from the temporal needs of the people to their deeper need of their relationship to God. The danger of this view is that mission runs the risk of making "rice Christians." Third, social activity not only follows evangelism as its consequences and aim, and precedes it as a bridge, but also accompanies it as its *partner*. Social activity and evangelism are carried out in tandem as the two blades of a pair of scissors or the two wings of a bird. Neither is the other but the one cannot be done without the other.[34]

With regard to the primacy of evangelization, the committee makes it clear that it refers to a *logical* primacy and not a *temporal* one, since in some situations social ministry may demand precedence. It is, of course, rare, if ever, that one has to choose between satisfying a person's temporal needs and his or her eternal salvation. Nevertheless, the committee affirms that "if we must choose, then we have to say that the supreme and ultimate need of all humankind is the saving grace of Jesus Christ and that therefore a person's eternal, spiritual salvation is of greater importance than his or her temporal or material well-being."[35]

From a practical point of view, it must be said that the recent emphasis on action on behalf of social justice and peace as an integral and constitutive element of the church's evangelizing mission represents a momentous reversal of the medieval paradigm of mission with its spiritualizing and individualizing concept of salvation. On the other hand, the affirmation of the non-identity between social action and evangelization is a necessary corrective to the Enlightenment's understanding and practice of mission with its emphasis on social transformation as the condition or result of the kingdom of God. However, the insistence on the priority of evangelization over social action, of eternal and spiritual salvation over temporal and material well-being, seems to me to be a relic of a dualistic mentality that has been plaguing both the Roman Catholic and evangelical churches. As long as one maintains the superiority of the salvation of the soul over the well-being of the body, one runs the risk of negating in practice the concept of "integral," "total," "comprehensive" salvation of the whole person and of all persons that is one of the great contributions of contemporary soteriology.

---

[33] The Lausanne Covenant, in *New Directions in Mission and Evangelization*, vol. 1, *Basic Statements 1974-1991*, ed. James Scherer and Stephen Bevans (Maryknoll, N.Y.: Orbis Books, 1992), 256.

[34] See ibid., 278-79.

[35] Ibid., 280.

However the precise relationship between evangelization and liberation is conceived, there is no doubt whatsoever that for the FABC the work for socio-political and economic liberation assumes a key priority in the church's activities in Asia, given the presence of massive and dehumanizing poverty among the Asian peoples. The emphasis on the "preferential love of the poor," on the duty of solidarity with the oppressed and marginalized, especially the migrants and refugees, overseas workers, tribal peoples, children, and women is a constant refrain sounding through all the FABC's documents. The Asian Synod and the ensuing apostolic exhortation of John Paul II return with insistence to the theme of human promotion and of building a "civilization of love, founded upon the universal values of peace, justice, solidarity and freedom, which find their fulfillment in Christ" (*EA*, no. 32). In particular, attention is drawn to the tasks of protecting the life of the unborn, providing health care, promoting education, fostering peace, preventing marginalization caused by globalization, canceling foreign debts, and safeguarding the environment (see *EA*, nos. 35-41).

Dialogue with Cultures and Mission

From its very beginnings Christian mission has always sought to incarnate the good news in the cultures of the peoples it evangelized. It did this not only by translating its sacred texts into their languages but also by "adapting" its message to their cultures. Popes such as Gregory the Great in the sixth century and Benedict XV in the twentieth century are widely known for their instructions on how missionaries should behave with regard to local cultures. Also of extraordinary significance is the instruction given in 1659 by the Sacred Congregation for the Propagation of the Faith (founded in 1622) to the vicars apostolic of Tonkin and Cochinchina (Bishops François Pallu and Lambert de la Motte, respectively). The instruction lists the qualities required of missionaries (especially the readiness to adapt themselves to the mentality and customs of others) and directs the bishops to prepare local clergy and even candidates for the episcopacy, to avoid introducing Western customs, and to practice evangelical poverty:

> Do not attempt in any way, and do not on any pretext persuade these people to change their rites, habits and customs, unless they are openly opposed to religion and good morals. For what could be more absurd than to bring France, Spain, Italy or any other European country to China? It is not your country but the faith you must bring, that faith which does not reject or belittle the rites or customs of any nation as long as these rites are not evil, but rather desires that they be preserved in their integrity and fostered. It is, as it were, written in the nature of all men that the customs of their country and especially their country itself should be esteemed, loved and respected above anything else in the world. . . . Never make comparisons between the customs of these peoples and those of Europe; on the contrary show your anxiety to become used to them. Admire and

praise whatever merits praise. As regards what is not praiseworthy, while it must not be extolled as is done by flatterers, you will be prudent enough not to pass judgement on it, or, in any case, not to condemn it rashly and exaggeratedly. As for what is evil, it should be dismissed by a nod of the head or by silence rather than by words, without losing the occasions, when souls have become disposed to receive the truth, to uproot it imperceptibly.[36]

These instructions are all the more remarkable because they were given at the height of colonialism. Sadly, the history of missions in East Asia as well as elsewhere shows that these instructions were not always followed, as is evidenced by what is known as the Chinese Rites Controversy. Protestant missions were not much better on this score, even though theoretically there was talk of the "three selfs" as the aim of mission, formulated by Rufus Anderson and Henry Venn, that is, self-government, self-support, and self-propagation.

But even when there was an attempt at indigenizing Christianity, such enterprise remained rather superficial. Expressions used for this process are adaptation and accommodation. Accommodation to local cultures still was predicated on the premise that Western theology should be regarded as the universal norm. It was a concession to native theologians to use some of the good or at best neutral elements of their cultures to express the faith. It was felt that the "young" churches alone need to undertake such adaptation and not the "older" churches that already possess a permanently valid theology and structures and therefore have nothing to learn from the former. In this process of accommodation only unessential elements of the faith (the "husk") can be changed, whereas the core (the "kernel") must remain unaltered. Lastly, the initiative was often taken by the benevolent missionaries and not the natives themselves.[37]

What has brought about a radical change in the understanding of the task of inculturating the gospel is the realization, fueled by the new sciences of sociology of knowledge and cultural anthropology, that every knowledge is contextualized, and hence every theology is a local theology. Today, it is widely accepted that every text is an interpreted text; that the text is not simply "out there" to be interpreted but "becomes" as we engage with it; that the reader, in some sense, "creates" the text in reading it; and that such a hermeneutic act is not only a literary but also a socio-political and an economic exercise.

It is this epistemological break, as this new approach to knowledge has been called, that lies at the basis of every contemporary attempt at contextualizing, indigenizing, localizing, or inculturating Christianity. Liberation theology itself can be regarded as a form of inculturating Christianity into the Third World in which the praxis of solidarity with the poor and the oppressed is an essential

---

[36] Joseph Neuner and Jacques Dupuis, eds., *The Christian Faith in the Doctrinal Documents of the Catholic Church* (New York: Alba House, 1982), 309-10.

[37] For a critique of this process of accommodation, see Bosch, *Transforming Mission*, 448-50.

element, indeed the first act, of the method of doing theology, which is the second act.

Besides liberation theology, which privileges the economic and socio-political aspects of human existence, there are other attempts at inculturating Christianity that, though not unsympathetic to liberation theology's starting point, focus more specifically on the cultures of the peoples. By *culture* we mean the entire complex of symbols and values (as well as those things not valued) that humans create in their relationship with nature, with each other, and with God. Culture is a dynamic and ever-changing reality, continually shaped and reshaped by the ongoing experiences of the people. Continually subjected to new developments, it is transmitted by tradition from generation to generation. At the heart of culture is religion, whereby people affirm or reject their relationship with God.[38]

The need for inculturating the gospel has been affirmed by recent popes. Pope Paul VI, who at first wavered between adaptation and inculturation, resolutely came down for the second alternative when he said: "Evangelization is to be achieved, not from without as though by adding some decoration or applying a coat of color, but in depth, going to the very center and roots of life. The Gospel must impregnate the culture and the whole way of life of man" (*EN*, no. 20).[39] John Paul II specifies further:

Through inculturation the church makes the gospel incarnate in different cultures and at the same time introduces peoples, together with their cultures, into her community. She transmits to them her own values, at the same time taking the good elements that already exist in them and renewing them from within. Through inculturation the church, for her part, becomes a more intelligible sign of what she is and a more effective instrument of mission.

Thanks to this action within the local churches, the universal church herself is enriched with forms of expression and values in the various sectors of Christian life such as evangelization, worship, theology and charitable works. . . . Missionaries, who come from other churches and countries, must immerse themselves in the cultural milieu of those to whom they are sent, moving beyond their cultural limitations. . . . It is not of

---

[38] For a discussion of culture, see Robert Schreiter, *Constructing Local Theologies* (Maryknoll, N.Y.: Orbis Books, 1985), 39-74; and Leonardo Boff, *New Evangelization*, 3-13.

[39] Also important is his earlier speech given to the African bishops assembled in Kampala, Uganda, in 1969. He says: "The expression, that is, the language and mode of manifesting this one Faith, may be manifold; hence, it may be original, suited to the tongue, the style, the genius, and the culture, of the one who professes this one Faith. From this point of view, a certain pluralism is not only legitimate, but desirable. An adaptation of the Christian life in the fields of pastoral, ritual, didactic and spiritual activities is not only possible, it is even favored by the Church. The liturgical renewal is a living example of this. And in this sense you may, and you must, have an African Christianity" *(Acta Apostolicae Sedis* 66 [1969], 57).

course a matter of missionaries renouncing their own cultural identity, but of understanding, appreciating, fostering and evangelizing the culture of the environment in which they are working (*RM*, nos. 52-53).

There is little doubt that the FABC has made inculturation one of the central concerns of the Asian churches. Document after document vigorously stresses the absolute necessity of a dialogue with Asian cultures as a way for the Christian churches to become local churches: "*True inculturation*, far from being a tactic for the propagation of the faith, belongs to the very core of evangelization, for it is the continuation in time and space of the dialogue of salvation initiated by God and brought to a culmination when he uttered his Word in a very concrete historical situation."[40]

In the previous chapter I listed agreements between Catholic and Protestant official documents on the nature and scope of inculturation. Here it may be helpful to expand them further by focusing on the Asian churches' understanding of inculturation as this is crystallized in the Asian Synod and the apostolic exhortation *Ecclesia in Asia*. Synthesizing the Asian bishops' discussion of this theme during the synod, John Paul II first of all emphasizes both the strict connection and distinction between evangelization and inculturation:

Evangelization and inculturation are naturally and intimately related to each other. The Gospel and evangelization are certainly not identical with culture; they are independent of it. Yet the kingdom of God comes to people who are fundamentally linked to a culture, and the building of the kingdom cannot avoid borrowing elements form human cultures (*EA*, no. 21).

Second, the pope reiterates a point that "was said repeatedly during the synod: that the Holy Spirit is the prime agent of the inculturation of the Christian faith in Asia" (*EA*, no. 21). This emphasis on the agency of the Holy Spirit not only allows the necessary freedom to carry out the project of inculturation but also "the Spirit's presence ensures that the dialogue unfolds in truth, honesty, humility and respect" (*EA*, no. 21).

Third, the Asian bishops and the pope envisage inculturation carried out in all areas of the church's life and activities, including theology, especially in the area of Christology, liturgy, biblical studies, and the formation of evangelizers. Here four criteria for an authentic inculturation are given: (1) "compatibility with the Gospel," (2) "communion with the faith of the universal church," (3) "full compliance with the church's tradition," and (4) "a view to strengthening people's faith" (*EA*, no. 22).

Finally, there is a strong emphasis on the necessity of the participation of all the people of God in the project of inculturation, in particular the laity: "A

---

[40] *For All the Peoples of Asia,* 1:94. See also "Dialogue Between Faith and Cultures in Asia: Towards Integral Human and Social Development," in *For All the Peoples of Asia,* 2:21-26.

wider inculturation of the gospel at every level of society in Asia will depend greatly on the appropriate formation which the local churches succeed in giving to the laity" (*EA*, no. 22).

Dialogue with Non-Christian Religions and Mission

The most recent challenge to evangelization, especially in Asia, is interreligious dialogue. The issue was not discussed by Paul VI in his important apostolic exhortation *Evangelii nuntiandi*. John Paul II was the first pope to deal with this issue, which he did in his December 1990 encyclical on mission, *Redemptoris missio* (nos. 55-57). Six months later the Pontifical Council for Inter-religious Dialogue and the Congregation for the Evangelization of Peoples issued *Dialogue and Proclamation*. Because the draft of *Redemptoris missio* was kept secret from the writers of the joint statement, there is no reference in the joint statement to the encyclical's teaching on interreligious dialogue and mission. Nevertheless, the document explicitly states that it must be read in light of the encyclical. Indeed, the statement offers a more detailed and nuanced treatment than the encyclical.

Vatican II's explicit acknowledgment of the presence of positive values in non-Christian religious traditions and attribution of these values to the active presence of God through the Word and the Spirit inevitably raise the question of whether evangelization has not been replaced by interreligious dialogue. In answer to this question John Paul II unequivocally affirms:

Interreligious dialogue is part of the church's evangelizing mission. Understood as a method and means of mutual knowledge and enrichment, dialogue is not opposed to the mission *ad gentes*; indeed it has special links with that mission and is one of its expressions. . . . Dialogue should be conducted and implemented with the conviction that the church is the ordinary means of salvation and that she alone possesses the fullness of the means of salvation (*RM*, no. 55).

Dialogue and Proclamation reinforces this position:

Interreligious dialogue and proclamation, though not on the same level, are both authentic elements of the Church's evangelizing mission. Both are legitimate and necessary. They are intimately related, but not interchangeable: true interreligious dialogue on the part of the Christian supposes the desires to make Jesus Christ better known, recognized and loved, proclaiming Jesus Christ is to be carried out in the Gospel spirit of dialogue. The two activities remain distinct but, as experience shows, one and the same local church, one and the same person, can be diversely engaged in both (*DP*, no. 77).

As mentioned above, interreligious dialogue can take four different forms: (1) the dialogue of *life*, in which people of different faiths bear witness before one another in daily life to their own human and religious values and in this way enrich one another's lives; (2) dialogue of *action*, in which Christians and others collaborate for the integral development and liberation of people; (3) dialogue of *theological exchange* in which experts seek to understand and appreciate the teachings of their respective religions; and (4) dialogue of *religious experience,* in which persons rooted in their own religious traditions share with one another their spiritual riches (see *RM,* no. 57; *DP,* nos. 42-46).

In this interreligious dialogue how should Christians look upon other religions? Current theological literature speaks of three possible positions: exclusivism, inclusivism, and pluralism.[41] The exclusivist position affirms that only in Jesus can true revelation and salvation be found, the Christ event being constitutive of any authentic encounter with God, always and everywhere. The inclusivist position affirms the uniqueness of Jesus without denying that God's saving presence may also be operative in other religions. Proponents of this view, however, insist that Christ includes other religions, either by being present in them anonymously or by fulfilling them as their goal. Jesus remains, if not constitutive of, at least normative for, all religious experience. Finally, the pluralistic position affirms that Jesus is unique, but his uniqueness includes and is included by other potentially equal religious founders. It views Jesus as neither constitutive of nor normative for authentic religious experience, but as theocentric, that is, as universally relevant manifestation, incarnation, and sacrament of God's revelation and salvation in history.[42]

My position is that neither the exclusivist nor the pluralist view does justice to the faith of the Catholic church. The former ignores the presence of the Spirit of Christ and divine grace in other religions explicitly recognized by Vatican II and other later magisterial documents. The latter suffers from relativism that vitiates the very enterprise of interreligious dialogue. The inclusivist position, in my judgment, holds in fruitful tension two basic truths of the Christian faith, namely, the universal salvific will of God and the necessary mediation of Jesus Christ in the salvation of every individual. It is also the position that makes interreligious dialogue possible, because on the one hand it commits the partners in dialogue to their respective faith traditions (hence it takes differences seriously, differences the partners try to understand and possibly overcome)

---

[41] See, for example, Alan Race, *Christians and Religious Pluralism: Patterns in the Christian Theology of Religions* (Maryknoll, N.Y.: Orbis Books, 1983); Paul F. Knitter, *No Other Names? A Critical Survey of Christian Attitudes toward the World Religions* (Maryknoll, N.Y.: Orbis Books, 1985); and Gavin D'Costa, *Theology and Religious Pluralism: The Challenge of Other Religions* (Oxford: Basil Blackwell, 1986). In a recent work Paul Knitter refines this threefold categorization by distinguishing four models of the theology of religions: the "replacement" model ("only one true religion"), the "fulfillment" model ("the one fulfills the many"), the "mutuality" model ("many true religions called to dialogue"), and the "acceptance" model ("many true religions: so be it") (see *Introducing Theologies of Religions* [Maryknoll, N.Y.: Orbis Books, 2002]).

[42] See Peter C. Phan, "Are There Other 'Saviors' for Other Peoples?" in *Christianity and the Wider Ecumenism*, ed. Peter C. Phan (New York: Paragon House, 1990), 163-80.

and on the other hand it recognizes that truth and goodness may be present in religious traditions other than one's own. Such an inclusivism will have to make a clear distinction between the claim for the universality and uniqueness of Jesus and that for the necessary instrumental role of the church, between the affirmation of Jesus as the universal and unique Savior as a faith-claim and the claim for the universality of Christianity as a historical and factual statement. Hence, there is the need to combine a "high" Christology with a "low" ecclesiology.[43] Furthermore, this "inclusivist pluralism," to use Jacques Dupuis's expression, needs to develop a robust trinitarian Christology and pneumatology as its theological underpinnings, as these have been developed by Dupuis himself.[44]

A final question must still be addressed: If interreligious dialogue and proclamation of the lordship of Christ are not mutually contradictory and if one does not supplant the other, is interreligious dialogue simply a means for evangelization or perhaps pre-evangelization, or is it evangelization itself? Following Jacques Dupuis, I would argue that interreligious dialogue is a form of evangelization in its own right and not merely a moment preceding or a means for evangelization. In certain situations it may be the only form of evangelization possible, besides personal witness to Jesus as Lord in one's daily life. Whether and when interreligious dialogue leads to an explicit proclamation of the lordship of Christ cannot be determined in advance by the Christian partners in dialogue but must be left to the guidance and action of the Holy Spirit.[45]

Finally, it must be pointed out that interreligious dialogue can also be a moment of mutual evangelization in the sense that not only the Christian partners in dialogue share their ideas and values with adherents of other religions but also the latter can challenge the former to purify and correct their own beliefs and values as well as enrich them with beliefs and values that may not be present in Christianity, at least not to the extent in which they are found in other religions.[46]

---

[43] See ibid., 163-80; see also Peter C. Phan, "The Claim of Uniqueness and Universality in Interreligious Dialogue," *Indian Theological Studies* 31/1 (1994), 44-66.

[44] See Jacques Dupuis, *Toward a Christian Theology of Religious Pluralism* (Maryknoll, N.Y.: Orbis Books, 1997); idem, "Le pluralisme religieux dans le plan divin du salut," *Revue théologique de Louvain* 29 (1998), 484-505; and idem, "L'Esprit-Saint répandu sur le monde: Fondement du dialogue interreligieux," *Lumen Vitae* 53 (1998), 57-66.

[45] See Jacques Dupuis, *Jesus Christ at the Encounter of World Religions* (Maryknoll, N.Y.: Orbis Books, 1991), 207-29.

[46] See ibid., 207-29.

3

Proclamation of the Reign of God as Mission of the Church

WHAT FOR, TO WHOM, BY WHOM, WITH WHOM, AND HOW?

The title of this chapter contains four key terms and the subtitle five questions. The answers to the five questions, at least prior to Vatican II, were obvious and simple, and could be given by any tolerably informed Catholic, or Protestant for that matter: Mission is (1) the church's work for the salvation of souls, (2) carried out for the benefit of the pagans abroad, (3) mainly by priests, religious brothers, nuns, and specially commissioned layfolk, mostly from Europe and America, (4) with the financial and spiritual support of the laity back home, and (5) by planting the church in these "mission fields." These answers were readily accepted as a matter of course because there was a common agreement on what was meant by *mission;* it was understood as the *foreign mission*, or *missio ad gentes*, to use a Latin expression, that is, mission in Africa, Asia, Latin America, and Oceania, all the continents except Europe and North America, which were considered already Christianized. To these foreign lands missionaries—generous and committed Christians with a romantic love of adventure, a heavy endowment of survival skills, and perhaps a touch of eccentricity—were sent (that is the meaning of *missionary* in Latin), and they would spend their entire lives there, amid the semi-literate and semi-clad natives, with an occasional trip home to regale their audiences with tales about conversions and mortal dangers, not averse to a bit of melodrama to shake loose the listeners' purses in support of the missions.

That was how mission was understood and practiced up to approximately thirty years ago. But now things have changed, and changed utterly. The change from the enthusiasm and optimism of the World Missionary Conference that met in Edinburgh, Scotland, in 1910—whose catchy slogan was "The evangelization of the world in this generation"—to the discouragement and even pessimism in today's missionary circles, Catholic and Protestant alike, is visible and palpable. The factors contributing to this widespread malaise are many. For one thing, geographical shifts in the 1950s and 1960s, especially the ending of European colonialism and the gaining of political independence by many African and Asian peoples, placed in serious jeopardy Christian mission, which began in massive numbers and in a systematic fashion in the sixteenth century and reached its apogee in the nineteenth and twentieth centuries, often marching in locked steps with the Western colonial enterprise. To the consternation of Western missionaries, the shout "Missionary, go home" was raised in the 1960s, to be followed a decade later by the demand for a moratorium on Christian missions from the West.

In addition to the political factors, the collapse of mission as we knew it was also caused by the unexpected resurgence of the so-called non-Christian religions, in particular Hinduism and Islam. The missionaries' rosy predictions of their early demise were vastly premature. Concomitant with this phenomenon is the current intense awareness of religious pluralism, which advocates several distinct, independent, and equally valid ways to reach the Divine and therefore makes conversion from one religion to another, which was considered the goal of mission, unnecessary. Last, and perhaps most important, there is the rise of what has been termed postmodernity, an umbrella label to describe sundry and diverse movements in contemporary thought that deconstruct and reject the claim to universal validity of any historical, philosophical, and theological system such as Christianity. Stripped of this claim Christianity—and for that matter, any religion with universalistic tendencies—would lose the raison d'être for its missionary endeavor.[1]

In what follows I will not focus on these extra-theological factors that have in one way or another contributed to the collapse of Christian mission. Rather, I contend that what has shattered our centuries-long consensus about mission and the conventional answers to the five questions raised above is a new theology of mission that views the relations among the four key terms—proclamation, reign of God, church, and mission—in a radically different way. This new way of conceiving the reciprocal relationships among these four theological realities is predicated upon a different way of conceiving their priorities. If a rather simplistic summary may be permitted, the "old theology" prioritizes these four realities in this descending order of importance: church, proclamation, mission, reign of God. The "new theology" prioritizes them in just the opposite order: reign of God, mission, proclamation, and church. Let it be noted at once that it is not a question of denying any of these four realities, whether in the old theology of mission or in the new. Indeed, all the four elements are present in both theologies, but in very different modes of emphasis and degrees of importance. Consequently, the answers to the five questions concerning Christian mission— what for, to whom, by whom, with whom, and how—are given very differently by the two theologies. And because they answer these five questions differently, the two theologies of mission are not harmless intellectual games. On the contrary, they determine, to descend to pedestrian matters, the way budgets are

---

[1] For a brief analysis of the factors contributing to the collapse of Christian mission, see Thomas Thangaraj, *The Common Task: A Theology of Christian Mission* (Nashville, Tenn.: Abingdon Press, 1999), 16-26; and Richard G. Cote, *Re-Visioning Mission: The Catholic Church and Culture in Postmodern America* (New York: Paulist Press, 1996), 3-19.

planned, which projects get funded, whether churches or social centers are built, and of course, how power is exercised and by whom.

I now delineate the ways in which these two theologies of mission conceive the relations among the four central realities of the Christian faith—reign of God, mission, proclamation, and church—and how within each theological purview the five questions concerning mission are answered. I illustrate my presentation with examples taken from the history of mission.

MISSION DEFINED BY CHURCH

In his monumental study of mission the late South African missiologist David Bosch argued that the Roman Catholic understanding of mission from 600 to 1500 was characterized by two basic concerns: saving souls and church extension.[2] The first goal of mission is dependent upon Augustine's view of humanity, which he developed in opposition to Pelagius, as radically corrupted by sin, both original and personal. This anthropology entails that missionaries focus their work on saving "lost souls," which in the mission fields are identical with the "heathens," that is, the unbaptized. In this perspective mission is narrowed down to ensuring the individual's eternal destiny, and other elements of the church's mission—such as the transformation of the economic, social, and political structures, dialogue with other religions, and engagement with the local cultures—are set aside as secondary or neglected.

Another Augustinian doctrine also determines the second goal of mission. In his dispute with the Donatists, who insisted that only those who were totally unblemished and perfect could be church members, Augustine emphasized that what is essential is not the personal moral and spiritual condition of Christians but the church and its official institutions. These are the means of salvation. This doctrine coheres well with an earlier teaching of Saint Cyprian, namely, there is no salvation outside the church *(extra ecclesiam nulla salus)*. Again, this ecclesiology entails that missionaries will concentrate their efforts on bringing as many "pagans" as possible into the church, the only ark of salvation, by blandishments and conquest if necessary. Baptism was changed from a process of the individual's gradual incorporation into the church after a long and arduous moral and spiritual training (the ancient catechumenate) into a rite of entrance of the mass, sometimes the whole tribe, into the church with a minimum of catechesis and often without real conversion. Once baptized, the new Christians become the objects of ecclesiastical control and guidance. Hence, it is necessary to set up church structures as soon as possible in the missionary fields, a process known as "planting the church" *(plantatio ecclesiae)*, which now becomes the second, and even the overriding goal of mission, on which most of the resources and energies of the missionary labor is spent. Consequently, the success of mission, not unlike the body count in war, is measured by the number

---

[2] See David Bosch, *Transforming Mission: Paradigm Shifts in Theology of Mission* (Maryknoll, N.Y.: Orbis Books, 1991), 214-19.

of the sacraments administered, dioceses established, churches built, and money collected.

There were, of course, missionaries who did not think that "saving souls" and "church planting" were the only or even the main goals of mission, and acted accordingly. My point here is not to evaluate the missionary enterprise of the last four centuries but to outline the theology of mission that served as its engine. In this theology, in which salvation is both individualized and ecclesiasticized, the center and heart of the missionary project is the church, and church understood primarily in the institutional model.[3] This is clear in both Protestant and Catholic circles. For example, Gustav Warneck (1834-1910), the foremost Protestant missiologist, has stated explicitly: "By Christian mission we understand the entire activity of Christendom that is directed to the planting and organization of the Church of Christ among non-Christians."[4] Similarly, even though he emphasized individual conversion, Josef Schmidlin (1876-1944), widely regarded as the first Catholic missiologist, believed that conversion is only a preliminary goal; the ultimate goal, for him, is to bring the individual into the organized church, which Schmidlin identified with the kingdom of God.[5] The planting of the church is also strongly emphasized in the so-called Louvain School (led by Pierre Charles and Jacques Masson), which viewed conversion as only the means to the goal of mission, which is the extension of the visible church.

In practice, the planting of the church in mission lands followed what has been called the "reduplication model."[6] That is, the missionaries sought to transplant or reproduce in another culture the type of church of their origins, with its organizational structure, laws, ways of worship, and theology. And since these elements of their original churches were tightly woven with European culture, mission often meant Europeanization. Even the enlightened Schmidlin thought that conversion of the natives required them to leave their cultures and adopt Western civilization, with its nobler "moral precepts," "better methods of work," and "higher culture." Already in the seventeenth century Jesuit missionary Alexandre de Rhodes noted, with deep regret, that Indian converts were required to dress like Portuguese and Chinese male converts to cut their long hair.[7]

In light of this mission theology we are in a better position to elaborate the answers it gave to the five questions mentioned above. (1) What is mission for? It is to save individual souls and to establish churches for this purpose in foreign lands, outside of Europe and North America. The emphasis was on their moral

---

[3] On the institutional model of the church, see Avery Dulles, *Models of the Church* (Garden City, N.Y.: Doubleday, 1974), 31-42.

[4] Gustav Warneck, *Evangelische Missionslehre: Ein missionstheologischer Versuch*, 3 vols. (Gotha: Friedrich Andreas Perthes, 1905), 1:1.

[5] See Josef Schmidlin, *Catholic Mission Theory*, trans. Matthias Braun (Techny, Ill.: Mission Press, S.V.D., 1931).

[6] See Wilbert R. Shenk, *Changing Frontiers of Mission* (Maryknoll, N.Y.: Orbis Books, 1999), 51-53.

[7] See Peter C. Phan, *Mission and Catechesis: Alexandre de Rhodes and Inculturation in Seventeenth-Century Vietnam* (Maryknoll, N.Y.: Orbis Books, 1998), 42-43, 81.

and spiritual welfare, even though their material well-being was not neglected, especially by means of education, health care, and social services. (2) To whom? Mission is to the "pagans," who were living outside the sphere of God's grace and on the way to eternal damnation. The "pagans" are the objects of the missionary's conversionary efforts (not the subjects with whom the missionary can enter into dialogue). Their religions are superstitions that they must abjure and reject in order to convert to the only true religion, that is, Christianity. (3) By whom? Mission is conducted mostly by special agents, such as priests, members of religious orders, both male and female, and some elite laity. All of these agents must be especially commissioned by the hierarchical church that sends and controls them, especially through the Sacred Congregation for the Propagation of the Faith (founded in 1622 by Pope Gregory XV, with a triple purpose: propagation of the faith, preservation of the Catholic faith, and dialogue with other Christian churches). (4) With whom? Certainly not with other Christians, especially Protestants, who are competing with Catholic missionaries for members among the pagans; not with the local churches, which are still immature. The immediate collaborators of the missionaries are the layfolk back home who support them with prayers and money and who try to raise other missionary vocations. Finally, (5) How? Mission means planting churches, that is, replicating the Western church models. (This strategy was adopted not only because Western culture was considered superior but also to ensure "unity," that is, uniformity, in the church).

From these answers it is clear that in this ecclesiocentric theology of mission the other three elements of the Christian faith—proclamation, mission, reign of God—were given short shrift. They were all subordinated to the church, which gave them meaning and purpose. Proclamation was subordinated, at least in Catholicism, to the sacraments, since it is the sacraments that admit the "pagans" into the church and make them dependent on the hierarchy. Ironically, mission too was neglected, since it is only an extremely small group of Christians that were missionaries; the church as a whole was not seen as missionary by nature, as Vatican II was to put it later on. Furthermore, the church was divided into the sending church and the receiving church, with the latter as the object of the former's missionary activities. Finally, the reign of God, especially its prophetic and eschatological dimensions, were practically forgotten; it was identified with the church in its current form.

CHURCH DEFINED BY MISSION

By the 1950s, with the colonial empires in ruins, independence movements in full swing, science and technology advancing, and with them, the worldwide process of secularization, and reform rumblings in the church, the old theology of mission underwent a severe crisis. It was seen as a model no longer suited for the emerging world order. For one thing, the frontiers that demarcated the "Christian" from the "non-Christian" lands, the "saved" from the "heathens," were becoming blurred. The "Christianized" West had become "dechristianized," so that in 1943 a book could be published with the shocking title *France: pays de mission?* Also, in the West Christians rub shoulders daily with Buddhists, Hindus, Muslims, and adherents of other religions. But a crisis is both danger and opportunity. The danger of extinction threatening the old theology of mission became an opportunity for a new theology of mission to be born, in which a quiet revolution took place. What had been at the periphery now occupied the central position. Or, to use another image, there was a topsy-turvy motion: What was on top fell to the bottom. What was first became last, and what was last became first, as a gospel saying goes.

First of all, there was a total reconfiguration of the relations among the four basic elements of the theology of mission. Now the central pillar sustaining the missionary edifice is the reign of God; it is the light that shines on all missionary activities of the church, which is now seen to be missionary by its very nature. Next, the mission of the church flows from the fact that it is a sign of and instrument for the reign of God, and therefore the church cannot be simply identified with the reign of God as such, in spite of the many links that unite the two. Then comes proclamation, which is seen as only *a part,* necessary but not dominant, of a complex of activities of the church. Last comes the church with its role as servant, not master, of mission. Like John the Baptist in front of Jesus, it has to say: "The reign of God must increase, and I must decrease."

Second, in light of this reconfiguration the five questions concerning mission receive different answers. (1) What for? For the full realization of the kingdom of God, which is already but not yet, present and future, realized and eschatological. (2) To whom? To the whole world in all its dimensions and arenas, including the cosmos, and to "pagans," who are not really pagan, and to "Christians," who are not really Christian. (3) By whom? By God, first of all, because the church's mission is nothing but a continuation of God's mission; and second, by all, hierarchy and laity, even though some are more engaged in "missionary" activities than others. (4) With whom? With all Christians, not only with Catholics, without denominational confrontation and competition; furthermore, with the followers of other religions as well, since they too are called to the reign of God, even though not all of them will join the church. Finally, (5) How? By personal witness and dialogue. A few words on each of the four elements of Christian mission in this new configuration and on each of these five answers are in order.

The Reign of God

Recent biblical scholarship has demonstrated the centrality of the reign of God in Jesus' ministry.[8] It is the heart of his preaching: "The time is fulfilled,

---

[8] For recent bibliography on the kingdom of God, see Peter C. Phan, "Kingdom of God: A Theological Symbol for Asians?" *Gregorianum* 79/2 (1998), 295-422. For a detailed study of the kingdom of God from the New Testament perspective, see John P. Meier, *A Marginal Jew: Rethinking the Historical Jesus,* vol. 2: *Mentor, Message, and Miracles* (New York: Doubleday, 1994), 237-506. For helpful reflections on the relationship between the kingdom of God and the church, see the works of John Fuellenbach, *The Kingdom of God: Jesus' Central Message* (Maryknoll, N.Y.: Orbis Books, 1995);

and the kingdom of God has come near, repent, and believe in the good news" (Mk 1:15). Many of his parables speak of the kingdom of God, and his miraculous deeds are signs that the kingdom of God that he was announcing had indeed arrived. This kingdom is said to be of God because its arrival signals the gracious, forgiving, and redeeming presence of Yahweh in the world; it is not the fruit of human efforts. This kingdom is open to all, and all are invited to enter into it, but it is given especially or "preferentially" to those who are marginalized, that is, the poor, the afflicted, the oppressed, the captives (Lk 4:18).

Jesus embodied in his person the reign of God he proclaimed: "Today this scripture has been fulfilled in your hearing," declared Jesus, referring to Isaiah 61:1-2, which he had just read from the scroll. In this sense the kingdom of God is a present reality. God's saving power and complete and perfect self-revelation in the future was already assured in the preaching, and above all, in the death and resurrection of Jesus. The eschatological events of Jesus' death/resurrection are a powerful validation by God of Jesus' message about God's power over sin, corruption, injustice, and violence. God's rule will be characterized by universal peace, justice, and love, and it is already here. In this sense the kingdom of God is professed to be "the eternal kingdom of our Lord and Savior Jesus Christ" (2 Pt 1:11), and to proclaim the kingdom of God is necessarily to proclaim the Christ-event. The two proclamations, which throw light on each other, cannot be separated.

On the other hand, there are sayings and gestures on Jesus' part that indicate that somehow this kingdom of God is still to come, or more precisely, that its full and complete self-realization and manifestation awaits a future time.[9] That is why he taught his disciples to pray for the coming of the kingdom. In his farewell dinner with his disciples he said that he had been longing to eat that Passover with them before he suffered, and that he would not eat it again "until it is fulfilled in the kingdom of God" and that he would not drink wine again "until the kingdom of God comes" (Lk 22:16-18). As a result his disciples and their immediate followers were acutely aware of Jesus' imminent return in glory, the parousia, perhaps within their lifetime. Even though the parousia did not occur in the way they anticipated, this expectation of Jesus' so-called Second Coming was not rejected. Indeed, the creed continues to proclaim that Jesus will "come again to judge the living and the dead." Needless to say, with the passage of time the fervor of the expectation did grow dim, and the symbol of the kingdom of God did eclipse and was eventually replaced by other less tension-filled and historically relevant images and ideas.[10]

---

idem, *Proclaiming His Kingdom* (Manila: Logos Publications, 1994); and idem, *Church: Community for the Kingdom* (Manila: Logos Publications, 2000).

[9] For various ways of understanding the time of the reign of God, see Peter C. Phan, *Eternity in Time: A Study of Karl Rahner's Eschatology* (Selinsgrove, Pa.: Susquehanna University Press, 1987), 26-31.

[10] Some of these ideas include: (1) the idea of the encounter of the dying with Christ the Judge in the afterlife. (2) the idea of a spiritual-mystical union between the immortal soul and Christ the Spouse; (3) the idea that the kingdom of God is a purely future, supernatural, otherworldly, and apolitical reality; and (4) the idea that the kingdom is identical with the historical church.

In a certain but true sense the mission that God has given to Jesus to perform is not yet completed, since history is still going on. The body of Christ is still growing and will continue to grow until the end of time. Like Paul, every Christian must say: "In my own flesh I am completing what is lacking in Christ's afflictions for the sake of his body, that is, the church" (Col 1:24). It is precisely in this in-between time, that is, between the ministry-death-resurrection of Jesus and his parousia, that the church was born, and it is within this time that its mission is to be carried out. The church has no self-identity except as rooted in and derived from the mission that Jesus received from his Father. And given the centrality of the reign of God in Jesus' mission, as we have observed above, it would be theologically wrong to subordinate the reign of God to the church, as was done in the old theology of mission. On the contrary, the church must be subordinated to and oriented toward the reign of God, which is its goal and raison d'être.

It is most interesting that in his 1990 encyclical *Redemptoris missio,* which together with Paul VI's *Evangelii nuntiandi* (1975), is widely regarded as the Magna Carta of Catholic mission, John Paul II places the theme of the reign of God immediately after speaking of Jesus as the only savior and devotes a long chapter to it, which by itself is a theologically significant departure from the old theology of mission. John Paul affirms that "the proclamation and establishment of God's kingdom are the purposes of his [Jesus'] mission" (*RM,* no. 13). Similarly, in his apostolic exhortation *Ecclesia in Asia,* which focuses on Christian mission in Asia, the pope also makes Jesus and his realization of the kingdom of God the starting point and ground of the church's mission in this continent. We will speak of the relationship between the church and the kingdom of God in due course, but there is no doubt that for John Paul II, as well as for most contemporary missiologists, the kingdom of God stands front and center in any theology of mission.

Mission

Another fundamental change introduced by the kingdom-centered missiology is that it is mission that defines the church and not vice versa.[11] Just as the kingdom of God is prior to mission, so mission is prior to the church. The church comes to be only because it has been called to mission. It exists for the sake of mission. Mission defines what the church is and what it must do.

Consequently, the whole church is missionary, or, as Vatican II declares in its *Decree on the Church's Missionary Activity (Ad gentes)*: "The pilgrim Church is missionary by her very nature, since it is from the mission of the Son and the mission of the Holy Spirit that she draws her origin, in accordance with the decree of God the Father" (*AG,* no. 2). The *Dogmatic Constitution on the Church*

---

[11] It is well known that the kingdom of God is given a central place in liberation theologies. See, for instance, Jon Sobrino's thesis that the starting point for Christology is the kingdom of God. See his *Jesus in Latin America* (Maryknoll, N.Y.: Orbis Books, 1987), 81-97, and *Jesus the Liberator: A Historical-Theological View,* trans. Paul Burns and Francis McDonagh (Maryknoll, N.Y.: Orbis Books, 1993), 67-134.

(Lumen gentium) affirms: "The obligation of spreading the faith is imposed on every disciple of Christ, according to his ability (*LG*, no. 17). Hence, it would be wrong to regard mission primarily as foreign mission and to believe that only an elite few are called to this mission. Pope John Paul II notes that "there is a new awareness that *missionary activity is a matter for all Christians,* for all dioceses and parishes, Church institutions and associations" (*RM*, no. 2). The hallowed distinction between the sending church and the receiving church is thereby invalidated.

This does not mean that the so-called foreign mission, the *missio ad gentes,* is no longer necessary, as John Paul II reminds us.[12] But it is not granted the almost exclusive right to mission. The pope recognizes the complex and ever-changing situation of the church, and to give due importance to all its aspects, he distinguishes three situations for the church's mission. The first is that of "peoples, groups and socio-cultural contexts in which Christ and his Gospel are not known, or which lack Christian communities sufficiently mature to be able to incarnate the faith in their own environment and proclaim it to other groups. This is the mission *ad gentes* in the proper sense of the term" (*RM*, no. 33). The second is that of "Christian communities with adequate and solid ecclesial structures. They are fervent in their faith and in Christian living. They bear witness to the Gospel in their surroundings and have a sense of commitment to the universal mission" (*RM*, no. 33). Here the mission of the church takes the form of "pastoral care of the faithful." Lastly, there is "an intermediate situation, particularly in countries with ancient Christian roots, and occasionally in the younger Churches as well, where entire groups of the baptized have lost their living sense of the faith, or even no longer consider themselves members of the Church, and live a life far removed from Christ and his Gospel" (*RM*, no. 33). Here we have a "new evangelization" or a "re-evangelization."[13]

Whatever may be thought about the accuracy and usefulness of this threefold distinction,[14] at least its basic point is well taken; namely, foreign mission does not constitute the entire mission of the church but is only a part, albeit necessary, of it. Furthermore, its principal goal is no longer "saving souls" and "church

---

[12] "To say that the whole Church is missionary does not preclude the existence of a specific mission *ad gentes,* just as saying that all Catholics must be missionaries not only does not exclude, but actually requires that there be persons who have a specific vocation to be 'life-long missionaries *ad gentes.*'" Indeed, the pope says that one of the purposes of his encyclical is "to clear up doubts and ambiguities regarding missionary activity *ad gentes,* and to confirm in their commitment those exemplary brothers and sisters dedicated to missionary activity and those who assist them" (*RM*, no. 2).

[13] The term *new evangelization* is confusing. It may mean evangelization for the first time; evangelization again, in the same modality; or evangelization again but in a different form.

[14] Ultimately, this threefold distinction is not very helpful. For one thing, it is impossible to find any local church that fully corresponds to the description given in this second situation. In addition, to call the church's mission in this second category "pastoral care of the faithful" blunts the very point of the encyclical; namely, mission pervades all the church's activities.

planting" but bearing witness to the kingdom of God. Nor is the field of mission *ad gentes* only the foreign lands; it also includes urban centers, the young, migrants and refugees, and what John Paul II calls "the modern equivalents of the Areopagus," namely, the world of communications, social justice, scientific research, and the world of consumerism and materialism (see *RM*, no. 37).

Proclamation

Among the many activities of the church's mission there must no doubt be proclamation. There was a rumor that at the Asian Synod, which met in Rome 19 April-14 May 1998, there was a fear that in Asia "dialogue" had replaced or at least overshadowed "proclamation." Perhaps for this reason, in his apostolic exhortation *Ecclesia in Asia*, the pope reaffirms not only the necessity but also the "primacy" of proclamation: "There can be no true evangelization without the explicit proclamation of Jesus as Lord. The Second Vatican Council and the magisterium since then, responding to a certain confusion about the true nature of the church's mission, have repeatedly stressed the primacy of the proclamation of Jesus Christ in all evangelizing work" (*EA*, no. 19).

What is meant by "proclamation" here? If past missionary practices are any guide, we tend to take it to mean *verbal* announcement of the good news, written and/or oral, Protestants mostly by means of the Bible, and Catholics mostly by means of the catechism. The emphasis is laid on the *verbal communication* of a message or a doctrine, and the preferred if not exclusive means are *words*. The main content of the proclamation is the truth that Jesus is "the only Savior," "the one mediator between God and mankind" (*RM*, no. 5).

Though this is admittedly the common meaning of *proclamation,* it is most interesting that John Paul II, in *Ecclesia in Asia*, where he reaffirms both the necessity and primacy of proclamation, nowhere emphasizes the exclusive use of *words* or *doctrinal formulas* to convey the message that Jesus is the only savior for all humankind. On the contrary, he says that "the presentation of Jesus Christ as the only Savior needs to follow a pedagogy that will introduce people step by step to the full appropriation of the mystery. Clearly, the initial evangelization of non-Christians and the continuing proclamation of Jesus to believers will have to be different in their approach" (*EA*, no. 20). As examples of these approaches, the pope mentions stories, parables, symbols, personal contact, and inculturation (see *EA*, nos. 20-22). More important, he also mentions "Christian life as proclamation," a life marked by "prayer, fasting and various forms of asceticism . . . renunciation, detachment, humility, simplicity and silence" (*EA*, no. 23). No less important is John Paul II's remark that in Asia "people are more persuaded by holiness of life than by intellectual argument" (*EA*, no. 42). Furthermore, the pope notes that in many places in Asia where explicit proclamation is forbidden and religious freedom is denied or systematically restricted, "the silent witness of life still remains the only way of proclaiming God's kingdom" (*EA*, no. 23). In sum, the pope recognizes that there is a "legitimate variety of approaches to the proclamation of Jesus, provided that the faith itself is respected in all its integrity" (*EA,* no. 23).

Church

Last, we come to the church, last not only in the chronological but also theological order. As has been said above, the church no longer occupies the center or the top position in the new theology of mission. It is, as John Paul II puts it, "effectively and concretely at the service of the kingdom of God" (*RM*, no. 20). It does so by "establishing communities and founding new particular Churches, and by guiding them into mature faith and charity in openness toward others, in service to individuals and societies, and in understanding and esteem for human institutions." Furthermore, the church serves the kingdom of God "by spreading throughout the word the 'Gospel values' which are an expression of the kingdom and which help people to accept God's plan." Finally, it serves the kingdom of God "by her intercession, since the Kingdom by its very nature is God's gift and work" (*RM*, no. 20).

Clearly, in this service of the church to the kingdom of God, "saving souls" and "church planting" still remain, but their meaning and scope have been fundamentally changed. Gone are the individualization and ecclesiasticization of salvation prevalent in the older theology; instead, concerns for the formation of a mature faith, the transformation of societal structures, and the valorization of and a genuine respect for human cultures are clearly in evidence.

By the same token, the church is not set in opposition to the reign of God and vice versa. John Paul II rejects the kind of "kingdom-centeredness" that leaves little or no room for Christ or the church: "The Kingdom cannot be detached either from Christ or from the Church" (*RM*, no. 18).

In light of this new theology of mission, it is useful to revisit the five questions given above.

1. *For what* is mission? Exclusively for the reign of God, or simply God. Anything else that is made into the goal of mission, even something as noble as church growth or salvation of souls, smacks of idolatry.

2. *To whom?* To the world, primarily. Mission is not primarily for the benefit of Christians; it is not inward but outward looking. This world is a complex reality and includes at least the three situations outlined by the pope. Mission is therefore not primarily, much less exclusively, mission *ad gentes*. The geographical frontiers that once served as useful markers between what is Christian and what is non-Christian are now superseded. Mission is in the midst of the Christian community.

3. *By whom?* By the whole community of believers, as we have said, but above all by God, or more specifically, by the Holy Spirit. In one of the best chapters of his encyclical, John Paul II affirms that the Holy Spirit is "the principal agent of mission." The Holy Spirit is said "to direct the mission of the church," to make "the whole church missionary," and to be "present and active in every time and place." It is here that we find one of John Paul II's most revolutionary statements about the mission of the church: "The Spirit's presence and activity affect not only individuals but also society and history, peoples, cultures and religions. Indeed, the Spirit is at the origin of the noble ideals and undertakings which benefit humanity on its journey through history" (*RM*, no.

28). If this statement is true, then Christian mission can no longer be what it was, a one-way proclamation of a message of salvation to a world of "pagans" totally bereft of God's self-revelation and grace. Rather, it is first of all a search for and recognition of the presence and activities of the Holy Spirit among the peoples to be evangelized, and in this humble and attentive process of listening, the evangelizers become the evangelized, and the evangelized become the evangelizers.

4. *With whom?* Of course, with all Catholics, each in his or her position in the church and the world. However, in mission oriented toward the kingdom of God and not to the growth of one's own church, missionary collaboration must not be limited to fellow Catholics. Rather, crossing denominational barriers, Catholic, Orthodox, and Protestant missionaries must abandon mutual antagonism and competition and work together in a common witness to the gospel. It is widely known that divisions within Christianity have been a scandal to non-Christians and a serious obstacle to a credible evangelization. There is no reason why church divisions, which are the results of internal quarrels among the Western churches, should be exported to the churches in the other parts of the world.

Furthermore, mission must be carried out in collaboration with followers of religion as well. Since these are not objects but rather subjects of the church's mission, they must be treated as responsible agents of the church's mission with whom missionaries must enter into dialogue of the various kinds described below. In addition, where the Christians form only a tiny minority of the population, for example, in Asia, the church's mission of promoting liberation and integral development cannot be carried out successfully without an effective collaboration of non-Christians.[15]

5. *How?* Because of the presence and activities of the Holy Spirit in every time and place, the most effective method of evangelization is dialogue. By *dialogue* is meant a fourfold activity: dialogue of *life*, that is, sharing of joys and sorrows; dialogue of *action*, that is, collaboration in furthering liberation and human development; dialogue of *theological exchange*, that is, deeper understanding of the religious heritages of others and better appreciation of their spiritual values; and finally, dialogue of *religious experience*, that is, sharing of spiritual riches through common prayer and other religious practices.[16]

This dialogical method in mission, which includes inculturation, liberation, and interreligious dialogue as an integral and intertwined process, therefore rejects the one-way replication model of the old theology of mission described above. But it also moves beyond what is called the indigenization model, in which Western Christendom is reproduced in another culture by drawing on the

---

[15] This point has been strongly stressed by Aloysius Pieris (see *An Asian Theology of Liberation* [Maryknoll, N.Y.: Orbis Books, 1988], esp. 69-86).

[16] See The Pontifical Council for Interreligious Dialogue and the Congregation for the Evangelization of Peoples, *Dialogue and Proclamation: Reflections and Orientations on Interreligious Dialogue and the Proclamation of the Gospel of Jesus Christ* (1991), no. 42. For more detailed discussion of this fourfold dialogue, see Chapter 2 herein.

resources of that culture. The original is still brought in from the outside, only this time it is clothed in the local garb. To vary the metaphor, the script remains the same, only the cast of actors has been changed, and the director is still the outside agent. In the dialogue described above, the way now is open for what has been called the contextualization model (I prefer *interculturation*), which is the "process whereby the gospel message encounters a particular culture, calling forth faith and leading to the formation of a faith community, which is culturally authentic and authentically Christian." Here, "control of the process resides within the context rather than with an external agent or agency." Finally, in this model, "culture is understood to be a dynamic and evolving system of values, patterns of behavior, and a matrix shaping the life of the members of that society."[17]

Mission understood in this way is both a gift and a task. Whether we are ready and willing to accept this gift and meet this challenge remains to be seen. But there is little doubt that if the mission of the church is to flourish in this new millennium, it must trod the path that the new theology of mission has outlined.

---

[17] Shenk, *Changing Frontiers of Mission*, 56.

4

Conversion and Discipleship as Goals of the Church's Mission

In his apostolic exhortation *Ecclesia in America* (1999) Pope John Paul II describes three paths leading to an encounter with Jesus Christ.[1] The first path is conversion; the other two are communion and solidarity. Of course, these paths are not parallel roads to Christ; rather they are convergent paths, or to change the metaphor, they are three skeins woven into a single rope binding us to Christ.[2]

While conversion, communion, and solidarity are all necessary for our union with Christ, it is highly significant that the pope places these three attitudes in that precise order in his exhortation, with conversion heading the list. Clearly, conversion is treated first because it is the foundation and the condition of possibility for communion and solidarity.[3] It is, as it were, the gate through which a person passes to meet Christ. Furthermore, it lends depth to communion and authenticity to solidarity. Without conversion, communion would be a mere feeling of empathy and sympathy, a sense of clubby fellowship of like-minded individuals, praiseworthy indeed, but lacking the dimension of personal union, the total gift of self, which is the hallmark of true communion as it has been exemplified by Jesus. Without conversion, solidarity risks being reduced to a simple sharing of common interests that binds together the members of a voluntary nonprofit association or a business corporation, necessary indeed for the well-being of a society, but still falling far short of the commitment to suffer

---

[1] For an English translation of *Ecclesia in America*, see *Post-Synodal Apostolic Exhortation Ecclesia in America of the Holy Father John Paul II* (Washington, D.C.: NCCB/USCC Publications, 1999).

[2] *Ecclesia in America* begins with the theme of encountering Christ in general (Chapter I) and in America in particular (Chapter II). It then discusses "the path of conversion" (Chapter III), "the path to communion" (Chapter IV), and "the path to solidarity" (Chapter V). Note the change of prepositions from "of" to "to" in the second and third paths. The exhortation ends with a discussion of the church's mission of new evangelization in America.

[3] This order is made clear by the pope: "Conversion leads to fraternal communion, because it enables us to understand Christ is the head of the Church, his Mystical Body; it urges solidarity, because it makes us aware that whatever we do for others, especially the poorest, we do for Christ himself" (no. 26).

with and for the marginalized, the poor and the oppressed, and to struggle with them to regain justice and human dignity.

As essential as it is for Christian life in general, conversion is even more central for mission. Indeed, for a long time it was taken to be the very goal of mission, since it is only through conversion that "soul saving" and "church planting"—considered the two purposes of mission—could be realized. The success of mission was often measured by the number of conversions it brought about. Of course, faith, hope and charity remain essential, but when it comes down to requesting funds for a particular missionary project, unless one can produce facts and figures of conversions likely to be achieved, there is little likelihood that a pragmatic and result-oriented foundation will dole out grants on the hope that the project will increase the three theological virtues.

Nevertheless, in recent theologies of mission the notion of conversion as the goal of mission, especially if it is understood as renouncing one religion or Christian denomination to join another, has been seriously questioned. Indeed, in the last four decades many if not most missiologists have rejected the long-held view that the purpose of mission is "soul saving" and "church planting."[4] "Soul saving" tends to individualize salvation, belittling the other aspects of the church's mission such as inculturation, interreligious dialogue, and liberation. "Church planting" tends to ecclesiasticize salvation, identifying the church with the kingdom of God and fomenting rivalries among Christian denominations.

Instead of this church-centered approach to mission, a kingdom-of-God-centered view has been proposed in which the church is made subservient to, though not separate from, the reign of God.[5] It is the reign of God that determines the church and its mission, and not the other way round. In terms of priority and intrinsic importance, the reign of God stands at the top, followed by mission, proclamation, and church. This is the order in which these four realities of the Christian faith should be understood and related to one another.[6] In this perspective, conversion in the sense of renouncing one religious tradition and joining the

---

[4] These two aspects of the church's mission form what David Bosch calls the "medieval Roman Catholic missionary paradigm" (see *Transforming Mission: Paradigm Shifts in Theology of Mission* [Maryknoll, N.Y.: Orbis Books, 1991], 214). Bosch refers to them as the "individualization" and "ecclesiasticization" of salvation, the former as the result of Augustine's doctrine of the total corruption of humanity in his debate with Pelagius, and the second as the result of his doctrine of the centrality of the institutional church in his debate with the Donatists. See the previous chapter for further elaboration.

[5] John Fuellenbach puts it tersely in *Church: Community for Kingdom* (Manila: Logos Publications, 2000), 217: "The mission of the Church must be seen and understood from this perspective: totally in the service of God's kingdom designed for the transformation of the whole of creation." Fuellenbach also makes it clear that the church is not identical with the kingdom of God; rather, it is the sign of and instrument for the kingdom. He describes well one of the temptations of the church: "One of the temptations for the Church in history is to claim the Kingdom for herself, to take over the management of the Kingdom, and even go so far as to present as the realized Kingdom of God vis-à-vis the world" (ibid., 79).

[6] This view of mission is elaborated in detail in the previous chapter.

Christian church still is a desirable outcome of mission, but it is not its main goal, let alone its sole purpose.

In light of this radical revisioning of mission, it is necessary to reexamine the concept of conversion and its place in mission. I first briefly review the biblical concept of conversion. Next, I place it in the wider context of the history of mission. Last, I relate it to the future of mission in Asia as this can reasonably be prognosticated.

CONVERSION AS "TURNING" TO JESUS CHRIST
AND TAKING UP HIS MISSION

That conversion occupied a prominent place in Jesus' preaching is beyond dispute. His message has been summarized in a terse sentence: "The time is fulfilled, and the kingdom of God has come near; repent and believe in the good news" (Mk 1:15). This message is composed of two parts: the first, a statement of fact; the second, a command. Jesus informed his audience that God's promise that God would intervene on their behalf was being fulfilled, and he used the symbol of God's kingdom or rule to describe this intervention. In other words, Jesus declared that they were living in the apocalyptic or end time. The old age had passed, and the new age was dawning. As the result of this epochal change, Jesus commanded his hearers to "repent and believe" the good news he was telling them. Repenting and believing were presented as two distinct but not separate acts; indeed, they were linked by the preposition "and" to indicate that they form a single process in which repenting leads to believing. This complex process is later called conversion.

Conversion as "Turning" to Jesus

The word *conversion* is associated with the Hebrew word meaning "turning" *(tešuva)* and the Greek word meaning "change of mind or direction" *(metanoia)*.[7] In neither Hebrew nor Greek is there a connotation of sorrow or regret or shame, much less the rejection of one religion in favor of another often associated with conversion. In the case of Jesus' announcement, there might be some feelings of sorrow or regret provoked by turning from one thing to another, as usually happens when one moves from one era to another, or from one place to another. However, the dominant feelings conjured by Jesus' proclamation were joy and happiness; after all, he was speaking of "good news"! At any rate, there was no question of abjuring one religion and joining another. At no time was Jesus advocating renouncing Judaism and

---

[7] For the biblical notion of conversion, see Beverly Roberts Gaventa, "Conversion," in *The Anchor Bible Dictionary*, ed. David Freedman (New York: Doubleday, 1992), 1:1131-33; idem, *From Darkness to Light: Aspects of Conversion in the New Testament* (Philadelphia: Fortress Press, 1986); and William L. Holladay, *The Root* šûbh *in the Old Testament* (Leiden: E. J. Brill, 1958).

joining another religion such as Christianity, if there had been such a thing then. Nor was Jesus seeking to establish a new religion in the way many religious founders did after him, laying out a constitution, bylaws, organizational structures, rituals, and so forth. After all, he continued to be a pious Jew and was even called a rabbi, observing most if not all of the Jewish laws, especially the Sabbath and the studying of the Torah.

On the other hand, for Jesus it was not Judaism as usual. In and through his words and deeds, and above all through his own person, something utterly new had happened that burst the bounds of Judaism, like the new wine bursting the old wineskin. This unexpected and total novelty consists precisely in the coming of what Jesus called the kingdom of God, which he himself ushered in. By this symbol Jesus understood the definitive coming of God in power to rule in the near future, to bring the present state of things to an end, and to establish God's full and victorious rule over the world in general and Israel in particular. This kingly reign of God would mean the reversal of all unjust oppression and suffering, the bestowal of the reward promised to faithful Israelites, and the joyful participation of believers—and even of some Gentiles—in the heavenly banquet with Israel's patriarchs.[8]

Because of this utterly new reality, Jesus taught with supreme authority, his own, unlike other rabbis and scribes, who had to depend on the Torah; dealt with the Mosaic law with sovereign freedom, breaking even its most sacred rules and regulations, when necessary, to demonstrate that God's kingdom had indeed arrived; criticized, at times very harshly, religious authorities such as the Pharisees and the Sadducees for failing to recognize the signs of the coming of God's reign; and performed miraculous deeds as signs of the coming of this kingdom.[9] Most important, in light of the coming of God's kingdom, Jesus related to God in a most unique and intimate way, calling God his Abba. No less important, because of the dawning of this kingdom, he included everyone into his circle, barring none, without any discrimination whatsoever. Rabbi though he was, he was known to share table with tax collectors and prostitutes, thereby defiling himself, but by the same act, showing them that God forgave them unconditionally. Rabbi though he was, he transgressed the impurity laws and touched and let himself be touched by women, menstruating and sinful women to boot, to let them know that they too were to be treated with dignity because the kingdom of God had arrived. And so the sinners, the impure, the sick, the poor, the women, the children (the "lost sheep of Israel"), even the pagans (goim)—whose faith amazed him and was praised by him—flocked to him, and he accepted them all.

---

[8] See John Meier, *A Marginal Jew: Rethinking the Historical Jesus*, 4 vols. (New York: Doubleday, 1991, 1994, 2001, forthcoming), 2:452: "The kingdom of God is not primarily a state or place but rather the entire dynamic event of God coming in power to rule his people Israel in the end time. It is a tensive symbol, a multifaceted reality, a whole mythic story in miniature that cannot be adequately grasped in a single formula or definition. This is why Jesus can speak of kingdom as both imminent and yet present."

[9] For a historical reconstruction of Jesus, see ibid.

That was, I submit, their conversion, that is, their "turning" to Jesus.[10] He was, as it were, the home to which they returned, an image evoked by the Hebrew word *(šûbh)*. They also changed their thinking about him, in the meaning of the Greek *metanoia*, because they believed that he was not just any other Jew but the embodiment of what the kingdom of God stood for, namely, the all-inclusive, gracious, forgiving, healing, saving, tender, motherly, fatherly love of Yahweh.

Lest we think that such a conversion is just a warm and fuzzy feeling, a hand-holding, body-swinging, hallelujah-shouting thing, Jesus' command to repent and believe was both urgent and radical. Urgent, because there was no possibility of tergiversating and procrastinating. Not even the sacred duty of burying one's own father could serve as an excuse: "Let the dead bury their own dead" (Mt 8:22). Radical, because conversion or turning to Jesus demands a total and absolute denial of self: "If any want to become my followers, let them deny themselves and take up their cross and follow me" (Mk 8:34). This is so because conversion is not getting a membership into a club, or changing a religious preference, not even joining a religious organization; it is becoming a disciple of Jesus.

The first and abiding consequence of turning to Jesus is becoming his disciple.[11] Accepting Jesus' call, and never on his or her own initiative, a disciple renounced possessions, abandoned familial and social ties, and literally followed Jesus in his wanderings. A disciple *(mathētēs)* is primarily one who "follows" or "walks behind" Jesus *(akolouthein)*. A disciple enters a lifelong relationship with him—"to be with him" (Mk 3:14)—and therefore can never aspire to become a master in his or her turn. A disciple is not just a student receiving instruction from a teacher. A disciple of Jesus is primarily an apprentice, learning by close observation and personal imitation, by *doing* what Jesus the Master does and by sharing his life.[12] As disciple of Jesus, a person will be persecuted,

---

[10] Interestingly, one of the important contemporary studies on religious conversion is entitled *Turning* (see Emilie Griffin, *Turning: Reflections on the Experience of Conversion* [New York: Doubleday, 1980]). Griffin sees "turning" as a process composed of four stages: desire or longing, dialectic or argumentative, struggle or crisis, and surrender. For helpful studies on conversion, see Stephen Happel and James J. Walter, *Conversion and Discipleship: A Christian Foundation for Ethics and Doctrine* (Philadelphia: Fortress Press, 1986); Walter Conn, *Christian Conversion* (New York: Paulist Press, 1986); and Hugh T. Kerr and John M. Mulders, eds., *Conversions: The Christian Experience* (Grand Rapids, Mich.: Eerdmans, 1983).

[11] For studies on discipleship, see Hans Weder, "Disciple, Discipleship," *The Anchor Bible Dictionary*, ed. David Freedman (New York: Doubleday, 1992), 2:207-10, and the helpful bibliography cited therein. John Meier summarizes discipleship as (1) the result of Jesus' initiative in calling; (2) leaving one's home and following Jesus physically; (3) risking danger and hostility (that is, losing one's life, denying oneself and taking up one's cross, and facing hostility from one's family). See Meier, *A Marginal Jew*, 3:47-73.

[12] For a theology of the church as a community of disciples, see Avery Dulles, *A Church to Believe In: Discipleship and Dynamics of Freedom* (New York: Crossroad, 1982).

as Jesus was, precisely because he or she must perform what Jesus did, namely, service to the kingdom.

Conversion as Continuing Jesus' Ministry

This brings me to the second aspect of conversion, namely, continuing the ministry of Jesus. When Jesus called disciples to himself, he did not just want them to keep him company. On the contrary, the call to discipleship is simultaneously a sending to the people of Israel for the sole purpose of proclaiming the approaching kingdom of God. Consequently, he sent them out on mission, to preach that "the kingdom of heaven has come near," and to "cure the sick, raise the dead, cleanse the lepers, cast out devils" (Mt 10:7-8). And, after his resurrection, on account of which all power in heaven and on earth was given to him, Jesus commanded them to go forth, teach all nations, and preach the gospel to all creatures, baptizing them in the name of the Father, the Son, and the Holy Spirit (Mt 28:19; Mk 16:15). Clearly, conversion is for the sake of mission.

This intrinsic orientation of discipleship to mission is particularly true in the case of the Twelve, who were the standing exemplars of what discipleship meant. The number twelve itself was symbolic; it stands for the twelve tribes of Israel. Furthermore, by sending the Twelve out on a prophetic mission to Israel during his lifetime, Jesus connected their mission with his own, which was to gather and reconstitute the tribes of Israel in the kingdom of God. As John Meier puts it concisely: "The creation of the Twelve thus coheres perfectly with Jesus' eschatological, people-centered message and mission: God is coming in power to gather and rule over all Israel in the end time."[13] In the particular case of the two brothers Peter and Andrew, Jesus promised to make them into "fishers of human beings."

I would like to suggest that even the command of Jesus at the Last Supper to his disciples to take up the bread and eat it and the cup and drink from it was also a command to take up his mission. I do not want to deny that at the Last Supper Jesus established a new ritual that would later be called the sacrament of the Eucharist, in which Jesus was really, truly, and as the Council of Trent was to say, substantially present. Unfortunately, the "real presence" of Jesus in the eucharistic species has often been understood in a static way. What I am suggesting is that the two expressions, body and blood, here mean not just the body and blood of Jesus in the physical sense. We know that in Hebrew thought *body* means the entire reality of the person, what we call today "body and soul" or the "self." Similarly, *blood* refers to the same entire reality of the person, and not something different from the body, but the very same "body and soul" as living, the self as a historical, evolving, living reality, since blood is the symbol of life. But the person of Jesus was more than his body and soul. What and who Jesus was, was determined by his relationship to his Father and what his Father assigned him to do. Jesus' self-identity cannot be restricted to his ontology or his two "natures." In other words, the body and soul of Jesus cannot be separated from the kingdom of God and his mission within it.

---

[13] John Meier, *A Marginal Jew*, 3:154.

Recall further that the Last Supper was "last" because it was a farewell dinner. Jesus knew he was going to be killed because of his message about and work for the kingdom of God. He also knew that he had not completed the mission entrusted to him by his Father; his life was to be cut short by those whose interests were threatened by his kingdom-of-God-oriented behavior. That was why he wanted to have a farewell dinner with his disciples. Now, in a farewell dinner, the one who is going away usually hands on something, perhaps the most precious and enduring thing, of herself or himself to those who remain behind. If a teacher, maybe a few words of wisdom; if a parent, a testament or will; if a friend, a token of abiding love. What was most important for Jesus was his mission; it had consumed his energies, been his passion and obsession, and made him who he was. So when he commanded his disciples to eat his body and drink his blood, he was effectively saying to his disciples: *You who are my followers, take over my mission and complete it for me, since I am prevented from completing it. By eating my body and drinking my blood, you are taking on my mission for the kingdom of God.* The Eucharist is therefore the sacrament of mission par excellence.

In sum, conversion means first of all turning to Jesus in a radical way, in a personal and absolute commitment to him, because he embodied the kingdom of God. Second, it means taking over and continuing his mission for that kingdom.

CONVERSION IN THE WIDER CONTEXT OF MISSION

If this is the essential meaning of conversion, when and why did it take on the further connotation of joining another religious organization, of becoming a member of the church? In a sense this new meaning is not totally alien to the original meaning of turning to Jesus and taking on his mission. Jesus did not call individuals qua individuals to conversion. While personal commitment to Jesus and his cause was required, his call to repent and believe in the good news was addressed to the people of Israel as a whole. It was the people of Israel, and not just individual Jews, that Jesus wanted to gather into the kingdom of God.

There was no evidence, however, that Jesus himself wanted to found a religious society—*religion* in the modern sense—apart from, much less opposed to Israel. Nor was he perceived to have done so by his contemporaries and even his followers. He and they continued to be and to behave as pious Jews, even though in several practices they did diverge from the official rules and norms. Rather, Jesus was seen as a new prophet who, as other prophets before him, attempted to give a new interpretation to the Torah and to purify contemporary Judaism of errors and abuses and bring it back to its authentic ideals. In other words, Jesus was perceived as starting a reform movement *within* Judaism itself.[14]

----

[14] The relationship between Judaism and Christianity has been the subject of much controversy, and the literature is immense. A very helpful introduction is Mary C. Boys, *Has God Only One Blessing? Judaism as a Source of Christian Self-Understanding* (New York: Paulist Press, 2000).

Jesus was not however a religious "Lone Ranger." As we have seen above, he called others to join him as a group in his mission for the kingdom of God, and he taught and trained them for this purpose. In this sense, whoever wanted to follow Jesus, to "convert" to him, necessarily had to join a new movement, a new group, a new community, albeit as yet not separate from and opposed to Israel. Conversion to Jesus was not simply an internal, spiritual experience, a response to his call, but required following him, physically, and joining the community of his disciples.

In this connection it may be useful to reflect briefly on the nature of Saul's (later known as Paul) so-called conversion. He was certainly one of the most celebrated converts to Jesus' movement and certainly *the* most influential one. Without his missionary labors and his many letters, Christianity as we know it would not have taken place. Yet we must be careful not to talk about his conversion as a rejection of his former religion, namely, Judaism, and joining a new religion called Christianity, as the word *conversion* is popularly used today (when we say that so-and-so is a "convert" from Judaism or from a Christian denomination to the Catholic church). Paul was and continued to be a religious Jew until the end. He was extremely proud of his religious heritage, even though he was deeply pained to see that some of his fellow Jews did not accept Jesus. Paul's so-called conversion was not joining a new religion but rather a change of brands of Judaism, switching from Pharisaic to Christian Judaism. It was an acceptance of a "call" from Jesus to proclaim that the kingdom of God, which had been addressed to the Jews, was now extended to the Gentiles as well. In other words, in his conversion Paul was not called to join a new religion but commissioned to proclaim that the "God of the Jews" is also the "God of the Gentiles."[15]

However, as the absolute novelty of Jesus' message about the kingdom of God dawned more fully on his disciples, and as the opposition to the new reform group on the part of some officials of Judaism gathered force and became more intense (Paul's persecution of the Christians was part of this opposition), the identity of Jesus' community as a separate social and religious entity grew. Indeed, at Antioch in Syria, the followers of Jesus were given the name Christians (Acts 11:26). This process of sociological and theological self-definition was accelerated by the fact that Jesus' followers were expelled from the synagogue, that certain practices functioned for them as entrance requirements and initiation rites (for example, baptism in the name of Jesus, or in the name of the Father, and the Son, and the Holy Spirit), and that some essential requirements of Judaism were abandoned (for example, circumcision).

---

[15] On Paul and his conversion, see the helpful essay by Hans Dieter Betz, "Paul," in *The Anchor Bible Dictionary*, ed. David Freedman (New York: Doubleday, 1992), 5:186-201, with an extensive bibliography. It is to be noted that even Paul, after his "conversion," had to join a community of Christians through baptism, namely, that of the Gentile church in Damascus. Indeed, it was from this community that he learned that righteousness came not from the Torah (as he had believed) but from faith in Jesus, whom he now confessed as Lord and Son of God.

Above all, the political events surrounding the destruction of the Temple of Jerusalem in A.D. 70 and the subsequent dispersion of the Jews from Palestine contributed mightily to the emergence of the Jesus movement as a separate "way" (Acts 9:2) and eventually a religion. This process of separation from the Jewish matrix and emergence into a distinct religion reached its apogee when Christianity was first accepted as a *religio licita* under Constantine and subsequently as the official religion of the Roman Empire under Theodosius. From then on the story of Christianity's extremely rapid, massive, and nothing short of miraculous expansion throughout the Roman Empire, not least by means of "mission," is too well known to need retelling here. Henceforward, conversion meant abandoning one religion and joining Christianity as another religion.[16]

To gain a better understanding of conversion I will place it in the wider context of past missionary endeavors. I will make use of the works of two noted missiologists, a Catholic and a Protestant, Anthony Gittins and Wilbert Shenk respectively.

Anthony Gittins, in his brief but illuminating study on conversion, speaks of it as a "complex and multifaceted" process. In a sense it may be described as a "religious experience."[17] But, as Gittins points out, for many peoples, especially the less technologically advanced ones, "religion is inextricable from life, embedded within its fabric. 'Religious' experiences are thus not entirely or always separable from what is conventionally labeled 'economic' or 'political' or 'social' activity."[18] Therefore, conversion must be seen in the total context of the people to be converted. In this way it is seen less as a sudden, dramatic event that happens to an individual, a breaking off from the past, though it is certainly that. It is much more, as Gittins notes, "a process rather than an event, part of life's unfolding."[19]

But being a process does not mean that conversion is not or must not be radical. However, Gittins again notes:

> Radical is not necessarily dramatic; conversion occurs through continuity as well as by discontinuity with earlier life. Radical disjunction certainly marks the lives of some individuals, particularly men, but does not necessarily characterize all communities, or many women. . . . Many women's experience is that lives may be lived authentically through commitment

---

[16] For a history of the spread of Christianity in the first centuries, see W. H. C. Frend, *The Rise of Christianity* (Philadelphia: Fortress Press, 1984); and Ramsay McMullen, *Christianizing the Roman Empire A.D. 100-400* (New Haven, Conn.: Yale University Press, 1984). For a brief presentation of the evolution from the Jesus movement to the institutional church, see Howard Clark Kee, "From the Jesus Movement toward Institutional Church," in *Conversion to Christianity: Historical and Anthropological Perspectives on a Great Transformation*, ed. Robert W. Hefner (Berkeley and Los Angeles: University of California Press, 1993), 47-63.

[17] Anthony J. Gittins, "Conversion," in *Dictionary of Mission: Theology, History, Perspectives*, ed. Karl Müller et al. (Maryknoll, N.Y.: Orbis Books, 1997), 87-89.

[18] Ibid., 87.

[19] Ibid., 88.

to daily routine, rather than by blazing new trails like explorers or pioneers.[20]

Finally, because conversion takes place within the total context of a person's life, it is necessarily related to the community or the culture to which the person belongs. Consequently, "mass conversion" should not be belittled or dismissed out of hand because of the contemporary emphasis on individual choice as the only truly free choice: "People in social groups frequently act precisely *as* a group, and the exercise of individual choice is subsumed into the group choice, as discerned or decided by appropriate authority."[21] Again, Gittins point out, "The conversion process represents the ultimate transformation of the community (and its members) in Christ. Missioners, especially, must discern the 'seeds of the Word' or 'gospel values,' or simply the presence of God, among people long before the arrival of Christian ministers."[22] Hence, the converts should not be detached from the community—neither the old community from which they come nor the new community to which they are now joined—because "the support of a community can legitimately endorse an individual's conversion and offer positive and negative sanctions to help it continue over time."[23]

Several points made by Gittins about conversion are confirmed by the history of mission. First of all, Gittins's warning against separating religious conversion from its social, economic, and political contexts is well taken. Only a very small number of the total of conversions that have taken place in mission fields have taken the form of a dramatic volte-face, such as Paul or Augustine, or of an intellectual discovery, such as Newman or Dulles. Rather, the majority occurred because of tribal membership (for example, in Taiwan, the highlands of Vietnam, and many other countries in Africa and Asia, where mass baptisms by legendary missionaries are still recalled with admiration and nostalgia); familial connections (for example, getting married to a Christian); educational contacts (for example, going to a Christian school); or, of course, through infant baptism (the overwhelming majority of cases). These modes of conversion do not differ substantially from those that were operative in the first five centuries of Christianity, both before and after the so-called Edict of Milan in 313.[24] These conversions, though dramatic and not purely religious at first, are not necessarily

---

[20] Ibid., 88-89.

[21] Ibid., 88.

[22] Ibid., 89.

[23] Ibid.

[24] As Ramsay McMullen points out in his study of Christian conversions in A.D. 100-400, there were "nonreligious factors" in these conversions, of which church leaders were quite well aware (see *Christianizing the Roman Empire A.D. 100-400*, 52-58). McMullen summarizes: "Emperors or ecclesiastical officers controlling the material benefits waved them in front of non-Christians obviously in the hope of changing their allegiance, or they handed out money and food (and advertised the fact) at the instant of change, or threatened to take money or food away from the already converted if they would not abide in their allegiance" (114-15). Of course, McMullen does not ignore cases of conversion through intellectual demonstration (68-73).

less radical, especially as time goes on and the individual is assisted in his or her faith growth in and by the community.

Second, Gittins's remark about group conversion is also to the point. One of the ironies of mission history is that whereas Western missionaries, especially of the evangelical tradition, emphasized the necessity of a "change of heart" and "rebirth" of each individual in the process of conversion, the great majority of conversions occurred in a group, for example, as the result of the conversion of the head of the tribe (who might have found conversion a politically and economically expedient act). As Wilbert Shenk notes, "Converts were drawn almost entirely from cultures in which the decision-making is communal. Personhood is defined in relation to one's group: 'I belong, therefore I am.' . . . The evangelical missionary message was directed to the individual, but that message was received through the eyes and ears that responded corporately, by a community that felt itself besieged."[25]

Wilbert Shenk provides an additional perspective on conversion in the wider context of mission. Canvassing the recent history of mission in Africa and Asia, he describes the context in which conversions occurred. He begins by noting that the world has become a *world system;* that is, "it has become increasingly interdependent through a series of subsystems: communications, financial, educational, political, religious, technological. At the heart of this system is a world economy held together by technology, which enables it to react to stimuli with great speed."[26] Religion, too, is now understood as a system, that is, as Clifford Geertz describes it, "(1) a system of symbols which acts to (2) establish powerful, pervasive, and long-lasting moods and motivations in men by (3) formulating conceptions of a general order of existence and (4) clothing these conceptions with such an aura of factuality that (5) the moods and motivations seem uniquely realistic."[27]

In light of this view of the world and religion as complex and interlocking systems, and from the history of mission, Shenk derives five postulates with regard to conversion. They may be summarized as follows: (1) As long as a group's world system and religions provide satisfactory answers to its various problems, there is little chance for large-scale conversion; conversely, large-scale conversion is likely to occur only if the group's world system and religions suffer a crisis. (2) The extent to which a world system and religions control the group determines the degree of success of a religion brought in from the outside in converting the members of the group. (3) In countries that have been colonized, there has been a coercive dimension in conversion, often overt, but real nonetheless, insofar as becoming a Christian in a colony was perceived as ensuring one's social and economic well-being; conversely, refusing to become a Christian could be seen as a patriotic act against colonialism. (4) Modernization

---

[25] Wilbert R. Shenk, *Changing Frontiers of Mission* (Maryknoll, N.Y.: Orbis Books, 1999), 101.

[26] Ibid., 87.

[27] Ibid. The quotation comes from Clifford Geertz, *The Interpretation of Cultures* (New York: Basic Books, 1973), 90.

and Westernization that missionaries brought with them were perceived as threats by traditional cultures. Hence, the Christian message, which could not be and was not separated from modernization and Westernization, was perceived to create social fragmentation. Consequently, conversion was increasingly confined to the "spiritual" realm. (5) Conversion occurs for a multiplicity of reasons and motives, some of which are reprehensible, while others can be used as bridges to build a more mature faith.[28]

As confirmation of these postulates Shenk highlights two significant facts of mission history: the vast majority of all conversions to Christianity have taken place (1) among small-scale ethnic, usually agrarian/subsistence societies, where there is no differentiation between religion and culture, not from the adherents of other world religions such as Hinduism, Buddhism and Islam and (2) from among the poor, those who are marginalized and oppressed by a powerful majority society, such as the Harijans in India.

The foregoing observations are not intended to belittle the importance of Christian conversion as a personal turning to Jesus and taking up his mission. Rather, they remind us that conversion is much more than renouncing one's former religion and joining another religion. Furthermore, the history of mission offers us useful insights into the nature and dynamics of conversion that, though a profoundly personal act in its intention, must be placed in the larger socio-political, economic and cultural context to be fully understood, especially in the work of evangelization. Let us now examine how these insights into conversion will play out in the future of mission, especially in Asia.

CONVERSION AND THE FUTURE OF MISSION

In concluding his study on mission David Bosch reflects on the question "Whither mission?" and ends with these words: "Mission is, quite simply, the participation of Christians in the liberating mission of Jesus . . . wagering on a future that verifiable experience seems to belie. It is the good news of God's love, incarnated in the witness of a community, for the sake of the world."[29] On his part, Wilbert Shenk, speaking of "the future of mission," suggests that any prognostication must use a twofold approach: "reflection on God's action in history, and reading with discrimination the signs of the times."[30]

God's action in history, I have argued above, is the establishment of his kingly rule on Israel and the world, which is referred to as the kingdom of God. God did this supremely through the incarnation, the cross, the resurrection, the ascension, Pentecost, and the parousia.[31] While these divine actions remain the theological constants, the "signs of the times" are by their very nature changeable and ever shifting. However difficult the reading of such signs, it is essential

---

[28] Shenk, *Changing Frontiers of Mission*, 87-91.
[29] Bosch, *Transforming Mission*, 519.
[30] Shenk, *Changing Frontiers of Mission*, 186.
[31] David Bosch refers to these six salvific events as the "faces of the church-in-mission" (*Transforming Mission*, 512).

for the future of mission. In the 1960s the signs were the shout "Missionary, go home!" from Asia and the call for a moratorium on Western missionary movement in Africa. Perhaps those signs of the times should be heeded since the church's missionary activities were at the time too enmeshed with Western colonialism and too preoccupied with self-preservation and self-aggrandizement.

Some thirty years later mission and missiology have experienced a significant revival, though in ways not anticipated or perhaps even desired by most missionaries of the past.[32] For one thing, the church is no longer the focus; in its stead the kingdom of God is given pride of place as the goal of mission, because the mission of the church is nothing more than the continuation of the *missio Dei* in Jesus and the Holy Spirit. Mission is, in the words of David Bosch quoted above, "quite simply, the participation of Christians in the liberating mission of Jesus." Instead of being defined by the church, mission now determines the identity and tasks of the church. Instead of viewing mission as something done by the "sending church" for the "receiving church," the church now is understood as missionary by its very nature; therefore, mission is incumbent upon every Christian. Furthermore, it is now maintained that mission is not only something that Christians carry out for the benefit of "pagans," but also something that the followers of other religions do for the benefit of the Christians, so that the evangelizers become the evangelized and the evangelized become the evangelizers. The *missio ad gentes* becomes a *missio inter gentes*. This is so because the divine Spirit is present and active in these cultures and religions and infuses them with the values of the kingdom.[33] Finally, the proclamation of the good news, which was considered the foremost activity of the church's mission, is now placed within a whole gamut of other, equally indispensable activities of the multifaceted ministry of the church: witness, worship, liberation, interreligious dialogue, inculturation, and so on.

In this new theology of mission, what place does conversion occupy? Certainly not the place of supreme honor assigned to it by the old theology of mission, namely, as the very goal of mission. As everything else, conversion is now made to serve the kingdom of God. Mission is not undertaken in the anxious fear that without baptism and incorporation into the church, "pagans" would be condemned to hell (mission as "soul saving"). The possibility of salvation outside the visible confines of the church is no longer in doubt.[34] Nor is "church

---

[32] Donal Dorr describes the older theology of mission, which was predominant from 1850 to 1960, as "the crusader model" or "the commando model" of mission. Its main image of mission is "sending out" missionaries. The alternative model of mission uses two complementary images of "gathering in" and "solidarity." See Donal Dorr, *Mission in Today's World* (Maryknoll, N.Y.: Orbis Books, 2000), 186-92.

[33] See Paul John Paul II's exceedingly important statement on the presence of the Holy Spirit not only in individuals but also in religions and cultures as such in his 1990 encyclical on mission, *Redemptoris missio:* "The Spirit's presence and activity affect not only individuals but also society and history, peoples, cultures and religions. Indeed, the Spirit is at the origin of the noble ideals and undertakings which benefit humanity on its journey through history" (*RM*, no. 28).

[34] On Vatican II's teaching on the possibility of salvation outside the visible confines of the church, though not without some connection with it, see *Lumen gentium*, no.16.

planting" rejected; rather, it is seen only as a part of the church's mission and is undertaken not in order to promote church extension but for the sake of the kingdom of God.[35]

Here it may be useful to take note of Pope John Paul II's rejection of some missionaries' practice of remaining silent about the call to conversion and of their separation of conversion from baptism. With regard to the first, the pope says: "Nowadays the call to conversion which missionaries address to non-Christians is put into question or passed over in silence. It is seen as an act of 'proselytizing'; it is claimed that it is enough to help people to become more human or more faithful to justice, freedom, peace and solidarity" (*RM*, no. 46). There is no doubt that conversion in the sense of turning toward Christ is the irreplaceable goal of Christian mission, and silence about it is not only unfaithful to the Christian message but also disingenuous. In this sense, works for justice and peace do not exhaust the mission of the church.

Not every silence about the call to conversion, however, is reprehensible, and to understand the pope's statement correctly, the following distinctions seem to be necessary.

1. If the call to conversion takes the form of "proselytizing" understood as any kind of manipulation of non-Christians to convert, by inducement or by threat (the so-called "rice Christians"), then the pope himself would condemn such an evangelizing strategy, since it infringes upon the convert's freedom of choice.

2. If the silence about the call to conversion is motivated by the concern that conversion has often been, especially in colonized countries, connected with psychological (most often covert but nonetheless real) coercion (see Wilbert Shenk's third postulate), then it is more than justified.

3. If it is claimed that "promoting and witnessing to the values of the reign of God may not be treated as though it were merely a means to achieve the end of building up the church; this work can be just as authentically missionary as building a church or preparing people for the sacraments,"[36] then such a claim is theologically valid.

If certain missionaries have been reticent about the call to conversion, it is perhaps because they see that conversion, which often is understood as renouncing one religion and joining the Christian church, has been made the be-all and end-all of mission. This brings us to the pope's second rejection, namely, that of the separation between conversion and baptism: "Not a few people, precisely in those areas involved in the mission *ad gentes*, tend to separate conversion to Christ from Baptism, regarding Baptism as unnecessary" (*RM*, no. 47). Again, it must be acknowledged that Christian tradition has consistently affirmed an intimate link between conversion and baptism. However, if the separation of

---

[35] Donal Dorr makes helpful distinctions between two kinds of missionaries, those engaged primarily in the building up of the church both as a community and in its institutional aspects and those primarily engaged in the promotion of "kingdom values" such as health care, education, human rights, ecology, and so on. The second kind of activities is no less mission than the first (*Mission in Today's World*, 193-201).

[36] Ibid., 198.

conversion from baptism is motivated by the concern that the number of conversions has been used as the yardstick to measure the success of mission, and that baptism has been administered without adequate spiritual preparation, then it is a salutary warning to missionaries that the temptation to make the church the center of mission is hard to resist.

Moreover, there is another reason why the call to conversion as the invitation to join the church has not been sounded in recent times, and that is, as far as Asia is concerned, the prospect of mass conversion to Christianity is extremely unlikely. The reason lies in Wilbert Shenk's first postulate mentioned above and is borne out by the fact that there have been few converts to Christianity from Hinduism, Buddhism, and Islam. The same point has also been made by Aloysius Pieris, who argues that Asian religions, which have penetrated deeply into the Asian soil, cannot be dislodged and replaced by Christianity. In other words, for most Asians, their religions do provide satisfactory answers to their existential problems, answers that Christianity cannot hope to improve upon, at least by theoretical arguments.[37] Missionaries in Asia must, calmly and soberly, face the fact that Christianity will remain forever a minority religion, despite Pope John Paul II's urgent appeal to direct the mission *ad gentes* to Asia in particular.[38] Moreover, this fact is not limited to Asia; rather, as Wilbert Shenk has noted, "the church of the future will be a minority church in most parts of the world."[39]

This minority status of the church is not something to be lamented over, however, nor should it be cause for missionary pessimism. Again, as Shenk suggests, "The prospect of a church stripped of the accouterments of privileges and power and committed to servanthood 'in the power of the Spirit' promises a real gain."[40] But such a promise can be fulfilled only if conversion is taken seriously in its twofold aspect of turning to Jesus as Lord and taking up his mission for the sake of the kingdom of God. Conversion as joining the Christian

---

[37] See Aloysius Pieris, *An Asian Theology of Liberation* (Maryknoll, N.Y.: Orbis Books, 1988), 54-55. Pieris distinguishes between "cosmic" (formerly called "animist") and "metacosmic" religiousness. Cosmic religiousness is an open-ended spirituality that is oriented toward its expression in metacosmic religiousness. The metacosmic religiousness is embodied in world religions and takes two forms: "agapeic" (such as Christianity) and "gnostic" such as Hinduism and Buddhism). Pieris acknowledges that Christianity still does have a chance of mass conversion in areas where cosmic religiousness remains intact, such as some tribal societies of India and Southeast Asia (as it had in the Philippines). See also Aloysius Pieris, *Love Meets Wisdom: A Christian Experience of Buddhism* (Maryknoll, N.Y.: Orbis Books, 1988) and *Fire and Water: Basic Issues in Asian Buddhism and Christianity* (Maryknoll, N.Y.: Orbis Books, 1996).

[38] See *RM*, no. 37 (a): "Particularly in Asia, toward which the Church's mission *ad gentes* ought to be chiefly directed, Christians are a small minority. . . . " The Pope also says that he is seeing a "new and promising horizon" for evangelization being fulfilled in Asia in his Apostolic Exhortation *Ecclesia in Asia*, no. 9. For an English translation of *Ecclesia in Asia*, see Peter C. Phan, ed., *The Asian Synod: Texts and Commentaries* (Maryknoll, N.Y.: Orbis Books, 2002), 286-340.

[39] Wilbert Shenk, *Changing Frontiers of Mission*, 188.

[40] Ibid., 189.

church is still a desirable outcome of mission, but it is made secondary to the turning to Jesus and taking up his mission.[41]

To better understand the role of conversion in mission, it would be helpful at this point to consider conversion in its psychological and anthropological aspects. Such a detailed study is, of course, beyond the purview of this chapter.[42] But if we only consider conversion in the strict sense, namely, the change of an individual from one religion to another, which mission *ad gentes* seeks,[43] and if we take into account the six stages of conversion as outlined by developmental psychology—crisis, quest, encounter, interaction, commitment, and growth[44]— it would seem proper, within the new theology of mission centered on the kingdom of God, to focus more on these six elements of conversion than on the individual's eventual act of joining the church through baptism or lack of it. Another way of explaining the role of conversion is to say that of the three components of religious conversion—"1) a change in denominational affiliation or status; 2) a movement *back* or to God through personal introspection or outward encounter; 3) a sense in which a person solves or resolves a religious identity crisis which integrates the personality and informs one's purpose,"[45] the focus should be placed on the last two components rather than on the first.

---

[41] For a very helpful study of the role of conversion in Roman Catholic theology of mission up to Vatican II, see Ronan Hoffman, "Conversion and the Mission of the Church," *Journal of Ecumenical Studies* 5 (1968), 1-20. Hoffman recommends dialogue as the way of mission and writes: "But if at the end of the dialogue, non-Christians wish to retain their religion, Catholics must not only give in gracefully but, even further, let them know that they would sincerely like them to be better followers of their chosen religion and leave all matters to Almighty God" (ibid., 19).

[42] For a brief study, see Lewis Rambo, "Conversion" in *Dictionary of Pastoral Care and Counseling*, ed. Rodney Hunter (Nashville, Tenn.: Abingdon Press, 1990), 228-30, with a useful bibliography; and Alan R. Tippett, "Conversion as a Dynamic Process in Christian Mission," *Missiology* (1977), 203-21.

[43] This type of conversion is called *tradition transition* (leaving one religion for another, e.g., Buddhism for Christianity) as distinct from *institutional transition* (leaving one community for another *within* the same religious system, e.g., Roman Catholicism for Lutheranism); *affiliation* (movement from no commitment to a nominal or strong commitment); and *intensification* (revitalization of the commitment to a religious body). See Rambo, "Conversion," 228; and V. Bailey Gillespie, *The Dynamics of Religious Conversion* (Birmingham, Ala.: Religious Education Press, 1991), 14-15.

[44] See Rambo, "Conversion," 229-30. I am modifying somewhat Rambo's categories. Persons undergoing conversion generally go through the following six stages: (1) In the stage of *crisis* they experience dissatisfaction with their lives, which they see as inauthentic and feel that change is demanded; (2) in the stage of *quest* they seek new ways of thinking, feeling, and acting; (3) in the stage of *encounter* they meet a person or group whose message seems to answer their needs; (4) in *interaction* they see that their needs are met by this person or group: needs for an intellectual system of meaning, for an emotional sense of belonging, for new modes of acting, and for a leader; (5) in *commitment* they decide to break with their past and accept the new way of life, often through some ritual; and (6) in *growth* they consider their new life as a pilgrimage supported by the community they have joined.

[45] Gillespie, *The Dynamics of Religious Conversion*, 63.

The reason for this shift of emphasis is that, given the little likelihood of many conversions to Christianity in Asia in the future in terms of receiving baptism and joining the church, the church's mission must focus on witnessing to the kingdom values by helping others cope with their personal crisis. This crisis may be caused by factors other than religious ones, such as material poverty, physical illness, psychological loneliness, political oppression, loss of loved ones, the breakup of relationships, and so forth. The purpose is not to exploit these vulnerable moments in a person's life and manipulate them into opportunities for evangelism and conversion. Rather, this work is part of the church's larger task of dialoguing with the local cultures (inculturation), with the poor (liberation), and with the indigenous religions (interreligious dialogue).[46] Through this triple dialogue not only individuals but also (and more importantly for Asia, since individual conversions will not be numerous) the cultural, political, social, and economic structures will be converted (Pope Paul VI's concept of "evangelization of culture"), that is, suffused with the gospel values of justice, peace, solidarity, reconciliation, harmony, forgiveness, sharing, and love.

Furthermore, in this triple dialogue not only the "pagans" and the cultures are converted but the "converters" as well. The evangelizers become the evangelized. Mission is never a monologue by the missionaries proclaiming the good news to those who have to listen to it; rather, it is a two-way movement in which, as in any effective communication, the sender becomes the receiver and the receiver becomes the sender in alternation. In this way conversion is no longer exclusively leaving one religion to join another but learning whatever is good from another religion so as to be a better follower of one's own religion. Conversion does not always take the form of tradition transition (leaving one religion for another) but is also that of "institutional transition," "affiliation," and "intensification," as explained in note 43.

Conversion then can mean, in its Latin etymology, "turning *with*" rather than simply turning *toward* something else. Christians and non-Christians can turn *together*, with one another, not toward a particular religious organization or church but toward the kingdom of God, and they can and must help each other in doing so. Just as in ecumenism, the model of "returning" of the "separated brethren" to the Catholic church is no longer adopted as the goal of church unity, so in mission in the future, especially in Asia where religious pluralism is the fact of life, conversion is not sought as the joining of the Christian church by, for example, ex-Buddhists or ex-Hindus or ex-Muslims (though that may happen from time to time, just as the other way round is also possible), but as the "turning" of all humans, together and with reciprocal assistance and encouragement, toward Christ, that is, to the way of life and the values that he embodied in his own person, and the "taking up of his mission" in the service of the kingdom of God.

---

[46] For more details on this triple dialogue, see Chapter 2 herein.

PART TWO

Worship and Prayer
in the Asian Way

5

Popular Religion
and Liturgical Inculturation

PERSPECTIVES AND CHALLENGES
FROM ASIA

POPULAR RELIGION IN RECENT THEOLOGIES

In the last three decades, and more specifically since the close of the Second Vatican Council, there has been, to judge from the avalanche of published literature, an intense interest in what is called popular piety, popular religiosity, popular religion, folk religion, common religion, or more narrowly, popular Catholicism.[1] Whereas popular religion—popular understood not in the sense of being fashionable or in vogue but in the sense of originating from and being practiced largely by the common people, as opposed to being codified, approved and propagated by the religious leaders—has always been present in human history, the widespread *interest* in and the scholarly *study* of this religious phenomenon are of recent vintage in the West. In the wake of cultural anthropology, sociology, psychology, and other sciences in the humanities, theology has

---

[1] For a helpful discussion of these terminologies and of popular religion in general, see Robert Schreiter, *Constructing Local Theologies* (Maryknoll, N.Y.: Orbis Books, 1985), 122-43. Popular religion is often contrasted to official religion, elite religion, and esoteric religion. Schreiter rightly notes the inadequacy of these approaches and calls for an adherence in the studies of popular religion to the following principles: "trying to listen to the culture on its own terms; adopting a holistic pattern of description; remaining attentive to the audience and the interest of the questioner in each event" (126). Other helpful discussions of popular religion are found in Peter W. Williams, *Popular Religion in America: Symbolic Change and the Modernization Process in Historical Perspective* (Urbana and Chicago: University of Illinois Press, 1980), 2-21; Charles H. Lippy, *Being Religious, American Style: A History of Popular Religiosity in the United States* (Westport, Conn.: Greenwood Press, 1994), 1-22; Michael Candelaria, *Popular Religion and Liberation: The Dilemma of Liberation Theology* (Albany, N.Y.: SUNY Press, 1990), 1-38; and Thomas Bamat and Paul Wiest, eds., *Popular Catholicism in a World Church: Seven Case Studies in Inculturation* (Maryknoll, N.Y.: Orbis Books, 1999), 1-16.

of late taken up a sustained investigation of popular religion and, with it, of popular culture.[2]

As is generally recognized, there was at Vatican II little discussion of popular religion as such. Rather, the council's concern was with what it called *pia exercitia*, that is, popular practices of devotion. These, it declares in the *Constitution of the Sacred Liturgy*, are to be highly recommended, "provided they conform to the laws and norms of the church." Moreover, "such devotions should be so drawn up that they harmonize with the liturgical seasons, accord with the sacred liturgy, are in some way derived from it, and lead the people to it, since in fact the liturgy by its very nature is far superior to any of them" (*SC*, no. 13).[3]

In the immediate post–Vatican II era, as the liturgical reform went into full swing, popular religion suffered a serious decline. All its four forms, as classified by Domenico Sartore, were affected: first, devotions to Christ, the Blessed Virgin, and the saints in the forms of pilgrimages, patronal feasts, processions, popular devotions, and novenas; second, the rites related to the liturgical year; third, traditional practices in conjunction with the celebrations of the sacraments and other Christian rites such as funerals; and fourth, institutions and religious objects connected with various forms of popular religiosity.[4]

Recently, however, there has been a noticeable resurgence of popular religion not only among the churches of the Third World,[5] but also among Christians of

---

[2] As evidence of this resurgence of popular religion in contemporary theological discourse, Anscar Chupungco cites the bibliography compiled by F. Trolese in 1979, which showed as many as 528 titles in Italian, French, and Spanish languages alone. See F. Trolese, "Contributo per una bibliografia sulla religiosità popolare," in *Ricerche sulla religiosità popolare* (Bologna: Dehoniane, 1979), 273-325, cited by Anscar Chupungco, *Liturgical Inculturation: Sacramentals, Religiosity, and Catechesis* (Collegeville, Minn.: Liturgical Press, 1992), 95. For works in German, see ibid., 95 n. 1. For a review of recent works on Hispanic popular religiosity, see Robert Wright, "Popular Religiosity: Review of Literature," *Liturgical Ministry* 7 (Summer, 1998), 141-46. The rise of this scholarly interest in popular religion may be a symptom of a diffuse malaise and disenchantment in Western societies with the ideals of scientific, value-free, and objective knowledge spawned by the Enlightenment. In the United States it has been accompanied by the adoption of some beliefs and practices of Eastern religions and some forms of Gnosticism such as New Age.

[3] This relative neglect of and suspicious attitude toward popular religion by Vatican II was one of the results of the triumph of the Liturgical movement, spearheaded by Dom Prosper Guéranger, at the council. The Liturgical movement saw popular religion as rooted in subjective and emotional piety, thus favoring the Enlightenment's individualist tendencies, which it wanted to combat. This belittling of "subjective" or "personal" piety and consequent rejection of "all other religious exercises not directly connected with the sacred Liturgy and performed outside public worship" were criticized by Pope Pius XII as "false, insidious, and quite pernicious" (*Mediator Dei*, no. 30). Papal condemnations notwithstanding, the Liturgical movement's negative assessment of popular religion found its way into article 13 of *SC*. See Patrick L. Malloy, "The Re-Emergence of Popular Religion among Non-Hispanic American Catholics," *Worship* 72/1 (1998), 2-4.

[4] See Chupungco, *Liturgical Inculturation*, 102, summarizing Domenico Sartore, "Le manifestazione della religiosità popolare," *Anamnesis* 7 (Genoa, 1989), 232-33.

[5] See Cristián Parker, *Popular Religion and Modernization in Latin America: A Different Logic*, trans. Robert Barr (Maryknoll, N.Y.: Orbis Books, 1996).

the First World.[6] One of the contributing factors to this comeback is the widespread dissatisfaction with the classical form of Vatican II's reformed rites characterized by Roman *sobrietas*, *brevitas*, *simplicitas* and linear rationality, which do not respond to the people's need for emotional and total involvement in liturgical celebrations.[7] This need is met by popular religion with its emphasis on spontaneity, festivity, joyfulness, and community.[8]

The stubborn persistence of devotional practices and the failure of certain liturgical reforms sparked a new interest among theologians and liturgists in the nature and function of popular religion. Among Latin American theologians there was a shift from an elitist and Marxist view of popular religion as Catholicism deformed by superstition and as the opiate of the masses, and hence an obstacle to liberation (represented by Juan Luis Segundo), to the view that popular religion as a mass phenomenon is an indispensable and powerful force for the liberation of the people, and hence something to be promoted (represented by Juan Carlos Scannone).[9]

Black Theology and Inculturation

In the United States the recovery of popular religion was spearheaded by black theology. In reaction to Joseph R. Washington Jr., who asserted in the 1960s that black congregations are not churches but religious societies to be integrated into the mainstream of American theology and that the Black Church

---

[6] See Malloy, "The Re-Emergence of Popular Religion among Non-Hispanic American Catholics," 5-8. On the resurgence of Marian devotion in the United States in particular, see Peter C. Phan, "Mary in Recent Theology and Piety: The View from the United States of America," *Ephemerides Mariologicae* 50 (October-December, 2000), 425-39.

[7] It is these characteristics that lie behind *SC*'s insistence on a "full, conscious, and active participation in liturgical celebrations" (no. 14). For a presentation of the critique of Vatican II's liturgical reform by four ideologically diverse theologians (Joseph Ratzinger, David Power, Francis Mannion, and Matthew Fox), see Malloy, "The Re-Emergence of Popular Religion among Non-Hispanic American Catholics," 12-20.

[8] For a description of the general traits of popular religion, see Chupungco, *Liturgical Inculturation*, 109-11. Chupungco quotes C. Valenziano's characterization of popular religion: "It is festive, felt, spontaneous; it is expressive, immediate, human; it is communitarian, collective, joyful, symbolic, traditional, alive" (109-10). See also C. Valenziano, "La religiosità popolare in prospettiva antropologica," in *Liturgia e religiosità popolare* (Bologna: Dehoniane, 1979), 83-110. Chupungco, in his analysis of Filipino popular religion, identifies the principal features of popular religion as follows: "These are, first, their literary genre, which is marked by a discursive and picturesque quality; second, their use of sacred images; third, their preference for such devices for participation as repetitiveness and communal recitation; and fourth, their use of dramatic forms that are often strongly mimetic or imitative" (119).

[9] For an exposition of these two opposing views of popular religion, see Candelaria, *Popular Religion and Liberation*. Candelaria highlights the double dimension of popular religion, already noted by Karl Marx, namely, its alienating effect and its liberating potential. For a detailed study of popular religion in Latin America, see Equipo Seladoc, *Religiosidad popular* (Salamanca: Ediciones Sístandardgueme, 1976); and Christian Smith and Joshua Prokopy, eds., *Latin American Religion in Motion* (London: Routledge, 1999).

has no theology,[10] black theology began to develop among Protestants.[11] Despite internal varieties and differences, black theology is rooted in the foundational experience of African Americans, namely, chattel slavery and its pervasive consequences in all areas of their lives. Besides drawing on the Bible and the writings of past black thinkers and activists (for example W. E. B. Du Bois, Henry M. Turner, Martin Luther King Jr., and Malcolm X), black theology makes extensive use of social analysis and even Marxist categories to frame its message of liberation. It also engages in a reinterpretation of cultural history, highlighting the cultural achievements of blacks. It mines the rich black spiritual tradition embodied in sermons, folktales, and music (for example, the spirituals and the blues).[12]

On their part, black American Catholics have also made a significant contribution to the development of black theology, with their own distinctive accents derived from the Roman Catholic tradition.[13] One of the contributions of immediate interest concerns liturgy. Clarence Rufus J. Rivers has pointed out that to have an authentically African American liturgy, it is necessary to shift from the one-dimensional "ocular" tradition of the West (and by implication, of the Roman liturgy), which emphasizes linearity and discursiveness, to the "oral-aural" African tradition, which involves the use of all the senses (in particular hearing and touch) and privileges the emotional, poetic, mythic, and dramatic dimensions of human knowing. The former is conducive to "liturgiology," the latter to "liturgy."[14] D. Reginald Whitt has provided an illuminating commentary on the Congregation for Divine Worship and the Discipline of the Sacraments' instruction *Varietates legitimae* and argued that the Roman instruction has only discouraged the use of liturgical inculturation to promote the emergence of new, non-Roman, ritual families other than the Ambrosian, Hispano-Mozarabic, and Roman in the Latin rite. But the document, he points out, does not rule out the possibility of the emergence of another ritual family. Hence, the door has not been closed on the

---

[10] See his *Black Religion: The Negro and Christianity in the United States* (Boston: Beacon Press, 1964). However, in his later books, *The Politics of God* (Boston: Beacon Press, 1967) and *Black Sects and Cults* (Garden City, N.Y.: Doubleday, 1972), Washington saw the necessity of joining political struggle with religion in the Black Church for survival and proposed a new program for black theology.

[11] Perhaps the most widely known black theologian is James Cone, whose prolific writings have exercised a profound influence on black liberation theology.

[12] See the works of James Cone, especially *The Spirituals and the Blues* (New York: Seabury Press, 1972); and Dwight N. Hopkins, *Shoes That Fit Our Feet: Sources for a Constructive Black Theology* (Maryknoll, N.Y.: Orbis Books, 1993).

[13] For a helpful introduction to black Catholic theology, see Diana L. Hayes and Cyprian Davis, eds., *Taking Down Our Harps: Black Catholics in the United States* (Maryknoll, N.Y.: Orbis Books, 1998).

[14] See Clarence Rufus J. Rivers, "The Oral African Tradition versus the Ocular Western Tradition," in Hayes and Davis, *Taking Down Our Harps*, 232-46. See also his other works: *The Spirit in Worship* (Cincinnati: Stimuli, 1973) and *Soulful Worship*, 2 vols. (Cincinnati: Stimuli, 1974).

study and discussion of an African American Catholic rite, including the adaptation of Roman liturgical books to the ethnic-religious heritage of African Americans, the erection of a particular Latin church jurisdiction for African American Catholics, or even the formation of a distinct African American canonical rite as part of a new Western church *sui iuris*, in addition to the twenty-one already existing churches.[15]

Hispanic/Latino Theology and Liturgical Inculturation

Hispanic/Latino theologians too have made significant contributions to the understanding of popular religion, and more specifically, popular Catholicism. In a very helpful essay James L. Empereur has surveyed the contributions of two prominent Latino theologians, Orlando Espín and Roberto Goizueto, to the theme of popular devotion as the privileged *locus theologicus* and as the embodiment of the aesthetic dimension of the Christian faith.[16] Other names should be added, such as Virgil Elizondo,[17] Allan F. Deck,[18] Alex García-Rivera,[19] Ana María Díaz-Stevens,[20] Anthony M. Stevens-Arroyo,[21] Timothy

---

[15] See D. Reginald Whitt, *"Varietates Legitimae* and an African-American Liturgical Tradition," in Hayes and Davis, *Taking Down Our Harps*, 247-80. To be noted also are two documents of the National Conference of Catholic Bishops: *In Spirit and Truth: Black Catholic Reflections on the Order of the Mass* (1988) and *Plenty Good Room: The Spirit and Truth of African American Catholic Worship* (1991).

[16] See James Empereur, "Popular Religion and the Liturgy: The State of the Question," *Liturgical Ministry* 7 (Summer, 1998), 105-10. The works examined are mainly Orlando Espín, *The Faith of the People: Theological Reflections on Popular Catholicism* (Maryknoll, N.Y.: Orbis Books, 1997), and Roberto Goizueta, *Caminemos con Jesús: Toward a Hispanic/Latino Theology of Accompaniment* (Maryknoll, N.Y.: Orbis Books, 1995).

[17] Among Virgil Elizondo's many works, the following should be mentioned: *Mestizaje: The Dialectic of Cultural Birth and the Gospel* (San Antonio, Tex.: Mexican American Cultural Center, 1978); *La Morenita: Evangelizer of the Americas* (San Antonio: Mexican American Cultural Center, 1980); *The Galilean Journey: The Mexican-American Promise* (Maryknoll, N.Y.: Orbis Books, 1983); *The Future Is Mestizo: Life Where Cultures Meet* (New York: Meyer-Stone, 1988); (with Timothy Mantovina), *Mestizo Worship: A Pastoral Approach to Liturgical Ministry* (Collegeville, Minn.: Liturgical Press, 1998), and *Guadalupe: Mother of the New Creation* (Maryknoll, N.Y.: Orbis Books, 1997).

[18] See *The Second Wave: Hispanic Ministry and the Evangelization of Cultures* (New York: Paulist Press, 1989).

[19] See *St. Martín de Porres: The "Little Stories" and the Semiotics of Culture* (Maryknoll, N.Y.: Orbis Books, 1995) and *The Community of the Beautiful: A Theological Aesthetics* (Collegeville, Minn.: Liturgical Press, 1999).

[20] See *Oxcart Catholicism on Fifth Avenue: The Impact of Puerto Rican Migration upon the Archdiocese of New York* (Notre Dame, Ind.: University of Notre Dame Press, 1993).

[21] See (with Ana María Díaz-Stevens), *Recognizing the Latino Resurgence in U.S. Religion: The Emmaus Paradigm* (New York: Westview Press, 1997).

Mantovina,[22] Marina Herrera,[23] María Pilar Aquino,[24] Jeanette Rodríguez,[25] and so on.[26]

Concerning Hispanic/Latino popular religion and liturgy in particular, a very substantial body of literature has been produced, and James Empereur has also provided a most helpful overview and critique.[27] Here the works of Arturo Pérez-Rodríguez,[28] Mark R. Francis,[29] Ricardo Ramírez,[30] Rosa María

---

[22] See "Liturgy, Popular Rites, and Popular Spirituality," *Worship* 63 (July 1989), 351-61; "Marriage Celebrations in Mexican American Communities," *Liturgical Ministry* 5 (Winter 1996), 22-26; and "Guadalupan Devotion in a Borderlands Community," *Journal of Hispanic/Latino Theology* 4/1 (August 1996), 6-26.

[23] See "Popular Religiosity and Liturgical Education," *Liturgy* 5/1 (1985), 33-37; and "Religion and Culture in the Hispanic Community as a Context for Religious Education: Impact of Popular Religiosity on U.S. Hispanics," *The Living Light* 21/2 (1985), 136-46.

[24] See *Our Cry for Life: Feminist Theology from Latin America* (Maryknoll, N.Y.: Orbis Books, 1993).

[25] See *Our Lady of Guadalupe: Faith and Empowerment among Mexican-American Women* (Austin, Tex.: University of Texas, 1994).

[26] For helpful general introductions to Hispanic/Latino theology, see Allan F. Deck, ed., *Frontiers of Hispanic Theology in the United States* (Maryknoll, N.Y.: Orbis Books, 1992); Roberto Goizueta, ed., *We Are a People! Initiatives in Hispanic American Theology* (Minneapolis: Fortress Press, 1992); Anthony Stevens-Arroyo and Ana María Díaz-Stevens, eds., *An Enduring Flame: Studies on Latino Popular Religiosity* (New York: CUNY, 1994); Jay Dolan and Allan Figueroa Deck, eds., *Hispanic Catholic Culture in the U.S.* (Notre Dame, Ind.: University of Notre Dame Press, 1994); Ana María Pineda and Robert Schreiter, eds., *Dialogue Rejoined: Theology and Ministry in the United States Hispanic Reality* (Collegeville, Minn.: Liturgical Press, 1995); Arturo Bañuelas, ed., *Mestizo Christianity: Theology from the Latin Perspective* (Maryknoll, N.Y.: Orbis Books, 1995); Allan F. Deck, Yolanda Tarango, and Timothy Mantovina, eds., *Perspectivas: Hispanic Ministry* (Kansas City: Sheed and Ward, 1995); Peter Casarella and Raúl Goméz, eds., *El Cuerpo de Cristo: The Hispanic Presence in the U.S. Catholic Church* (New York: Crossroad, 1998); Orlando Espín and Miguel H. Díaz, eds., *From the Heart of the People: Latino/a Explorations in Catholic Systematic Theology* (Maryknoll, N.Y.: Orbis Books, 1999); Eduardo Fernandez, *La Cosecha: Harvesting Contemporary U.S. Hispanic Theology* (Collegeville, Minn.: Liturgical Press, 2000); and Miguel H. Díaz, *On Being Human: U.S. Hispanic and Rahnerian Perspectives* (Maryknoll, N.Y.: Orbis Books, 2001). In addition, there are two important documents of the NCCB: The 1983 pastoral letter *The Hispanic Presence* and the 1987 *National Plan for Hispanic Ministry*. Finally, there is the journal of the Academy of Catholic Hispanic Theologians of the United States (ACHTUS), *Journal of Hispanic/Latino Theology*, which publishes essays related to Hispanic theology and ministry. *New Theology Review* 3/4 (November 1990) is devoted entirely to United States Hispanic Catholicism.

[27] See "Popular Religion and the Liturgy," 111-20.

[28] See *Popular Catholicism: A Hispanic Perspective* (Washington, D.C.: The Pastoral Press, 1988).

[29] See *Liturgy in a Multicultural Community* (Collegeville, Minn.: Liturgical Press, 1991); "Building Bridges between Liturgy, Devotionalism, and Popular Religion," *Assembly* 20/2 (1994); "Popular Piety and Liturgical Reform in a Hispanic Context," in Pineda and Schreiter, *Dialogue Rejoined*, 162-75; and "The Hispanic Liturgical Year: The People's Calendar," *Liturgical Ministry* 7 (Summer, 1998), 129-35.

[30] See *Fiesta, Worship, and Family* (San Antonio, Tex.: Mexican American Cultural Center, 1981).

Icaza,[31] Raúl Gómez,[32] Angela Erevia,[33] Gilbert Romero,[34] Jose Aviles,[35] Juan Sosa,[36] and Karen Mary Dávalos[37] may be mentioned, especially the practical and helpful book *Primero Dios: Hispanic Liturgical Resource* by Arturo Pérez-Rodríguez and Mark Francis.[38]

Elsewhere I have surveyed black and Hispanic/Latino theologies in the context of theological inculturation in the United States.[39] In this chapter I join in the conversation about popular devotion and liturgical inculturation, already carried out ably by black and Hispanic/Latino theologians, from the perspective of the Christian mission in Asia and Asian theologies. As a launching pad for my reflections, I begin with a summary exposition and evaluation of two official documents, one Protestant, the other Catholic, on liturgical inculturation. In the second part I present some insights of Asian theologies on liturgical inculturation, with special reference to popular religion. Finally, I consider some of the most difficult theological issues underlying liturgical inculturation from the perspective of Christian mission in Asia.

LITURGICAL INCULTURATION AND POPULAR RELIGION: OFFICIAL POSITIONS

A quick glance at the documents of the Roman Catholic magisterium since the Second Vatican Council, especially those of Pope John Paul II, shows that

---

[31] See "Prayer, Worship, and Liturgy in a United States Hispanic Key," in Deck, *Frontiers of Hispanic Theology in the United States*, 134-53 and " Do We Have Inculturated Liturgies?" in *Misa, Mesa y Musa: Liturgy in the U.S. Hispanic Church*, ed. Kenneth Davis (Schiller Park, Ill.: World Library Publications, in association with Instituto de Liturgia Hispana, 1997), 17-24.

[32] See "Celebrating the *Quinceañera* as a Symbol of Faith and Culture," in Davis, *Misa, Mesa y Musa*, 104-15; "The Day of the Dead: Celebrating the Continuity of Life and Death," *Liturgy* 14/1 (Spring, 1997), 28-40; and (with Heliodoro Lucatero and Sylvia Sánchez), *Don y Promesa: Costumbres y Tradiciones en los Ritos Matrimoniales Hispanas/Gift and Promise: Customs and Traditions in Hispanic Rites of Marriage* (Washington, D.C.: Instituto de Liturgia Hispana, 1997).

[33] See *Quince Años: Celebrando una tradición/Celebrating a Tradition* (San Antonio, Tex.: Missionary Catechists of Divine Providence, 1985).

[34] See *Hispanic Devotional Piety: Tracing the Biblical Roots* (Maryknoll, N.Y.: Orbis Books, 1991).

[35] See "Order for the Blessing of a *Quinceañera*," unpublished manuscript, discussed in James Empereur, "Popular Religion and Liturgy," 119-20.

[36] See "Illness and Healing in Hispanic Communities," *Liturgy* 2 (1982), 62-67; and "Hispanic Weddings: A Family Affair," *Liturgia y Canción* 7/3 (1996), 5-13.

[37] See "*La Quinceañera*: Making Gender and Ethnic Identities," *Frontiers* 16/2-3 (1996), 101-27.

[38] Mark R. Francis and Arturo J. Pérez-Rodríguez, *Primero Dios: Hispanic Liturgical Resource* (Chicago: Liturgical Training Publications, 1997).

[39] See Peter C. Phan, "Contemporary Theology and Inculturation in the United States," in *The Multicultural Church: A New Landscape in U.S. Theologies*, ed. William Cenker (New York: Paulist Press, 1996), 109-30, 176-92.

inculturation, including liturgical inculturation, has been a major concern.[40] Among Protestants, too, even though the term *inculturation* has rarely been used, it has recently been a subject of intense debate, especially in the context of mission and evangelization.[41] For the purpose of comparison I focus only on the Lutheran World Federation's Nairobi Statement on Worship and Culture (1996) and the Pontifical Council for Culture's *Toward a Pastoral Approach to Culture* (1999). Because space does not permit a detailed examination and evaluation of these two documents, only their main positions are highlighted.

The Nairobi Statement on Worship and Culture

The 1996 Nairobi Statement on Worship and Culture is the result of a four-year study, beginning in 1992. In the first phase of the study, the Department for Theology and Studies of the Lutheran World Federation (LWF) organized an international study team of about twenty-five scholars and church leaders (including three ecumenical participants, Anglican, Roman Catholic, and Methodist) who met for two consultations, first in Cartigny, Switzerland (1992) and then in Hong Kong (1994). The Cartigny statement and the papers and reports of these two consultations were published in 1994 as *Worship and Culture in Dialogue*.[42] This book served as the text for the second phase of the study, involving regional and subregional research around the world. The reports of that research, in turn, provided the material for the third phase, which was the gathering of the study team in Nairobi, Kenya, in 1996. The reports and papers of

---

[40] For a brief overview of the recent church teaching on inculturation, see Aylward Shorter, *Toward a Theology of Inculturation* (Maryknoll, N.Y.: Orbis Books, 1988), 179-238; and Michael Paul Gallagher, *Clashing Symbols: An Introduction to Faith and Culture* (New York: Paulist Press, 1998), 36-55. Important magisterial documents on inculturation include Paul VI's *Africae terrarum* (1967) and *Evangelii nuntiandi* (1975); John Paul II's *Catechesi tradendae* (1979), *Slavorum apostoli* (1985), *Redemptoris missio* (1993) and *Fides et ratio* (1998); the final statements of the assemblies of the Latin American Episcopal Conference (CELAM) at Medellín (1968), Puebla (1979), and Santo Domingo (1992); the International Theological Commission's *Faith and Inculturation* (1988); the Congregation for the Clergy's *General Directory for Catechesis* (1997); John Paul II's post-synodal apostolic exhortations following the special assemblies of the Synod of Bishops for Africa (1994), Asia (1998) and Oceania (1999); the Pontifical Council for Culture's *Toward a Pastoral Approach to Culture* (1999) and the numerous statements of the Federation of Asian Bishops' Conferences (FABC) since 1970. In liturgical matters there is the Congregation for Divine Worship and the Disciplines of the Sacraments' *Inculturation of the Roman Liturgy within the Roman Rite* (1994).

[41] Of special interest are the Lutheran World Federation's Nairobi Statement on Worship and Culture (1996); the World Council of Churches' Jerusalem statement "On Intercultural Hermeneutics" (1995); and the Report from the WCC-WCME Ecumenical Conference in Salvador, de Bahia, Brazil (1996). These texts are available in James A. Scherer and Stephen B. Bevans, eds., *New Directions in Mission and Evangelization,* vol. 3, *Faith and Culture* (Maryknoll, N.Y.: Orbis Books, 1999), 177-234.

[42] Geneva: LWF, 1994.

the Nairobi consultation were published in the volume entitled *Christian Worship: Unity in Cultural Diversity.*[43]

With regard to the relationship between worship and culture, the Nairobi Statement makes four basic affirmations. The first is that worship is *transcultural.* The source of the transculturality of Christian worship is said to be Christ's resurrection, and the meanings and fundamental structure of Christian worship, which are shared across the globe, are said to reside in the Eucharist: "The people gather, the Word of God is proclaimed, the people intercede for the needs of the Church and the world, the eucharistic meal is shared, and the people are sent out into the world for mission."[44] Other transcultural elements of Christian liturgy include readings from the Bible, the ecumenical creeds and the Our Father, and baptism in water in the Triune Name. The preservation of this core liturgical structure and the use of the transcultural elements of the liturgy in local congregational worship are "expressions of Christian unity across time, space, culture, and confession."[45]

Second, worship is *contextual,* and the model and mandate for the contextualization of Christian worship is said to be the mystery of Christ's incarnation. The method recommended for contextualization is dynamic equivalence, which involves "re-expressing components of Christian worship with something from a local culture that has an equal meaning, value, and function."[46] This method of dynamic equivalence is composed of four steps:

> First, the liturgical *ordo* (basic shape) should be examined with regard to its theology, history, basic elements, and cultural backgrounds. Second, those elements of the *ordo* that can be subjected to dynamic equivalence without prejudice to their meaning should be determined. Third, those components of culture that are able to re-express the Gospel and the liturgical *ordo* in an adequate manner should be studied. Fourth, the spiritual and pastoral benefits our people will derive from the changes should be considered.[47]

In addition to the dynamic equivalence method, the Nairobi Statement suggests that local churches might consider "the method of creative assimilation." This method goes beyond re-expressing some elements of the liturgical *ordo* by "adding pertinent components of local culture to the liturgical *ordo* in order to enrich its original core."[48] As examples of this creative assimilation, the Nairobi

---

[43] For information on this three-phase study, see the introduction to the Nairobi Statement by S. Anita Stauffer, study secretary for Worship and Congregational Life, Department for Theology and Studies, LWF. See Scherer and Bevans, *New Directions in Mission and Evangelization,* 3:177-80.

[44] Scherer and Bevans, *New Directions in Mission and Evangelization,* 3:181.

[45] Ibid., 3:182.

[46] Ibid.

[47] Ibid.

[48] Ibid.

Statement cites the addition to baptismal rituals of the practices of giving white garments and lighted candles to the neophytes of ancient mystery religions.

One important criterion for both dynamic equivalence and creative assimilation is that

> sound or accepted liturgical traditions are preserved in order to keep unity with the universal Church's tradition of worship, while progress inspired by pastoral needs is encouraged. On the side of culture, it is understood that not everything can be integrated with Christian worship, but only those elements that are connatural to (that is, of the same nature as) the liturgical *ordo*. Elements borrowed from local culture should always undergo critique and purification, which can be achieved through the use of biblical typology.[49]

Third, worship is *counter-cultural*. Every culture contains elements that are sinful and contradictory to the values of the gospel, and these require transformation: "Contextualization of Christian faith and worship necessarily involves challenging of all types of oppression and social injustice wherever they exist in earthly cultures."[50] In addition to these sinful elements, the Nairobi Statement mentions the "cultural patterns" themselves, which are imprinted by individualism and consumerism at the expense of the community and the care of the earth and its poor. The model for the transformation of the patterns and sinful elements of culture is the mystery of Christ's passage from death to eternal life.

Fourth, worship is *cross-cultural;* that is, all the elements of Christian worship taken from various cultures should be shared by all the churches across the cultural and denominational divides. This cross-cultural and ecumenical sharing "helps enrich the whole church and strengthen the sense of the *communio* of the Church."[51] The reason for this cross-culturality is the universality of Christ as the savior of all people.

In many ways the affirmations of the Nairobi Statement on Worship and Culture are akin to those of the Congregation for Divine Worship and the Discipline of the Sacraments' instruction *Inculturation of the Liturgy within the Roman Rite* (1994), even though the latter is focused on the narrower scope of providing the guidelines for the implementation of articles 37-40 of Vatican II's *Constitution on the Sacred Liturgy*.[52] The instruction decides to abandon the term *adaptation* of Vatican II in favor of *inculturation* in order to emphasize the double movement of the process: incarnating the gospel in different cultures

---

[49] Ibid., 3:182-83.

[50] Ibid., 3:183.

[51] Ibid.

[52] The official Latin text is "De Liturgia romana et inculturatione. Instructio quarta ad exsecutionem Constitutionis Concilii Vaticani Secundi de Sacra Liturgia recte ordinandam (ad Const. Art. 37-40)," published in *Notitiae* 30 (29 March 1994), 8-115. Its English text, under the title *Inculturation of the Liturgy within the Roman Rite*, was published by Vatican Press in 1994. Henceforth, *Inculturation*.

and introducing cultures into the gospel. Though the four categories of the Nairobi Statement are not used, there is little doubt that the Roman instruction shares its fourfold concern. First, implicit in the instruction is the transculturality and universal relevance not only of the Christian faith but even of the Roman rite itself.[53] Second, the very purpose of the instruction is to promote a greater contextualization of the Roman rite.[54] Third, the instruction also emphasizes the counter-culturality of the liturgy, rejecting elements of the culture that are contrary to the gospel.[55] Fourth, the instruction is also sensitive to the cross-culturality of liturgy, highlighting the varieties of cultural situations and the differences between traditional culture and an urban and industrial culture (see esp. nos. 29-30).

Furthermore, even the methods of inculturation advocated by the Nairobi Statement and the Roman instruction closely parallel each other. The former's "method of dynamic equivalence" is by and large the same as that of adaptation of the latter, minus, of course, the question of the authority supervising and approving the proposed changes proper to the Roman Catholic Church.[56] Whereas the Nairobi Statement speaks of the necessity of preserving the "meanings and fundamental structure," or the *ordo* of Christian worship, the Roman instruction makes the maintenance of the "substantial unity of the Roman rite" imperative in inculturation.

According to the Roman instruction, as long as the "typical editions of liturgical books, published by authority of the Supreme Pontiff, and . . . the liturgical books approved by the Episcopal Conferences for their areas and confirmed by the Apostolic See" are followed, adaptations in language, music and singing, gesture and posture, and art are possible. Besides textual adaptations that are envisaged in the typical Latin editions, adaptations in rituals are especially called for in the rites of Christian initiation, the marriage rite, funerals, blessings, the Liturgical Year, and the Liturgy of the Hours (see nos. 53-61).

In sum, both the Nairobi Statement and the Roman instruction envisage inculturation as no more than adaptation of a previously existing rite, whether

---

[53] "So the liturgy of the Church must not be foreign to any country, people or individual, and at the same time it should transcend the particularity of race and nation" (*Inculturation,* no. 18).

[54] "Inculturation thus understood [as penetration of the gospel into the culture and insertion of the culture into the gospel] has its place in worship as in other areas of the life of the Church. It constitutes one of the aspects of the inculturation of the Gospel, which calls for true integration, in the life of faith of each people, of the permanent values of a culture, rather than their transient expressions" (*Inculturation,* no. 5).

[55] "Fidelity to traditional usages must be accompanied by purification and, if necessary, a break with the past. . . . Obviously the Christian liturgy cannot accept magic rites, superstition, spiritism, vengeance or rites with a sexual connotation" (*Inculturation,* no. 48).

[56] "Adaptations of the Roman rite, even in the field of inculturation, depend completely on the *authority* of the Church. This authority belongs to the Apostolic See, which exercises it through the Congregation for Divine Worship and the Discipline of the Sacraments; it also belongs, within the limits fixed by law, to Episcopal Conferences, and to the diocesan bishop" (*Inculturation,* no. 37).

Lutheran or Roman, by way of translating official liturgical texts as well as modifications and additions of nonessential rituals. As the Roman instruction puts it clearly: "The work of inculturation does not foresee the creation of new families of rites; inculturation responds to the needs of a particular culture and leads to adaptations which still remain part of the Roman rite" (no. 36).

It is true that more than the Nairobi Statement's "method of creative assimilation," the Roman instruction does envisage, in accord with *SC,* no. 40, that "in some places and circumstances, an even more radical adaptation of the liturgy is needed and this entails greater difficulties" (no. 63).[57] We are warned however that these "more profound adaptations do not envisage a transformation of the Roman rite but are made within the context of the Roman rite" (no. 63).[58] Examples of these more radical adaptations are not given in the instruction. However, they are said to go beyond those "envisaged by the *General Instructions* and the *Praenotanda* of the liturgical books" and are to be undertaken only after "an Episcopal Conference has exhausted all the possibilities of adaptation offered by the liturgical books" (no. 63). The experimental nature of these more radical adaptations is strongly emphasized, and a detailed procedure is laid out for their proposal, experimentation, and final approval (see nos. 65-69).

With regard to popular religion and devotional practices in particular, the Nairobi Statement has very little to say, except to affirm that these cultural practices, such as the giving of white vestments and lighted candles, rituals taken from ancient mystery religions, can enrich the liturgical *ordo*, though the elements of the *ordo* itself, the statement warns, should not be culturally re-expressed, but only enriched by adding new elements from local culture. Similarly, the approach toward popular devotions in the Roman instruction is equally restrictive:

> The introduction of devotional practices into liturgical celebrations under the pretext of inculturation cannot be allowed "because by its nature, (the liturgy) is superior to them." It belongs to the local Ordinary to organize such devotions, to encourage them as supports of the life and faith of Christians, and to purify them, when necessary, because they need to be constantly permeated by the Gospel. He will take care to ensure that they do not replace liturgical celebrations or become mixed up with them (no. 45).

A more appreciative understanding of popular piety is present in the 1988 International Theological Commission's *Faith and Inculturation*: "Without any

---

[57] In some respects, however, the Nairobi Statement is more flexible than the Roman instruction, since it insists only on the preservation of the liturgical *ordo* and not substantial unity with any particular rite.

[58] It is interesting to note that the phrase "within the context of the Roman rite" is used in reference to these more radical adaptations, rather than "the substantial unity of the Roman rite," which has been used for adaptations allowed by the typical editions of liturgical books and the liturgical books approved by the episcopal conferences for their areas and confirmed by the Apostolic See. Whatever their precise meanings, their differences appear intentional.

doubt whatsoever, popular piety can bring an irreplaceable contribution to a Christian cultural anthropology which would permit the reduction of the often tragic division between the faith of Christians and certain socioeconomic institutions, of quite different orientation, which regulate their daily life" (no. 7). However, *Faith and Inculturation* states, the general evaluation of popular religion is still overwhelmingly negative:

> The limits of popular piety have often been condemned. They stem from a certain naïveté, are a source of various deformations of religion, even of superstitions. One remains at the level of cultural manifestations without a true adhesion to faith at the level where this is expressed in the service on [*sic*] one's neighbor. Badly directed, popular piety can even lead to the formation of sects and thus place true ecclesial unity in danger. It also risks being manipulated, be it by political powers or by religious forces foreign to the Christian faith (no. 6).

Toward a Pastoral Approach to Culture

An almost diametrically opposite evaluation of popular religion was given in the 1999 document of the Pontifical Council for Culture titled *Toward a Pastoral Approach to Culture*.[59] The aim of popular religion is to reflect on the contemporary challenges to the church's task of evangelization and to propose concrete ways to inculturate the Christian faith into cultures. As *Toward a Pastoral Approach to Culture* puts it:

> The primary objective of the pastoral approach to culture is to inject the lifeblood of the Gospel into cultures to renew from within and transform in the light of revelation the visions of men and society that shape cultures, the concepts of men and women, of the family and of education, of school and university, of freedom and of truth, of labor and leisure, of the economy and of society, of the sciences and of the arts (nos. 27-28).

To fulfill this mission, the church must have what John Paul II calls "a cultural project."[60] The "ordinary" ways in which this project is carried out, says *Toward a Pastoral Approach to Culture*, are popular piety and the parish.

It is highly significant that among the various concrete proposals that the document suggests, popular religion obtains primacy of place. The lengthy statement on popular piety needs to be quoted in full so that its radical volte-face from earlier magisterial documents can be appreciated:

---

[59] An English translation is available from Pauline Books & Media, Boston. The Pontifical Council for Culture was instituted by John Paul II in 1982. In his *Letter Instituting the Pontifical Council for Culture*, the pope says: "A faith that does not become culture is a faith not fully accepted, not entirely thought out, not faithfully lived" (in *Acta Apostolicae Sedis* 74 [1982], 683-88).

[60] John Paul II, *Address to the Pontifical Council for Culture* (1997), 405.

It is a fact that, in what are known as "Christian" countries, from one generation to the next there had developed a whole way of understanding and living the faith which eventually, to a greater or lesser degree, permeated people's individual and social lives: local feasts, family traditions, various celebrations, pilgrimages and so on. This created a whole culture which effectively included everyone, a culture built on faith and organized around it. Such a culture appears to be particularly threatened by secularism. It is important to support the better efforts which have been made to revive such traditions. However, this must not be left to specialists in folk heritage or politics, whose aims are often alien, if not hostile, to faith; pastoral workers, Christian communities and qualified theologians should also be involved.

If they are to touch people's hearts, proclaiming the Gospel to the young and to adults and celebrating salvation in the liturgy demand not only a profound knowledge of the faith, but also a knowledge of the cultural environment. When people love their culture as the special part of their life, it is in that culture that they live and profess their Christian faith. Bishops, priests, men and women religious and lay people need to *develop* a sensitivity to this culture, in order to protect and promote it in the light of the Gospel values, above all when it is a minority culture. Such attention to culture can offer those who are in any way disadvantaged a way to faith and to a better quality of Christian life at the heart of the Church. Men and women who have integrated a deep faith with their education and culture are living witnesses who will help many others to rediscover the Christian roots of their culture.

Religion is also memory and tradition, and *popular piety* is one of the best examples of genuine inculturation of faith, because it is a harmonious blend of faith and liturgy, feelings and art, and the recognition of our identity in local traditions. Thus, "America, which historically has been, and still is, a melting pot of peoples, has recognized in the *mestizo* face of the Virgin of Tepeyac, in Blessed Mary of Guadalupe, an impressive example of a perfectly inculturated evangelization" (*Ecclesia in America*, 11). Popular piety is evidence of the osmosis that takes place between the innovative power of the Gospel and the deepest levels of a culture. It is one of the foremost opportunities for people to meet the living Christ. There needs to be a constant pastoral discernment of popular piety as it evolves, in order to discover its genuine spiritual values and bring them to fruition in Christ "so that . . . it might lead to a sincere conversion and a practical exercise of charity" (cf. ibid., 16). Popular piety is the way a people expresses its faith and its relationship to God and his Providence, to Our Lady and the saints, to one's neighbor, to those who have died or to creation, and it strengthens its belonging to the Church. Purifying and catechizing expressions of popular piety can, in certain regions, be a decisive element of in-depth evangelization to support and to develop a true community awareness in the sharing of faith, particularly through the demonstration of the religiosity of the people of God as in the celebration of major feasts (cf. *Lumen Gentium*, 67).

These humble means are available to everyone, and allow the faithful to express their faith, be strong in hope and demonstrate their love. Daily life in many lands is colored by a strong sense of the sacred. A valid pastoral approach should promote and make the most of holy places, sanctuaries and pilgrimages, holy days and holy nights, liturgical vigils and adoration, holy things or sacramentals, remembrances and the sacred seasons of the liturgy. Several dioceses and university chaplaincies organize, at least one a year, a journey on foot to a sacred place, following in the footsteps of the Hebrews who sang the *Canticles of Ascent* with real joy as they drew near Jerusalem.

Popular piety naturally cries out for artistic expression. Those with pastoral responsibility must encourage creativity in all areas: ritual, music, song, decoration, etc. . . . They should also see to it that these things are of good cultural and religious quality (nos. 27-28).

A long way has been traveled from Vatican II's *Sacrosanctum concilium* to this 1999 document of the Pontifical Council on popular religion. It may be useful to elaborate briefly this new appreciation of popular religion:

1. Popular religion is "a whole way of understanding and living the faith." It is therefore none of the following: (1) a debased form of Catholicism (the elitist interpretation), (2) a false consciousness imposed by the ruling class upon the proletariat (the Marxist interpretation), (3) the foundational and original religiosity that cannot be totally absorbed by world religions (the base-line interpretation), (4) the genuine religion of the poor and simple folk skewed by the church and the clergy (the romanticist interpretation), (5) the survival of pre-Christian religion (the remnant interpretation), (6) a form of resistance of the dominated class against the ruling class (the subaltern interpretation), or (7) a response to the people's social-psychological needs in interaction with the economic and political conditions (the social-psychological interpretation).[61]

2. Popular religion is all-inclusive; everyone is welcome to participate in this culture built on faith and organized around faith.

3. Everyone in the church must develop a sensitivity to the surrounding culture, in particular the cultures of minority groups, to protect and promote them in light of gospel values, because cultures provide, especially to those who are disadvantaged, a way to live the Christian faith.

4. Popular religion is "one of the best examples of genuine inculturation of faith," because it is "a harmonious blend of faith and liturgy, feeling and art," and because it recognizes a people's identity in local traditions.

5. Popular religion is a powerful instrument for evangelization, "one of the foremost opportunities for people to meet the living Christ," "a decisive element

---

[61] For an explanation of these seven approaches to popular religion, see Schreiter, *Constructing Local Theologies*, 131-39.

for an in-depth evangelization," because it is the osmosis between the transformative power of the gospel and the deepest levels of a culture.

6. Popular religion is the way people establish their relationships not only to God, Mary, and the saints but also to their neighbors, their ancestors, the material environment, and the church.

7. The church should therefore promote holy places, sanctuaries, and pilgrimages, holy days and holy nights, liturgical vigils and adoration, holy things and sacramentals, remembrances and the sacred seasons of the liturgy. It should encourage creativity in areas such as ritual, music, song, decorations, and so on.

Clearly, these statements on popular piety or religion (and not simply popular devotions, the *pia exercitia* of Vatican II) are a far cry from the minimalist, legalistic, and overwhelmingly negative approach of *Sacrosanctum concilium*, the International Theological Commission's *Faith and Inculturation*, the instruction on liturgical inculturation, and even the Nairobi Statement. From the context, it is clear that *Toward a Pastoral Approach to Culture*, when speaking about the various expressions of popular religion, is referring to existing Christian devotional practices. Nevertheless, its explicit intention is to urge an encounter among the gospel and the cultures and the popular religions of non-Christian people. How this encounter should be carried out, the document does not specify, except for recommending "purifying and catechizing" expressions of popular piety.[62] To find an answer to this question, we turn to the missionary experiences in Asia and Asian theologies.

LITURGICAL INCULTURATION AS DIALOGUE

Born in Asia, Christianity soon moved to the West, but its early presence in Asia should not be forgotten.[63] One prominent characteristic of this early Asian Nestorian Christianity was its remarkable openness to dialogue with other cultures and religions. Never a majority, Christians learned how to live as a community of believers among other communities of believers, especially Buddhists and Manichaeans. The ethnic diversity of these Christian communities is illustrated by a tenth-century mural on a church wall in Kocho, near the ancient city of Turfan, west of the Great Wall, depicting a Sogdian priest, holding a chalice, addressing two Turkish men and a Chinese woman. We have reliable evidence that Buddhists, Christians, and Manichaeans read one another's writings and even collected them in their libraries. They also collaborated in translation projects, and there was mutual influence in the ways each group believed and expressed their faiths.[64] The borrowing of concepts and terminology, while

---

[62] It is interesting to note that not once does *Toward a Pastoral Approach to Culture* cite *Inculturation of the Liturgy within the Roman Rite*, though obviously liturgical inculturation is one of the concrete and most effective ways in which a pastoral approach to culture is realized.

[63] See Chapter 2 herein.

[64] For an account of how the Christian Nestorian Bishop Adam helped the Indian Buddhist missionary to China translate the Buddhist texts into Chinese and how he might have influenced the two famous Japanese Buddhist monks, Kobo Daishi (the founder of

maintaining basic Christian orthodoxy, was particularly evident in the early documents from China, where Chinese Christians borrowed Buddhist terms to formulate their understanding of God and Jesus.[65] So pronounced was this inter-religious exchange along the Silk Road and in China that, in the words of two recent scholars, Ian Gillman and Hans-Joachim Klimkeit, "one could almost speak of a Christian-Buddhist dialogue being conducted in Central Asia 1000 years ago, Christians and Buddhists not only living together, but being in constant interaction."[66]

This openness to dialogue with the local religions and cultures also marked the missionary enterprise of the Jesuits to China, India, and Vietnam. The names of Matteo Ricci (1552-1610) in China, Roberto de Nobili (1577-1656) in India, and Alexandre de Rhodes (1593-1660) in Vietnam eloquently testify to the Society of Jesus's commitment to what we call today inculturation.[67]

Unfortunately, the history of the so-called Chinese Rites Controversy is a tragic testimony to how the spirit of respectful dialogue toward cultures and religions, which characterized the early Nestorian missionary enterprise in the seventh century and the Jesuit mission in the seventeenth century, is not something that can be taken for granted but must be carefully and sedulously cultivated.[68]

It is in this spirit of dialogue, I submit, that inculturation, and by implication, liturgical inculturation, should be understood and undertaken. In Chapter 3 I have shown how, for the FABC, the church that is not only *in* but also *of* Asia must carry out its evangelizing mission in the mode of dialogue, indeed, in a triple dialogue, with the Asian poor, their religions, and their cultures. This new way of being church requires that the church be a "communion of communities," a participatory church, a living witness to the risen Christ, and a prophetic sign of the reign of God.

It is only in light of the Asian church's attempt to find a new way of being church, becoming a fully local church, a church which is a participatory "communion of communities," integrally engaged in the triple, intrinsically interconnected dialogue with the Asian poor, their cultures, and their religions, that, in my judgment, liturgical inculturation can be correctly understood. In this connection it is very interesting to note that in the thirty years of its existence and its abundant theological production, the FABC has devoted very few pages to the explicit theme of liturgical inculturation.[69] This lacuna, I believe, is not an

---

Japan's sect of Tantric Buddhism), and Dengyo Daishi (the founder of the Tendai school of Japanese Buddhism), see Moffett, *A History of Christianity in Asia*, 1:301-2.

[65] For a discussion of theological syncretism in the early Chinese Christian texts, see ibid., 1:305-13.

[66] Ian Gillman and Hans-Joachim Klimkeit, *Christians in Asia before 1500* (Ann Arbor, Mich.: University of Michigan Press, 1999), 206.

[67] Ricci and de Nobili are better known than de Rhodes. On the latter, see Peter C. Phan, *Mission and Catechesis: Alexandre de Rhodes and Inculturation in Seventeenth-Century Vietnam* (Maryknoll, N.Y.: Orbis Books, 1998).

[68] On the Chinese Rites Controversy, see Chapter 7 herein.

[69] One important text on liturgical inculturation, however, is FABC, *Theses on the Local Church: A Theological Reflection in the Asian Context*, FABC Papers, no. 60 (Hong Kong: FABC, 1991), thesis 8.

oversight. Rather, it is due to the FABC's overarching and fundamental insight that inculturation, liturgical or otherwise, is not something to be pursued for its own sake or to make worship palatable to Asian aesthetic and religious tastes. Instead, it must be subordinated to the task of becoming an Asian church through the essential mode of dialogue with the Asian poor, their cultures, and their religions.

Of course, it is not the task of the FABC to devise concrete forms or programs of liturgical inculturation. These fall within the competence of each bishop and each conference of bishops. The FABC recognizes that the church in Asia still "remains foreign in its lifestyle, in its institutional structure, in its worship" and that "Christian rituals often remain formal, neither spontaneous nor particularly Asian."[70] Hence, it urges, in general terms, a renewal of all aspects of the church's prayer life, including "its liturgical worship, its popular forms of piety, prayer in the home, in parishes, in prayer groups."[71] One step of this renewal is the use of "venerable books and writings" of other religions for prayer and spirituality.[72]

With regard to Asian popular religion in particular, the FABC recognizes that its world view is heavily influenced by Confucian and Taoist thought, which emphasizes that "the human person is a spiritual being living in a spirit-filled, mutually interacting and interdependent world" and that "the underlying aim of customs, ritual, worship, etc. is the maintenance of harmony between humankind and the natural world."[73]

In spite of these rather general indications, the FABC does provide two very useful guidelines for an authentic liturgical inculturation. First, liturgical inculturation must be undertaken always in conjunction with and as an intrinsic component of interreligious dialogue and the work for human liberation. Without interreligious dialogue, liturgical inculturation would operate in the void, at least in Asia, since it would lack the context into which it can insert Christian worship, on the one hand, and would have nothing to bring into Christian worship, on the other, as the twofold movement of inculturation implies. This inculturation of Christian liturgy must be carried out in two areas: the metacosmic

---

[70] Gaudencio Rosales and C. G. Arévalo, eds., *For All the Peoples of Asia: Federation of Asian Bishops' Conferences. Documents from 1970 to 1991,* vol. 1 (Maryknoll, N.Y.: Orbis Books; Quezon City: Claretian Publications, 1992); Franz-Josef Eilers, ed., *For All the Peoples of Asia: Federation of Asian Bishops' Conferences. Documents from 1992 to 1996,* vol. 2 (Quezon City: Claretian Publications, 1997); and Franz-Josef Eilers, ed., *For All the Peoples of Asia: Federation of Asian Bishops' Conferences. Documents from 1997 to 2002,* vol. 3 (Quezon City: Claretian Publications, 2002), 2:195.

[71] Ibid., 1:34.

[72] "We believe that with deeper study and understanding, with prudent discernment on our part and proper catechesis of our Christian people, these many indigenous riches will at last find a natural place in the prayer of our churches in Asia and will greatly enrich the prayer-life of the Church throughout the world" (ibid., 1:35). For the FABC's theology of liturgical inculturation, see Jonathan Tan Yun-ka, "Constructing an Asian Theology of Liturgical Inculturation from the Documents of the Federation of Asian Bishops' Conferences (FABC)," *EAPR* 36/4 (1999), 383-401.

[73] *For All the Peoples of Asia,* 2:163.

religions or soteriologies (Hinduism, Buddhism, Taoism, Confucianism, Islam, Shintoism, and so on) with their official forms of worship and prayer, and the cosmic religion that is often embodied in popular devotions commonly practiced at home and in the family. The separation of religion from culture, which is often made in the West and which permits an inculturation of liturgy into culture without facing the religious issues, makes no sense in Asia, where culture and religion form an indivisible whole.

Furthermore, as a form of interreligious dialogue, liturgical inculturation will not be undertaken simplistically as the "incarnation" of a culture-free gospel or culture-free liturgy into another culture, which at times the model of incarnation for inculturation seems to suggest. As Michael Amaladoss and Aylward Shorter have reminded us, inculturation is always *interculturation*. It is an encounter among at least three cultures—the Bible, the Christian tradition, and the people to whom the gospel is proclaimed.[74] I will broach the dynamics of power in this intercultural encounter in the last part of my essay; here, suffice it to note that liturgical inculturation without an adequate sensitivity to its intercultural dimension runs the risk of imposing onto others a particular culture, for example, that which is implicit in the Roman rite.

Without the struggle for human liberation, liturgical inculturation runs the risk of being an elitist enterprise, perhaps with a purely aesthetic and archeological interest.[75] Worse, it may be a disguised form of cultural chauvinism, especially when the culture into which the liturgy is inculturated is that of the dominant class.[76] For instance, *Dalit* and tribal theologians in India have consistently argued that Brahminic Hinduism is not the only culture and religion of India, and therefore liturgical inculturation cannot assume it to be the only partner with which it must dialogue.[77] Similarly, *minjung* theologians of Korea have chosen the "people"—that is, the mass that is politically oppressed, economically exploited, socially alienated, religiously marginalized, and culturally kept

---

[74] See Michael Amaladoss, *Beyond Inculturation: Can the Many Be One?* (Delhi: Society for Promotion of Christian Knowledge, 1998), 20-23; and Shorter, *Toward a Theology of Inculturation*, 13-16.

[75] For the FABC's theology of human liberation, see Peter C. Phan, "Human Development and Evangelization: The First to the Sixth Plenary Assembly of the Federation of Asian Bishops' Conference," *Studia Missionalia* 47 (1998), 205-27.

[76] *Varietates legitimae* reminds the bishops that "they should not ignore or neglect a minority culture with which they are not familiar" (no. 49).

[77] The *Dalits* (literally, "broken") are considered too polluted to participate in the social life of Indian society; they are the untouchable. Between two-thirds and three-quarters of the Indian Christian community are *Dalits*. On *Dalit* theology, see Sathianathan Clarke, *Dalit and Christianity: Subaltern Religion and Liberation Theology in India* (New Delhi: Oxford University Press, 1998); James Massey, *Dalits in India: Religion as a Source of Bondage or Liberation with Special Reference to Christians* (New Delhi: Mahohar, 1995); and M. E. Prabhakar, *Towards a Dalit Theology* (Madras: Gurukul, 1989). On tribal theology, see Nirmal Minz, *Rise Up, My People, and Claim the Promise: The Gospel among the Tribes of India* (Delhi: ISPCK, 1997). See also R. S. Sugirtharajah, ed., *Frontiers in Asian Christian Theology: Emerging Trends* (Maryknoll, N.Y.: Orbis Books, 1994), 11-62.

uneducated by the dominant group of the society—as the embodiment of the Messiah.[78] Among Asian theologians no one has argued more forcefully for the unity between inculturation and liberation than the Sri Lankan Jesuit Aloysius Pieris who insists that the church *in* Asia, in order to be *of* Asia, must undergo a double baptism in the river of the "religiousness of the Asian poor" and the "poverty of religious Asians."[79]

If this coupling of liturgical inculturation with liberation and interreligious dialogue is objected to on the ground that it is made into an exceedingly complicated affair, then my point has been understood. Indeed, we should disabuse ourselves of the notion that liturgical inculturation consists mainly in the adaptation of local language, music and singing, gestures and posture, and art while maintaining the "*substantial unity* of the Roman rite," as *Varietates legitimae* insists. In fact, in such a strategy there is a serious danger of what Aloysius Pieris calls "theological vandalism"; that is, picking and choosing elements of non-Christian religions, and "baptizing" them for Christian use, with no reverence for the wholeness of non-Christians' religious experience.[80]

The second important insight of FABC on liturgical inculturation concerns popular religion. By focusing on dialogue with the Asian poor, the FABC sees popular religion primarily as the religion of the poor people. This popular religion or cosmic religiosity in Asia is characterized, according to Pieris, by seven features: it has a this-worldly spirituality, it is animated by a sense of total dependence on the divine, it longs for justice, it is cosmic, it accords women a key role, it is ecological, and it communicates through story.[81] By engaging with and retrieving this popular religion, liturgical inculturation will tap into its potential for human liberation. In popular religion believers seek immediate satisfaction of physical and material needs, they feel God as a close liberating presence, they appeal to the spirits for protection and deliverance, they accord equal roles to women and men in their rituals, and their religious symbols can function

---

[78] On *minjung* (literally, "people") theology, see *An Emerging Theology in World Perspective: Commentary on Korean Minjung Theology* (Mystic, Conn.: Twenty-Third Publications, 1988) and Peter C. Phan, "Experience and Theology: An Asian Liberation Perspective," *Zeitschrift für Missionswissenschaft und Religionswissenschaft* 77/2 (1993), 118-20.

[79] See Aloysius Pieris, *An Asian Liberation Theology* (Maryknoll, N.Y.: Orbis Books, 1988), 45-50.

[80] See ibid., 41-42, 53, 85.

[81] See Aloysius Pieris, "An Asian Paradigm: Inter-religious Dialogue and Theology of Religions," *The Month* 254 (1993), 131-32. Michael Amaladoss offers a comprehensive discussion of popular Catholicism in "Toward a New Ecumenism: Churches of the People," in Bamat and Wiest, *Popular Catholicism in a World Church,* 272-301. He sees popular Catholicism as characterized by the desire for a good earthly life, a concern to ward off evil, a connection with the world of spirits and ancestors, an inclination toward sacramentality and community, and a suspicion of modern ideologies. For a presentation of Catholic popular devotions with respect to Asia, see José M. de Mesa, "Primal Religion and Popular Religiosity," *EAPR* 37 /1 (2000), 73-82; Kathleen Coyle, "Pilgrimages, Apparitions and Popular Piety," *EAPR* 38/2 (2001), 172-89; and Chapter 6 herein.

as rallying points for the masses. An example of this liberative power of popular religion, from the Christian perspective, is the People Power in the Philippines, which has demonstrated the power of popular devotions to unite the people in their effort to overthrow dictatorship and, recently, to remove corruption.

THEOLOGICAL ISSUES IN LITURGICAL INCULTURATION

Liturgical inculturation, clearly, is an extremely complex affair. It is even more complicated when it takes non-Christian popular religion into account. However, in my judgment, the process of liturgical inculturation is often impeded or is forced to remain at a superficial level, not because of the rejection by Roman authorities of more or less avant-garde proposals from the periphery, but because of the lack of agreement on fundamental theological issues. For example, underlying the Chinese Rites Controversy were at least six theological issues, namely, the salvific nature of non-Christian religions, the universal presence of the Holy Spirit, Christ as the universal and unique savior, the relationship between the local churches and the universal church, the nature of ancestor worship, and the nature and function of popular religion.[82] Other issues could be added, such as syncretism and the nature and scope of liturgical inculturation itself. I highlight here, in summary fashion, only two items that bear a direct relation to liturgical inculturation.

Culture as Ground of Contest in Relations and Popular Religion

The first fundamental theological issue regards the dynamics of power in inculturation. It seems both the Nairobi Statement and the Roman instruction are still operating with the concept of culture as an integrating and integrated whole, an anthropological concept that emerged as a theoretical construct after the 1920s, especially on the American scene.[83] This anthropological approach to culture tends to view it as a human universal. This universal is realized, however, in particular forms by each social group as its distinct way of life. Culture is constituted by the conventions created by the consensus of a group into which its members are socialized. Given this notion of culture as group-differentiating, holistic, non-evaluative, and context-dependent, anthropologists commonly perceive the culture of a social group as a whole, as a single albeit complex unit, and distinguish it from the social behaviors of its members. Culture is seen as the ordering principle and control mechanism of social behaviors without which human beings would be formless. Above all, culture is seen as an integrated and

---

[82] See Chapter 7 herein.

[83] For a history of the concept of culture, see Alfred A. Kroeber and Klyde Kluckhohn, *Culture: A Critical Review of Concepts and Definitions* (Cambridge, Mass.: Papers of the Peabody Museum of American Archeology and Ethnology, Harvard University, 1952). For a brief overview, see Kathryn Tanner, *Theories of Culture: A New Agenda for Theology* (Minneapolis: Fortress Press, 1997), 3-24. Tanner surveys the meaning of *culture* as it was used in France, Germany, and Great Britain before its current usage in anthropology.

integrating whole whose constituent elements are functionally interrelated to one another. These elements are thought to be integrated into each other because they are perceived as expressing a fundamental, overarching theme, style, or purpose. Or they are thought to be consistent with or imply one another. Or they are supposed to operate according to laws or structures, not unlike grammatical rules in a language. Or, finally, they are supposed to function with a view to maintaining and promoting the stability of the social order.

In recent years this modern concept of culture has been subjected to a searing critique.[84] The view of culture as a self-contained and clearly bounded whole, as an internally consistent and integrated system of beliefs, values, and behavioral norms that functions as the ordering principle of a social group and into which its members are socialized, has been shown to be based on unjustified assumptions.[85] Against this conception of culture it has been argued that (1) it focuses exclusively on culture as a finished product and therefore pays insufficient attention to culture as a historical process; (2) that its view of culture as a consistent whole is dictated more by the anthropologist's aesthetic need and the demand for synthesis than by the lived reality of culture itself; (3) that its emphasis on consensus as the process of cultural formation obfuscates the reality of culture as a site of struggle and contention; (4) that its view of culture as a principle of social order belittles the role of the members of a social group as cultural agents; (5) that this view privileges the stable elements of culture and does not take into adequate account its innate tendency to change and innovation; and (6) that its insistence on clear boundaries for cultural identity is no longer necessary, because it is widely acknowledged today that change, conflict, and contradiction are resident *within* culture itself and are not simply caused by outside disruption and dissension.[86]

Rather than as a sharply demarcated, self-contained, homogeneous, and integrated whole, culture today is seen as a ground of contest in relations and as a historically evolving, fragmented, inconsistent, conflicted, constructed, ever-shifting, and porous social reality. In this contest of relations the role of power in the shaping of cultural identity is of paramount importance, a factor that the modern concept of culture largely ignores. In the past, anthropologists tended to

---

[84] For the following reflections on the postmodern concept of culture, see Tanner, *Theories of Culture*, 40-56; Peter C. Phan, "Religion and Culture: Their Places as Academic Disciplines in the University," in *The Future of Religions in the Twenty-first Century*, ed. Peter Ng (Hong Kong: Centre for the Study of Religion and Chinese Society, 2001), 321-53.

[85] See Pierre Bourdieu, *Outline of a Theory of Practice* (Cambridge: Cambridge University Press, 1977); James Clifford, *The Predicament of Culture* (Cambridge, Mass.: Harvard University Press, 1988); George Marcus and Michael Fischer, *Anthropology as Cultural Critique* (Chicago: University of Chicago Press, 1986); Ulrich Beck, *Risk Society: Toward a New Modernity* (London: Sage, 1992); Homi K. Bhabha, *The Location of Culture* (London: Routledge, 1994); Jonathan Friedman, *Cultural Identity and Global Process* (London: Sage, 1994); and Mike Featherstone, *Undoing Modernity: Globalization, Postmodernism and Identity* (London: Sage, 1995).

[86] For a detailed articulation of these six objections against the anthropological concept of culture, see Tanner, *Theories of Culture*, 40-56.

regard culture as an innocent set of conventions rather than a reality of conflict in which the colonizers, the powerful, the wealthy, the victors, the dominant can obliterate the beliefs and values of the colonized, the weak, the poor, the vanquished, the subjugated, so that there has been, in Serge Gruzinski's expression, "la colonization de l'imaginaire."[87] This role of power is, as Michel Foucault and other masters of suspicion have argued, central in the formation of knowledge in general.[88] In the formation of cultural identity the role of power is even more extensive, since it is constituted by groups of people with conflicting interests, and the winners can dictate their cultural terms to the losers.

This predicament of culture is exacerbated by the process of globalization, in which the ideals of modernity and technological reason are extended throughout the world (globalization as *extension*), aided and abetted by a single economic system (neoliberal capitalism) and new communication technologies.[89] With globalization, geographical boundaries, which at one time helped define cultural identity, have now collapsed. Even our sense of time is largely compressed, with the present predominating and the dividing line between past and future becoming ever more blurred (globalization as *compression*). In this process of globalization a homogenized culture is created, consolidated by a "hyperculture" based on consumption, especially of goods exported from the United States, such as clothing (for example, tee-shirts, denim jeans, athletic shoes), food (such as McDonald's and Coca Cola), and entertainment (for example, films, video, and music).

Such a globalized culture is not accepted by local cultures hook, line and sinker. Between the global and the local cultures there takes place a continuous

---

[87] Serge Gruzinski, *The Conquest of Mexico* (Cambridge: Polity, 1993).

[88] See Michel Foucault, *The Archaeology of Knowledge*, trans. A. M. Sheridan Smith (New York: Pantheon Books, 1972); idem, *Discipline and Punish: The Birth of Prison*, trans. Alan Sheridan (New York: Vintage Press, 1975); Michael Kelly, ed., *Critique and Power: Recasting the Foucault/Habermas Debate* (Cambridge, Mass.: MIT Press, 1994); Michel Foucault, *Madness and Civilization: A History of Insanity in the Age of Reason*, trans. Richard Howard (New York: Vintage Books, 1988); idem, *Language, Counter-Memory, Practice: Selected Essays and Interviews*, ed. Donald Bouchard and trans. Donald Bouchard and Sherry Simon (Ithaca, N.Y.: Cornell University Press, 1977); idem, *Power/Knowledge* (New York: Pantheon Books, 1987); Lawrence D. Kritzman, ed., *Politics, Philosophy, Culture: Interviews and Other Writings*, trans. Alan Sheridan (New York: Routledge, 1988).

[89] For a discussion of the historical development of globalization, see the works of Immanuel Wallerstein, *The Modern World-System I: Capitalist Agriculture and the Origins of the European World-Economy in the Sixteenth Century* (New York: Academic, 1974), idem, *The Modern World-System II: Mercantilism and the Consolidation of the European World-Economy, 1600-1750* (New York: Academic, 1980); Anthony Giddens, *Modernity and Self-Identity: Self and Society in the Late Modern Age* (Stanford, Calif.: Stanford University Press, 1991); and Roland Robertson, *Globalization: Social Theory and Global Culture* (London: Sage, 1992). In general, Wallerstein attributes an exclusively economic origin to globalization; Giddens sees it as rooted in four factors, namely, the nation-state system, the world military order, the world capitalist economy, and the international division of labor; and Robertson highlights the cultural factors in globalization.

struggle, the former for political and economic dominance, the latter for survival and integrity. Because of the powerful attraction of the global culture, especially for the young, local cultures often feel threatened by it, but they are far from powerless. To counteract its influence, they have devised several strategies of resistance, subversion, compromise, and appropriation. And in this effort religion more often than not has played a key role in alliance with local cultures.

Moreover, globalization affects not only non-Western countries but also, like a boomerang, returns to hit the thrower. This is seen, for example, in France, Britain, and Portugal, where people of their former colonies have come to live and thereby created a multicultural and multi-ethnic situation unknown hitherto. The same situation occurs also in the United States, where because of economic and political pressures, people from South America, Latin America, and Asia have come in recent decades to settle in large numbers, as legal or illegal immigrants, and thus diversify the ethnic and cultural composition of the population.[90]

In light of this postmodern and postcolonial understanding of culture, it is easy to appreciate popular devotion as a form of resistance and subversion, as well as compromise and appropriation of the official religion. Keith Pecklers, in the wake of Latin American theologians, highlights the ways in which popular devotion has opened up alternative access to the divine, especially in the Marian devotion and different forms of blessing, and has privileged the role of women as domestic priestesses.[91] David Power has also argued that liturgical inculturation must be aware of the fact that "people who in the celebration of the sacraments have known a cultural domination, linked with the economic and political suppression of their lives, bring that history with them to the liturgy. It is this domination which is at issue, and not only the retrieval of values and expressions of ancient cultures previously ignored."[92]

In this context the concept of liturgical inculturation as proposed by the Nairobi Statement on Worship and Culture as well as, and perhaps especially, the Roman instruction *Varietates legitimae*, I submit, is inadequate for the task of carrying out a fruitful dialogue between the gospel and culture. With reference to the Roman document in particular, it must be said that it is not sufficiently

---

[90] For a brief discussion of globalization, see Robert Schreiter, *The New Catholicity* (Maryknoll, N.Y.: Orbis Books, 1997), 4-14. Social scientist Arjun Appadurai lists five factors that have contributed to the "deterritorialization" of contemporary culture: "ethnoscape" (the constant flow of persons such as immigrants, refugees, tourists, guest workers, exiles), "technoscape" (mechanical and informational technologies), "finanscape" (flow of money through currency markets, national stock exchanges, commodity speculation), "mediascape" (newspapers, magazines, TV, films), "and "ideoscape" (key ideas such as freedom, welfare, human rights, independence, democracy). See his "Disjuncture and Difference in the Global Economy," *Public Culture* 2/2 (1990), 1-24.

[91] See Keith Pecklers, "Issues of Power and Access in Popular Religion," *Liturgical Ministry* 7 (Summer, 1998), 136-40.

[92] David Power, "Liturgy and Culture Revisited," *Worship* 69/3 (1995), 232-33.

sensitive to the fact that inculturation is interculturation. It ignores the fact that the Roman rite is itself already a specific cultural product, and that when it insists that inculturation maintain "the *substantial unity* of the Roman rite," however this ambiguous phrase is interpreted, it de facto demands that other cultures submit themselves to the culture embodied in the Roman rite, especially if the unity of the Roman rite is seen to reside in the typical editions of liturgical books.[93] Put differently, inculturation understood as a project that "leads to adaptations which still remain part of the Roman rite" (no. 36) produces just that, "adaptations," in spite of the terminological switch to "inculturation." That is, it is external tinkering that is only skin-deep and never penetrates the deeper levels of culture and therefore fails in the church's mission of evangelizing cultures.

Liturgy of Life, Official Liturgy, and Popular Religion

Another theological issue that needs reexamination is the teaching that the liturgy, in particular the Eucharist, is the *culmen et fons* (summit and font) of the church's life. Elsewhere I have argued that this phrase, which has become something of a mantra among post–Vatican II liturgists, can lead to theological and pastoral distortions, including the triple dichotomy between spirituality and liturgy, between spirituality and socio-political involvement, and between socio-political involvement and liturgy. Instead of privileging the official liturgy, I suggest that theological priority be assigned to the "liturgy of life"—the experiences of God's gracious self-communication, available to all human beings, in the midst of life and in all concrete situations, from the most sublime to the most mundane, both positive and negative.[94]

This liturgy of life is structurally trinitarian, since it is a gift originating from God the Father, culminating in Jesus' ministry, death, and resurrection; and now poured upon the whole world by the Holy Spirit. Though it is diffuse, unstructured, and therefore easily unnoticed, this liturgy of life is the source of fecundity and effectiveness of the liturgy of the church.[95] Indeed, in Rahnerian terminology, official or church liturgy is the "Realsymbol" of the liturgy of life. As the symbolized and its symbol, the liturgy of life and church liturgy constitute

---

[93] The ethnocentrism of the Roman instruction is evident in its remark about the translation of liturgical books to the effect that "certain Christian expressions can be transmitted from one language to another, as has happened in the past, for example in the case of: *ecclesia, evangelium, baptisma, eucharistia*" (no. 53). This may be true of Indo-European languages, but is such transliteration possible and desirable for the languages of other families such as Chinese and Vietnamese?

[94] See Peter C. Phan, "The Liturgy of Life as the 'Summit and Source' of the Eucharistic Liturgy: Church Worship as Symbolization of the Liturgy of Life?" in *Incongruities: Who We Are and How We Pray*, ed. Timothy Fitzgerald and David A. Like (Chicago: Liturgy Training Publications, 2000), 5-33.

[95] In the language we have been using in this essay, the liturgy of life is the "cosmic religiousness" or popular religion, which is partially embodied in the "metacosmic soteriologies" of religions and partially in devotional practices of the people.

an ontological and indissoluble unity, and yet cannot be reduced to each other. Furthermore, because it is diffuse and unstructured, the liturgy of life needs to be brought to our consciousness by being symbolized in the concrete and explicit rituals and prayers of church worship and the sacraments. Hence, in its liturgical celebrations the church does not perform worship *in addition to* the liturgy of life or unconnected with it; rather, it makes explicit and intensifies through words and rituals the liturgy of life. It is by symbolizing the liturgy of life, that is, by way of formal and not efficient causality, that church liturgy acquires its innate effectiveness, or as we used to say, *ex opere operato*.

On the other hand, popular devotions are also a parallel symbol of this liturgy of life. Since the liturgy of life cannot by its very nature be exhaustively symbolized by church liturgy, it finds other outlets for self-expression. Hence, popular devotions are not necessarily antagonistic to official religion or liturgy. Nor should they be, by the same token, somehow made "to harmonize with the liturgical seasons," "accord with the sacred liturgy," to be "in some way derived from it, and lead the people to it," not because, as *Sacrosanctum concilium* and the Roman instruction put it, "the liturgy by its very nature is far superior to them," but because they have their own efficacy as symbols of the liturgy of life.

Patrick Malloy has arrived at the same conclusion with regard to popular religion when he argues that as the liturgy is an *anamnesis*, not a historical reproduction *(mimesis)* of the events of Jesus' life, death, and resurrection, so popular devotions can exist along the same line of "anamnetic intent." He concludes: "To set the liturgy up, therefore, as the arbiter of popular devotion is ill conceived. The only possible results are the death of popular religion as it tries to be what it is not, or a rebellion by popular religion as it rejects outright intolerable constraints."[96]

Let me conclude these reflections on liturgical inculturation and popular religion with a true story. A Vietnamese priest by the name of Pio Ngo Phuc Hau recounts one of his pastoral experiences in 1965:

> *Legio Mariae* [Legion of Mary] asked me to go and visit a sick person. She was an old woman over eighty. She asked to be baptized. I asked her about a few doctrines that the catechism used to call "the fundamental and necessary teachings." After the baptism, she looked at me with imploring eyes:
> —Father, I have been a Buddhist since a child. I love the Buddha greatly. Now that I have accepted Jesus, would you please allow me to keep my altar to the Buddha?
> I was only 29 years old, and only a year as a priest. I was quite perplexed by such a request. Suddenly I recalled what my professor Luke Huy had

---

[96] Patrick Malloy, "Christian Anamnesis and Popular Religion," *Liturgical Ministry* 7 (Summer, 1998), 121-28. Malloy sets up two criteria for both liturgy and popular devotions: (1) How anamnetic are they of Jesus? (2) How focused are they on Jesus?

VIETNAMESE MARIAN PIETY:
HISTORICAL ROOTS AND CHARACTERISTICS

Marian devotion entered Vietnam for the first time with Catholic missionaries in the early seventeenth century.[3] Its characteristics and practices were those prevalent in these missionaries' Catholicism, which was late-medieval Iberian Christianity.[4] Most missionaries to Vietnam in the first half of the seventeenth century were Portuguese Jesuits, with a few Italians, Japanese, and French (among the latter was the most outstanding figure of the history of the Vietnamese mission, Alexandre de Rhodes, who was a citizen of the Papal State of Avignon).[5] The reason for the overwhelmingly Portuguese presence was that at that time Vietnam, as part of China and Macao, along with India, Malacca, and Japan, was under the Portuguese *padroado*.[6] These Portuguese missionaries, just as the Spanish ones, brought with them their own brand of Iberian Catholicism wherever they went to evangelize, whether in Latin America or in Asia, and transmitted it to their converts.

Marian devotion, see Martin Le Ngoc An, "La Dévotion Mariale au Viêt Nam," S.T.D. dissertation, Facoltà Pontificia Teologica Marianum, Rome, 1977. See also older works, such as Joseph Terrès, "Le culte de la Sainte Vierge au Tonkin Oriental," in *Compte-rendu du Congrès marial à Fribourg en Suisse, du 18 au 21 août 1902*, vol. 2 (Blois: Imprimerie C. Migault, 1903), 141-65; and F. Parrell, "Le culture de Marie au Viêt-nam," *Bulletin de la Société des MEP*, 2d series, 71 (1954), 657-61. Because potential readers of this essay probably do not read Vietnamese, no reference will be made to writings in Vietnamese.

[3] On the history of early Catholic mission in Vietnam, see Peter C. Phan, *Mission and Catechesis: Alexandre de Rhodes and Inculturation in Seventeenth-Century Vietnam* (Maryknoll, N.Y.: Orbis Books, 1998). Older works that are still valuable include Henri Chappoulie, *Aux origins d'une Église. Rome et les Missions d'Indochine au XVIIè siècle*, 2 vols. (Paris: Bloud et Gay, 1943, 1948); Adrien Launay, *Histoire de la Mission de Cochinchine (1658-1823), Documents Historiques*, vol. 1, *1658-1728* (Paris: Anciennes Maisons Charles Douniol et Retaux, Pierre Téqui, successeur, 1923); and Nguyen Huu Trong, *Les origines du clergé vietnamien* (Saigon: Tinh Viet, 1959). For a history of Christianity in Vietnam, see Peter C. Phan and Violet James, "Vietnam," in *A Dictionary of Asian Christianity*, ed. Scott W. Sunquist (Grand Rapids, Mich.: Eerdmanns, 2001), 876-80.

[4] On medieval Iberian Christianity, especially with regard to Marian devotion, see Richard Kieckhefer, "Major Currents in Late Medieval Devotion," in *Christian Spirituality: High Middle Ages and Reformation*, ed. Jill Raitt (New York: Crossroad, 1988), 89-93; W. A. Christian, *Apparitions in Late Medieval and Renaissance Spain* (Princeton, N.J.: Princeton University Press, 1981); and W. A. Christian, *Local Religion in Sixteenth-Century Spain* (Princeton, N.J.: Princeton University Press, 1981).

[5] On Alexandre de Rhodes, see Phan, *Mission and Catechesis.*

[6] On the *padroado* system in Asia, see Chappoulie, *Aux origins d'une Église*, 1:42-54; António da Silva Rego, *Le Patronage portugais de l'Orient, aperçu historique* (Lisbon: Agência Geral do Ultramar, 1957); Adelhelm Jann, *Die katholischen Missionen in Indien, China und Japan: Ihre Organization und das portugiesische Patronat, vom 15. bis ins 18. Jahrhundert* (Paderborn: Ferdinand Schöningh, 1915); and Teotonio R. de Souza and Surachai Chumsriphan, "Padroado," in Sunquist, *Dictionary of Asian Christianity*, 623-27.

It is generally recognized that this Iberian Catholicism was pervaded with what is now termed popular religion, in which devotion to Mary assumed a prominent place.[7] Furthermore, Iberian Christianity was largely popular Catholicism, in the sense that it was the form of faith believed and practiced by the common folk, not the intellectual and hierarchical elite, and it displayed a predilection for the visual, the oral, and the dramatic as the means of communicating the gospel.[8] With regard to the place of Marian devotion in this popular Catholicism, Richard Kieckhefer writes: "Relics, shrines, and pilgrimages, feast days, hymns, motets, legends, plays, paintings and statues, patronage of churches and monasteries, sermons, devotional treatises, visions, theology—in all these areas Mary was not merely present but vitally important."[9]

To this first Iberian layer of Christian spirituality was added another, French in flavor. When Alexandre de Rhodes was sent back to Rome in 1645 to request more personnel and material assistance for his society's mission in China, he conceived the bold idea of having a hierarchy established in Vietnam, with bishops appointed as "vicars apostolic," directly responsible to the Propagation of the Faith, to bypass the Portuguese *padroado*. His plan was well received by the Propagation, which had been founded in 1622 to undertake Christian mission independently from the *padroado* system, and de Rhodes was charged with recruiting candidates for the episcopacy. In 1652 de Rhodes left for Paris, where he found three priests worthy of the episcopacy. Eventually, in 1659, over the strenuous protest of the Portuguese crown, François Pallu (1626-84) and Pierre Lambert de la Motte (1624-79) were appointed vicars apostolic "in partibus infidelium," for Tonkin and Cochinchina respectively.[10] Desirous to extend mission work to secular clergy, and not to let it be restricted to religious, the two bishops founded a society dedicated to mission, especially for Asia, known as Société des Missions-Étrangères de Paris (MEP). Though Pallu was not able to come to Vietnam, his companion de la Motte and a large number of missionaries of MEP labored in Vietnam from the seventeenth century to 1975; they have left an indelible mark on the character of Vietnamese Catholicism, and by extension, as will be shown later, on Vietnamese Marian piety.[11]

The third significant influence on Vietnamese Marian devotion was exerted by the return of the mendicant orders and the coming of new religious congregations, both male and female, all bringing with them their distinct forms of

---

[7] As Richard Kieckhefer puts it, "If there is any principle that applies to Marian devotion in the later Middle Ages, it is that of accumulation. Virtually anything that could be said, sung, displayed, or thought in Mary's honor found its place in the mélange" (see "Major Currents in Late Medieval Devotion," in *Christian Spirituality: High Middle Ages and Reformation*, 89).

[8] On popular Catholicism, see Orlando Espín, *The Faith of the People: Theological Reflections on Popular Catholicism* (Maryknoll, N.Y.: Orbis Books, 1997), 69-71.

[9] Kieckhefer, "Major Currents in Late Medieval Devotion," 89.

[10] For brief biographies of de la Motte and Pallu, see Sunquist, *Dictionary of Asian Christianity*, 231-32 and 633-34 respectively.

[11] Ten MEP (two bishops and eight priests) who were martyred in Vietnam were canonized on 19 June 1988.

Marian devotion. The Dominicans from the Province of the Most Holy Rosary in the Philippines, whose devotion to Mary, especially with the practice of Rosary recitation, is well known, came back to Tonkin in 1676, and several dioceses were eventually entrusted to their care.[12] From the Philippines, too, Franciscans returned, especially to Cochinchina, in 1719, to carry out their mission. Among the newcomers, two male religious congregations merit special mention because of their strong influence on Vietnamese Marian devotion. The Redemptorists came to Vietnam from Canada in 1925 and, through their highly successful preaching in novenas and retreats and their widely circulated periodical *Our Lady of Perpetual Help*, spread devotion to Mary under this title. The Salesians of Don Bosco came to Hanoi in 1952 and, through the education of poor youth, promoted their devotion to Mary Help of Christians. Among the female religious orders, of special significance for Marian devotion were the Chanoinesses de Saint Augustin (also known as Couvent des Oiseaux), the Daughters of Charity, the Franciscan Missionaries of Mary, and in particular, the indigenous congregation called Lovers of the Cross (Amantes de la Croix), founded by Pierre Lambert de la Motte in 1669.

Lastly, an indigenous male congregation, whose very name is indicative of its Mariology and spirituality, deserves special notice, namely, the Congregation of Mary Co-Redemptrix. Founded by a Vietnamese priest, Fr. Tran Dinh Thu, on 4 April 1941, on the feast of the Seven Sorrows of the Blessed Virgin Mary, to honor Mary as collaborator with Christ in the work of redemption through her sufferings, it was approved by Rome on 15 December 1952. After the fall of South Vietnam in 1975, some 170 priests and brothers left Vietnam and were settled in Carthage, Missouri, in the United States. Every August, to celebrate the feast of the Assumption, the congregation organizes days of prayers in honor of Mary at its headquarters. Fifty thousand Vietnamese participate in these prayer days.

From this brief survey it is clear that Marian piety in Vietnamese Catholicism has had a long history and different layers, and that, given its historical roots in Portugal, Spain, and France, it is marked by most of the characteristics associated with the Marian cults in these countries. Before describing its major features, it will be helpful to examine in some detail the late-medieval Mariology that was first presented to the Vietnamese Catholics by one of the most important Jesuit missionaries in Vietnam, Alexandre de Rhodes. One of the great achievements of the early Jesuit missionaries in Vietnam was to make use of the Latin alphabet and diacritical marks to transcribe the Vietnamese language, in addition to using the Chinese characters *(chu nho)* and the demotic script *(chu*

---

[12] Eleven Spanish Dominicans (six bishops and five priests) who were martyred in Vietnam were also canonized on 19 June 1988. The Vietnamese have ninety-six canonized martyrs and one blessed. They were killed between 1644 and 1883. Thirty-seven were priests (twenty-six secular, eleven Dominicans) and sixty were lay (one of whom was a woman). Clearly, at least from the point of view of martyrdom, the Dominicans have had a significant impact on Vietnamese Catholicism. On martyrdom in Asia, see Francis X. Clark, *Asian Saints* (Quezon City, Philippines: Claretian Publications, 2000).

nom). This Romanized script is now used as the national script *(chu quoc ngu)*.[13] The person most instrumental in perfecting and promoting this new script was Alexandre de Rhodes, and the first printed works in this script were his *Cathechismus* and his *Dictionarium*.[14]

It is in de Rhodes's *Cathechismus* that we have the earliest extant teaching on Mary in Vietnam. The author does not present Mary in a separate section of his catechism but weaves his presentation of the mother of God into his narrative of the life of Jesus, beginning with the incarnation. It is impossible to quote at length here the passages in which de Rhodes mentions Mary.[15] Suffice it to say that de Rhodes mentions all the Marian dogmas, including Mary's divine motherhood,[16] her perpetual virginity,[17] and even the immaculate conception[18] (though not the assumption). The full title that de Rhodes gives to Mary in Vietnamese, summarizing in a nutshell his Mariology, is "Rat thanh dong than Duc Chua Ba Maria la Me Chua Troi" (literally, The Very Holy Virgin, the Noble Sovereign Mary, the Mother of the Noble Lord of Heaven).

De Rhodes is not satisfied with a mere doctrinal presentation of Mary to the catechumens. He recommends that catechists follow their lecture on Mary with an act of devotion to her:

> At this point, we should show a beautiful image of the Blessed Virgin Mary carrying her infant son Jesus, our Lord, so that people may adore him humbly by bowing their heads to the ground. First, a triple adoration

---

[13] For a brief explanation of these scripts, see Phan, *Mission and Catechesis*, 28-35.

[14] The catechism is entitled *Cathechismus pro iis, qui volunt suscipere Baptismum, in Octo dies divisus. Phep giang tam ngay cho ke muan chiu phep rua toi, ma beao dao thanh duc Chua Bloi. Ope sacrae Congregationis de Propaganda Fide in lucem editus. Ab Alexandro de RHODES è Societate Jesu, ejusdemque Sacrae Congregationis Missionario Apostolico* (Rome, 1651). Henceforth: *Cathechismus*.

The dictionary is entitled *Dictionarium annamiticum, lusitanum, et latinum ope Sacrae Congregationis de Propaganda Fide in lucem editum ab Alexandro de Rhodes è Societate Jesu, ejusdemque Sacrae Congregationis Missionario Apostolico* (Rome, 1651). It comprises three parts: the first part, with a separate pagination (31 pages) is an essay on Vietnamese grammar entitled *Linguae Annamiticae seu Tunchinensis brevis declaratio*; the second part is the dictionary proper, entitled *Dictionarium Annamiticum seu Tunchinense cum Lusitana, et Latina declaratione*; and the last part, unpaginated, is entitled *Index Latini sermonis* and is an index of Latin words followed by the numbers of the pages in which they occur in the second part.

[15] For the most important passages, see *Mission and Catechesis*, 264-71.

[16] "The Lord of heaven chose to take flesh from her who is at the same time truly the mother of God and a virgin. Her name would be Mary" (Phan, *Mission and Catechesis*, 264). "The Blessed Virgin was chosen by the *Sanctissima Trindade* to be the true mother of God, and the only Son of God, true God, would have to take flesh from her flesh" (ibid., 265).

[17] "Thus, the most holy Mary Mother of God is a virgin before, during, and after parturition, and she who remained intact after parturition did not experience any pain during parturition" (ibid., 269).

[18] "After receiving this happy message, the spouses [Joachim and Anna] in their humility gave thanks to God with all their strength and they gave birth to a daughter, a flower of virginity, conceived, according to the teaching of many doctors, without the sin that Adam transmitted, because God, who would come into the world to restore the human race, had chosen her as his mother before the ages" (ibid., 264).

should be made to the three divine persons in the one divine essence, thus confessing the mystery of the divine Trinity by this external adoration. The knees should be bent only once, to confess the one divine essence. The head should be bowed to the ground three times, demonstrating our adoration to the three divine persons, imploring each of them to forgive our sins. The head should be bowed once more to render reverence and adoration to the Lord Jesus Christ, man and mediator, humbly asking him to make us worthy to receive the fruits of his abundant redemption and to forgive all our sins.

Lastly, reverence should be shown to the Blessed Virgin by bowing the head to the ground once more, though we know that the Blessed Virgin is not God, but because she is the mother of God, all-powerful over her son, we hope to obtain pardon for our sins through her holy intercession.[19]

Several interesting points should be noted here. First, the passage presumes that there were at that time in Vietnam holy pictures of Mary (probably brought in from Europe), and that de Rhodes's preferred representation was that of the madonna and child, which indicates the inseparability between Christology and Mariology in his theology (as is also clear from the way he integrates his presentation of Mary into his narrative of Jesus' life). Second, in a move reminiscent of Matteo Ricci's attempt at inculturation, de Rhodes was concerned with adopting the typically Asian kowtow to express the Christian sentiments of worship and reverence. Third, in prescribing this gesture of profound reverence, de Rhodes was careful to make a distinction between the honor rendered to the Trinity and that rendered to Mary, even though the same gesture is performed for both. Fourth, one of the reasons for the cult of Mary is her efficacious ("all-powerful") influence over her Son through her intercession. Finally, in this cult what we ought to seek is not material benefits but spiritual ones ("pardon for our sins").

In concluding his catechism, de Rhodes also mentions Mary's presence during the passion and death,[20] resurrection and apparitions,[21] and ascension of Jesus,[22] and at Pentecost.[23] In sum, we have in de Rhodes's *Cathechismus* the

---

[19] Ibid., 270-71.

[20] "At the foot of the *crux* of the Lord Jesus stood his deeply anguished mother, the Virgin Mary. She witnessed all this, her soul so afflicted with incredible pain at the death of her only and beloved son that she was almost lifeless" (ibid., 289).

[21] "The Lord Jesus raised from the dead appeared in all his glory first of all to the Virgin his mother who had been crushed by unspeakable sorrows at the atrocious death of her only and beloved son. He gladdened her with a heavenly consolation proportionate to her sorrows" (ibid., 293). Needless to say, this statement is rooted in de Rhodes's personal piety and not in the gospel account of Jesus' apparitions.

[22] "He [Jesus] led his disciples out of Jerusalem and departed for Mount Olivet. He said goodbye to the Virgin Mother and the others with tender and loving words; then he raised his hands and blessed them" (ibid., 294-95).

[23] "After the Lord Christ had ascended into heaven, the apostles and the other disciples, together with the Virgin Mother and other pious women, altogether about 120, returned to Jerusalem, entered the room where the Lord, before bidding them goodbye, had eaten the *coena* with his disciples, and remained together in prayer, as the Lord had commanded" (ibid., 295).

basic contents of Mariology that would be presented to Vietnamese Catholics for the next three hundred years, until the Second Vatican Council enriched it further with newer insights.

As for the contribution of the MEP to Marian devotion in Vietnam, it is well known that its founders had a deep devotion to Mary. François Pallu, before becoming a bishop, was an active member of the Marian association Société des Bons Amis, founded by the Jesuit Jean Bagot with the express purpose of cultivating a special devotion to Mary. Later, in 1668, as bishop, Pallu demonstrated his deep love for our Lady when he courageously defended a book by his friend, Henri-Marie Bourdon, *Le saint esclavage de l'Admirable Mère de Dieu*, which was being condemned by Rome, paving the way for the work of Saint Grignion de Montfort.[24] Furthermore, both Pallu and Lambert de la Motte were greatly influenced by Cardinal Pierre de Bérulle, who promoted the practice of consecrating oneself as a slave to Mary, and by St. Jean Eudes, whose spirituality was deeply Marian.

As a consequence, there has been among the members of MEP a strong tradition of deep devotion to Mary; this was then transmitted to the Vietnamese Catholics.[25] It is no wonder, then, that the first official consecration to Mary in the history of the Vietnamese Catholic church was done by Bishop Paul Puginier, a member of MEP, who consecrated his diocese of Hanoi and his personal ministry to Mary on the feast of the Presentation of Mary in the Temple, 21 November 1868. This practice of consecrating dioceses to Mary was later followed by many Vietnamese bishops. The most solemn act of consecration to Mary, however, was performed during the first National Marian Congress in 1959, when Vietnam was consecrated to the Immaculate Heart of Mary. This consecration was repeated a year later on the occasion of the establishment of the ecclesiastical hierarchy in Vietnam by Pope John XXIII.

Last, other forms of Marian devotion were either strengthened or introduced into Vietnam by the mendicant orders and other religious congregations. Mention has already been made of the recitation of the Rosary, a distinctive Dominican practice, and of the widespread devotion to Our Lady of Perpetual Help, a specialty of the Redemptorists, and to Our Lady Help of Christians, a specialty of the Salesians of Don Bosco.

The nineteenth and twentieth centuries have been rightly called the Marian Age of the Catholic church; this is true also of the Vietnamese church. With the coming of new religious orders into Vietnam during these two centuries, new Marian devotions were introduced. Of the many new titles, "Our Lady of . . . "s, the ones of La Salette, Lourdes, and Fatima, for obvious reasons, are the most popular. The practices of honoring Mary during the month of May with flower offerings, songs, and dance, and during October with the recitation of the Rosary,

---

[24] See Jean Guennou, "Monseigneur Pallu et la Sainte Vierge," *Bulletin de la Société des MEP*, 2d series, 80 (1955), 433-38.

[25] See C. Cesselin, "La Société des Missions-Étrangères et le culte de la Très Sainte Vierge," in *MARIA, Études sur la Sainte Vierge*, vol. 4, ed. Hubert du Manoir (Paris: Beauchesne, 1956).

are widely adopted. The practice of wearing medals, scapulars, and rosaries is widespread, as well as making pilgrimages to several Marian sanctuaries (for example, Bai Dau, Gia Vien, and Binh Trieu) and participating in processions. Marian associations such as Legio Mariae and the Blue Army were also instituted and were extremely active. Indeed, a plethora of mariological writings were either translated into or composed in Vietnamese, and all things Marian in France, Canada, and Portugal were imported into Vietnam and well received. In due course Marian devotion began to influence Vietnamese Catholic literature, arts, architecture, music, and philately.[26]

Before moving on to Marian apparitions in Vietnam, it will be helpful to summarize the main characteristics of Vietnamese Marian piety. It is, first of all, traditional in the sense that it is deeply rooted in the teachings of the church regarding Mary. De Rhodes's explanation of the Marian dogmas, in particular Mary's divine motherhood, perpetual virginity, and immaculate conception (and after 1950, the assumption), served a solid basis for Vietnamese Marian piety. Second, it is also traditional in the sense that it has inherited most if not all Marian practices of the West, as these were imported into Vietnam by various waves of missionaries, beginning with the Portuguese Jesuits, followed by the Spanish Dominicans and Franciscans, then by the French MEP, the Canadian Redemptorists, the Italian Salesians of Don Bosco, and other male and female religious orders. Third, Marian devotion is popular in the sense of being widespread and practiced by the common Catholic folk for whom Mary serves as the gateway to God. Fourth, though popular (that is, practiced by the people), it is enthusiastically endorsed and encouraged by the hierarchy as well, especially through the official consecration of Vietnam to our Lady. Fifth, though imported from the outside, Marian devotion has sunk roots into the Vietnamese soil, as testified by Marian congregations founded by the native clergy, such as the Congregation of Mary Co-Redemptrix.

MARIAN APPARITIONS AND MARIAN SITES

Like many other countries, Vietnam claims to have had Marian apparitions. So far there are two locations where our Lady is said to have appeared, La Vang and Tra Kieu, the former by far the more famous of the two.[27] Compared with other Western apparitions, such as Lourdes and Fatima, there is no historical documentation for these two apparitions but only unverifiable oral tradition. Furthermore, our Lady did not appear to identifiable individuals (such as Bernadette Soubirous or Lucia, Francesco, and Jacinta) but to a large group of

---

[26] For a discussion of the influence of Marian devotion in these areas, see Le Ngoc An, *La Dévotion Mariale au Viet Nam*, 264-350.

[27] There is another Marian sanctuary in the parish La Ma (literally, Rome) in the south of Vietnam, some fifty miles south of Saigon (Ho Chi Minh City). This site in honor of Our Lady of La Ma is not due to an apparition of Mary, however, but to an alleged reappearance of the faces of Our Lady of Perpetual Help and Jesus on a wooden faded picture that had been lost in a river. The discovery by Mr. Nguyen Van Hat and his fourteen-year-old son occurred on 7 October 1950.

anonymous people. Nor was there a doctrinal message conveyed (such as Mary's immaculate conception) or a spiritual practice recommended (for example, reform of life, recitation of the Rosary, devotion to the heart of Mary). Both alleged apparitions have one thing in common; namely, our Lady is said to have appeared during the persecution of Catholics and to have promised them maternal protection.[28]

Our Lady of La Vang

The years 1798-1800, under the reign of King Canh Thinh (1792-1802), were very hard for Catholics. The king suspected that his opponent, Nguyen Anh, was being assisted by the French bishop Pigneau de Béhaine (1741-99), who had recruited French officers and arms to help Nguyen Anh reestablish his dynasty. Fearful that Catholics would collude with his enemies, the king ordered them to be killed as a preventive measure. La Vang was a small Catholic village, with about 150 inhabitants, about eighty miles north of Hue, the ancient imperial capital, in the Quang Tri province.[29] There are two accounts, one Catholic, the other Buddhist, of why the village became a Marian site.[30]

According to the Catholic version, during Canh Thinh's persecution several Catholics from a nearby parish fled to La Vang. There, in spite of severe sufferings, they gathered every evening under a banian tree to recite the Rosary. One evening, according to the tradition, a lady of great beauty appeared to them, clad in white and surrounded by light, holding the infant Jesus in her arms, with two charming boys, each holding a torch, standing beside her. The lady walked back and forth several times in front of the Christians, her feet touching the ground. Even the non-Christians who were there saw the vision. Then the lady stopped and addressed them in a sweet voice: "My children, what you have asked of me, I have granted you, and henceforth, whoever will come here to pray to me, I will listen to them." Then she vanished.

The Buddhist version, called "The Pagoda of the Three Villages," runs as follows. There were three villages near La Vang, namely, Co Thanh, Thach Han, and Ba Tru. The Buddhists there heard that a lady called Thien Mu (literally, The Heavenly Lady) had appeared in La Vang under the banian tree (which is considered a sacred tree), and that those who went to pray there were miraculously healed. During the persecution of Catholics under Emperor Ming Mang (1820-40) the Buddhists took over the place and built a pagoda in honor of the

---

[28] For a detailed account of these two apparitions, see Le Ngoc An, *La Dévotion Mariale au Viet Nam*, 225-54.

[29] The word *La Vang* may have two meanings: (1) a loud shout, and (2) the name of a tree whose leaves are medicinal. The first meaning refers to the custom of village inhabitants making loud noises to chase away roaming tigers and other animals; the second to the medicinal tree that grows abundantly in this area.

[30] The oldest extant document referring to Our Lady of La Vang is an anonymous article by a missionary of MEP, "Notre Dame de La Vang," *Annales de la société des MEP* 24 (1901), 273-77.

Buddha. The night after the dedication of the pagoda, so the story goes, the leaders of the three villages had a dream in which the Buddha appeared to them and told them to remove his statue from La Vang, because, he said, there was a lady more powerful than he occupying the place. The following day they went to the pagoda and saw that the Buddha statue and its ornaments had been moved outside, and so they brought them in. That night they had the same dream and received the same message. As a result, the Buddhists donated the pagoda to the Catholics, who converted it into the first chapel of Our Lady of La Vang.[31]

What historical validity is to be attached to both accounts is impossible to determine. The Vietnamese hierarchy has not officially pronounced on the historicity of Mary's apparition at La Vang. Nevertheless, there is no doubt that Vietnamese Catholics regard La Vang as sacred land. In 1901 a small chapel was built there and was blessed by Louis Casper, bishop of Hue, during a solemn procession in which, somewhat incongruously, a statue of the French Notre-Dame des Victoires was honored.[32] Since then, every three years there has been a pilgrimage to La Vang, except when impeded by war. In 1924 a larger sanctuary was built to replace the chapel, now too small for the huge crowd. In 1959 it was raised to the rank of minor basilica by Pope John XXIII and became the national Marian center of pilgrimage. Under the current communist government, travels to La Vang have been severely restricted. Nevertheless, the bicentennial commemoration in 1998 of our Lady's apparition at La Vang was attended by a huge number of Catholics, from both North and South, with Cardinal Phan Dinh Tung, archbishop of Hanoi, presiding as the special legate of Pope John Paul II.

Our Lady of Tra Kieu

In 1885 the Vietnamese Catholic church was inflicted with another wave of persecution. After the death of Emperor Tu Duc (1883), a pro-royal movement called Can Vuong (For the Defense of the King) was initiated by the young emperor Ham Nghi, who acceded to the throne in 1884, to fight against the French colonial power. The movement, composed mainly of court officials sharing Ham Nghi's liberation program, ended when Ham Nghi was arrested by the French in 1888 and exiled to Algeria.

Another movement, called Van Than (the Literati movement), many members of which joined the Can Vuong movement, instigated a campaign of "Binh Tay Sat Ta," literally, destroying the West and killing the false religion, code words for the French and the Vietnamese Catholics, respectively. Tra Kieu, a small village of some nine hundred inhabitants in the province of Quang Nam, south of Hue, had a tiny Catholic parish.

---

[31] See M. Bernard, "La Vierge Marie au Viet Nam," *Revue du Rosaire* 6 (1969), 162-90.

[32] A painting and statue of our Lady of La Vang have been designed, reflecting the Vietnamese culture.

According to the account given by M. Geffroy,[33] on 1 September 1885 the parish, with its pastor, Father Bruyère, was surrounded by the Van Than army. The army, however, did not attack until the following day. The Catholics were desperate, outnumbered three to one, and with very few weapons. Father Bruyère urged them to place their confidence in Mary by putting a statue of Mary on the table with a candle on each side. While the young men went out to fight, old people, women, and children recited the Rosary. The Van Than army was held at bay for several days. Frustrated, the Van Than decided to bring in cannons and began shooting at the church. However, all their cannons, to the Van Than's consternation, missed their easy mark. A military mandarin later confessed that he saw a beautiful lady, dressed in white, standing on top of the church, and that he tried to hit her with the cannons but always missed. The soldiers said that for two days this lady stood on top of the church, and, try as they might, they could never hit her.

On 21 September the Van Than decided to carry out a final assault on the parish. The Catholics, on their part, decided that the best defense was offense, in spite of great risks due to their numerical inferiority and lack of weapons. They made a sortie and attacked the Van Than troops, who were occupying the two hills overlooking the village. The Van Than tried to use elephants to attack the Catholics, but the animals refused to move. The riders explained that the elephants were terrified because there were thousands of children, dressed in white and red, coming down from the bamboo trees and marching with the Catholics toward them. Then one of the Catholics shot and killed one of the literati in charge of the Van Than troops, which caused them to run away in total disarray. The Catholics attributed their improbable victory to the protection of Mary.

As with La Vang, there is no way to validate the Van Than's vision of the lady dressed in white and standing on top of the church to protect it or of troops of children dressed in white and red coming down from the bamboo trees to join forces with the Catholics at Tra Kieu. Nevertheless, Vietnamese Catholics did not hesitate to attribute to Mary's miraculous intervention their victory over their enemy, whose number and weapons were overwhelming. In 1898 a chapel was built in Tra Kieu, dedicated to Mary Help of Christians, and in 1959 and 1971 pilgrimages to this Marian sanctuary were organized with a large number of participants.

MARY, MOTHER OF MERCY: TOWARD A VIETNAMESE MARIOLOGY

As with any theological treatise, Mariology underwent an extensive reconstruction as the result of Vatican II's *aggiornamento*.[34] Questions were raised

---

[33] See M. Geffroy, "Une page de la persécution en Cochinchine," *Les Missions catholiques* 900 (1886), 428-30. See also two earlier reports: "Sauvetage de 900 chrétiens de la province de Phú Yên (Cochinchine orientale)," *Les Missions catholiques* 870 (1886), 61-65, and 871 (1886), 75-77.

[34] For a helpful analysis of contemporary trends in Mariology, see the annual reports by Eamon Carroll published in *Marian Studies*. See also the essays published in *Ephemerides Mariologicae*.

about its fundamental approaches (for example, christological, pneumatological, and ecclesial). Certain mariological dogmas have been targeted for revision (for example, Mary's virginity). Feminist theology has had an extensive impact on reconfiguring Mary. Ecumenical dialogue has made its contributions as well. Recent developments in trinitarian theology related Mary more intimately to the Trinity. In addition, the role of Marian devotional practices has been reexamined in a much more positive light.[35]

Cut off from the theological world, since 1954 for the North and since 1975 for the South, Vietnam has not been able to keep up with recent trends in Mariology. Despite Vatican II's reforms, Vietnamese Catholicism, especially in the North, has remained immune to changes and developments, not least because of the oppressive economic and political situation of the country. In particular, with regard to Mariology, the Vietnamese theology of Mary has remained "Mariology of privileges," as is clear from the theological orientations implied in the name of the indigenous Congregation of Mary Co-Redemptrix mentioned above.

Nevertheless, Vietnamese history and culture do offer very useful resources for constructing a Mariology that is both meaningful to the Vietnamese people and harmonious with the biblical and theological traditions about Mary as critically retrieved in contemporary scholarship. Here I can only paint a theological portrait of Mary in very broad strokes, and what emerges is not *the* Vietnamese Mariology but only one of the many ways of imagining Mary in accord with certain trends of the Vietnamese culture.

Persecution

As is clear from the above narratives, Mary's alleged apparitions at La Vang and Tra Kieu both occurred in the context of persecution, which is very different from other major Marian apparitions, such as those at Lourdes and Fatima. Mary appeared at La Vang and Tra Kieu as a protective mother, full of love and mercy for her suffering children. She had no message containing the threat of apocalyptic divine punishment if the Vietnamese people did not repent, nor did she require them to do anything in return for her favors. On the contrary, out of gratuitous and merciful love she liberated them and promised to listen favorably to those who would pray to her. In other words, she is the figure of pure mercy and compassion. She suffered with and protected the Vietnamese Catholics because they suffered.

It is perhaps this figure of Mary as the embodiment of divine mercy that powerfully attracts the Vietnamese, Christian and non-Christian alike, to her. It is well known that the Buddha is often presented as a man of infinite compassion for suffering humankind and that it was out of this compassion that he taught the Eightfold Path that would lead humans out of suffering and toward enlightenment. Three of the four divine attitudes or virtues *(brahmavihās)* that

---

[35] See Peter C. Phan, "Mary in Recent Theology and Piety: The View from the United States of America," *Ephemerides Mariologicae* 50 (2000), 425-40.

the Buddha stresses as necessary to achieve Buddhahood or enlightenment have to do with this quality of mercy and compassion: *mettā*, sometimes translated as "friendship," is a selfless, universal, all-expansive love; *mudita* is an altruistic joy in the success or welfare of others; and *karunā* is compassion for all living beings in their suffering, with no sense of superiority over them. This *karunā* is not an emotional sympathy, a mere feeling of pity or a helpless vicarious suffering for others, but rather a compassion that leads to positive action on behalf of one's fellow sufferers. In Vietnam, where mahāyanā Buddhism is prevalent, the virtue of *karunā* is highly stressed, equal to wisdom *(prjñā)*. It is in this tradition that we have the figure of Avalokiteśvara, a bodhisattva who, out of infinite compassion for suffering beings, postpones personal freedom from suffering and delusion until all other beings are saved from suffering as well. This is not the place to discuss the historical origins and the different manifestations of this extremely popular Buddhist figure, in India as well as in China, Japan, and Korea.[36] Suffice it to point out that in Vietnam, as well as in China, Japan and Korea, there is the female figure of Kwan-Yin (in Japan, Kannon), much beloved not only by Buddhists but also by the general populace. She is thought to be like mother, sister, friend, and queen, always listening to the cries for help (the word *Kwan-Yin* means "regarder of sounds," that is, the voices of the suffering). She is the first bodhisattva to whom lay people turn in time of trouble, and whom they seek to worship in gratitude for blessings received. Her statue is displayed in all Buddhist pagodas as well as in Taoist temples. In Vietnam she is represented as a woman holding a child and crushing a toad with her right foot.[37]

---

[36] For a presentation of Avalokiteśvara, see John Blofield, *Bodhisattva of Compassion: The Mystical Tradition of Kuan Yin* (London: Allen & Unwin, 1977); *Kuan Yin: Myths and Revelations of the Chinese Goddess of Compassion*, ed. Martin Palmer, Jay Ramsay, and Kwok Manho (London: Thorsons, 1995); Sandy Boucher, *Discovering Kwan Yin, Buddhist Goddess of Compassion* (Boston: Beacon Press, 1999); and Chun-Fang Yu, *Kwan Yin: The Chinese Transformations of Avalokiteśvara* (New York: Columbia University Press, 2001).

[37] Kwan-Yin is known in Vietnamese as Quan Âm Thi Kính. There are different stories about this goddess of compassion. In Vietnam, the story runs as follows: Thi Kính, a reincarnation of a man who still needed purification before achieving enlightenment, was a young woman wrongly accused of wanting to kill her husband. She left her husband, disguised as a man, and joined a Buddhist monastery. A young girl by the name of Thi Mâu, struck by the beauty of Thi Kính and thinking that she was a man, fell in love with her, but her love was rebuffed. Disconsolate, she gave herself to a man and conceived a child. When the child was born, she carried him to the pagoda and accused Thi Kính of being the father. When Thi Kính saw the child, out of maternal instincts, she reached for him and cradled him. Her gesture was judged to be the confirmation of the accusation, and she was sent out of the monastery in disgrace. For the rest of her life she was despised by the village, but she took care of the child and bore her unjust sufferings in silence, with patience, and with compassion for all. At her death people discovered that she was a woman in disguise and realized the injustices done to her. During her funeral, the Buddha himself appeared to reveal that she was the boddhisattva of compassion who listens to the cries of distress of all beings. Thi Mâu, for her punishment, was turned into a toad. See Pham Duy Khiem, *Légendes des terres sereines* (Paris: Mercure de France, 1953), 25-29.

Given this cultural and religious context, it is no wonder that Vietnamese Catholics readily see in Mary the figure who embodies divine compassion and mercy and who is always ready to assist them. Love of and devotion to Mary as Mother of Mercy, for Vietnamese Catholics, is a natural extension of their love of and devotion to the merciful Quan Âm Thi Kính.[38] Interestingly, Pope John Paul II, in his encyclical *Dives in misericordia* on God the Father, describes Mary as the "Mother of divine mercy" who has "the deepest knowledge of God's mercy. She knows its price, she knows how great it is. In this sense, we call her the Mother of mercy: our Lady of mercy, or Mother of divine mercy" (no. 9).

Furthermore, this Mariology echoes well the concerns of feminist theology that sees in Mary a Jewish woman who makes "an option for the poor" and whose Magnificat is a Magna Carta for the liberation of humans from all forms of oppression, especially patriarchalism and androcentrism.[39] This view is confirmed by Pope John Paul II, who, in his encyclical *Redemptoris Mater*, sees Mary's Magnificat as an expression of her love for the poor:

The Church's love of preference for the poor is wonderfully inscribed in Mary's Magnificat. . . . Drawing from Mary's heart, from the depth of her faith expressed in the words of the Magnificat, the Church renews ever more effectively in herself the awareness that the truth about God who saves, the truth about God who is the source of every gift, cannot be separated from the manifestation of his love of preference for the poor and humble, that love which, celebrated in the Magnificat, is later expressed in the words and works of Jesus (no. 37).

Power

The second component of a Vietnamese Mariology is the issue of power. From the accounts of the two Marian apparitions in Vietnam it is clear that Mary's merciful interventions were powerful and effective. The beleaguered Vietnamese Catholics were delivered from their persecutors. Mary showed herself a merciful mother but not a weak one. Mercy, as has been said above, is not a mere sense of pity or a sentimental sympathy (suffering with). Rather, it moves the compassionate person to action. Mercy without powerful action on behalf of the suffering is empty and demeaning. Conversely, power without mercy, which "has the interior form of the love that in the New Testament is called agape" (*Dives in misericordia*, no. 6), runs the risk of turning into dictatorship.

---

[38] On the role of mercy in Christian theology, see Jon Sobrino, *The Principle of Mercy: Taking the Crucified People from the Cross* (Maryknoll, N.Y.: Orbis Books, 1994), especially pp. 15-26.

[39] On feminist Mariology, see especially the works of Elizabeth Johnson, for instance, "The Marian Tradition and the Reality of Women," *Horizons* 12/1 (1985), 116-35; "Mary and the Female Face of God," *Theological Studies* 50 (1989), 500-526; and "Mary, Friend of God and Prophet: A Critical Reading of the Marian Tradition," *Theology Digest* 47/4 (Winter 2000), 317-25.

This figure of a powerful woman has much to recommend it to the Vietnamese people and is well represented in Vietnamese history and culture. This may explain why Marian devotion is also widely popular with Vietnamese men. It is true that Confucian morality, which was imposed on the Vietnamese by the Chinese during their thousand-year-long domination, is heavily patriarchal and androcentric. Women in a Confucian society are bound by the Three Submissions *(tam tong)*: when a child, she must submit to her father; in marriage, to her husband; in widowhood, to her eldest son. Women's behavior is to be guided by the Four Virtues *(tu duc)*, which are designed to restrict their role to the sphere of domesticity: assiduous housewifery *(cong),* pleasing appearance *(dung)*, appropriate speech *(ngon)*, and proper conduct *(hanh)*.[40]

Daily life and history in Vietnam, however, present a far different picture. Vietnamese history is replete with female political and military leaders, among whom the most celebrated and beloved are the Trung sisters, Trung Trac and Trung Nhi, who led a revolution against the Chinese in A.D. 42.[41] Another famous female leader is Trieu Au, who led an uprising against the Chinese in A.D. 248.[42] Indeed, historians have argued that in the earliest Vietnamese society, called the Lac or Dong Son civilization (from the seventh century B.C. to the first century A.D.), women occupied a high position.[43] Legally, Vietnamese women, compared with their Chinese counterparts, were in a far more favorable situation, accorded as they were many important rights.[44] In family life women exert a far greater authority than their husbands; in fact, they are called *noi*

---

[40] See Hue-Tam Ho Tai, *Radicalism and the Origins of the Vietnamese Revolution* (Cambridge, Mass.: Harvard University Press, 1992), 52-53; and David G. Marr, *Vietnamese Tradition on Trial 1920-1945* (Berkeley and Los Angeles: University of California Press, 1981), 190-99.

[41] See Keith Weller Taylor, *The Birth of Vietnam* (Berkeley and Los Angeles: University of California Press, 1983), 37-41, 334-39.

[42] "The Vietnamese remembered Lady Trieu's uprising as the most important event of the time. Her leadership appealed to strong popular instincts. The traditional image of her as a remarkable yet human leader, throwing her yard-long breasts over her shoulders when going into battle astride an elephant, has been handed down from generation to generation. After Lady Trieu's death, her spirit was worshiped by the Vietnamese. We owe our knowledge of her to the fact that she was remembered by the people" (ibid., 90).

[43] "Women enjoyed a relatively high status in Lac society. . . . When the Lac lords eventually rose up against increasing Chinese influence, they were led by women. According to Vietnamese tradition, the children of Lac Long Quan and Au Co were divided into two groups, with half following their father back to the sea and half going into the mountains with their mother. This division of the children into two groups appears to reflect a bilateral family system in which inheritance rights could be passed on through maternal and paternal lines" (ibid., 13).

[44] See the important studies by Ta Van Tai, especially "Protection of Women's Civil Rights in Traditional Vietnam: A Comparison of the Code of the Lê Dynasty (1428-1788) with the Chinese Codes," in *Law and the State in Traditional East Asia: Six Studies on the Sources of East Asian Law*, ed. Brian E. McKnight (Hawaii: University of Hawaii Press, 1987), 37-72. For studies on the role of Vietnamese women in general, see Nguyen Huu Tan, "La femme vietnamienne d'autrefois à travers les chansons populaires," *Bulletin de la Société des Études Indocinoises*, new series, 45/1 (1970): 3-13; My-Van Tran, "The Position of Women in Traditional Vietnam: Some Aspects," in

tuong (internal general). The contributions of women to Vietnamese "high" culture are also notable, especially in literature.[45]

Needless to say, given the central position of women in Vietnamese culture and history and in spite of the deeply ingrained Confucian patriarchalism and androcentrism, the figure of Mary as a powerful woman has profound implications for the struggle of Vietnamese women for equal rights and full human dignity. A Mariology that highlights the powerful role of Mary as a woman, together with her mercy and compassion, will be appealing to Vietnamese women and men.

Interreligious Dialogue

The third component of a Vietnamese Mariology is interreligious dialogue. It is most interesting that in the Buddhist version of the origins of the Vietnamese devotion to Our Lady of La Vang it was the Buddhists who, at the Buddha's behest, voluntarily offered their pagoda to the Catholics, who turned it into a Marian shrine. The relations between Buddhists and Catholics were apparently very amicable. Furthermore, according to this account, the statue of the Buddha was, as far as we know, not smashed as an idol but simply moved to another place. In addition, in the Tra Kieu story, our Lady was not seen by the Catholics of the village but by the "pagans" who attacked them. In M. Geffroy's account of the Tra Kieu incident, it is explicitly said that the Catholics saw nothing. Ironically, it was only through the testimony of the "unbelievers" that the "believers" knew that Mary had appeared and defended them! In a certain sense Vietnamese Catholics owe their devotion to Mary to the "pagans," at least at Tra Kieu.

Vietnamese Catholics form but a minority of Vietnam's population of seventy-five million (approximately 6 to 8 percent). Dialogue with the followers of other faiths (mainly Buddhist, Confucian, Taoist, and some other indigenous religions) is not a luxury but an absolute necessity for Vietnamese Catholics. Indeed, it is an essential component of Christian mission in Vietnam, along with inculturation and liberation. This triple dialogue has been recognized by the FABC to be the mode of Christian mission in Asia.[46]

Essays in Asian History, Past and Present, ed. K. M. de Silva et al. (New Delhi: Vikas Publishing House, 1990), 274-83; Stephen O'Harrow, "Vietnamese Women and Confucianism: Creating Spaces from Patriarchy," in *"Male" and "Female" in Developing Southeast Asia*, ed. Wazir Jahan Karim (Oxford/Washington, D.C.: Berg Publishers, 1995), 161-81; *Vietnam's Women in Transition*, ed. Kathleen Barry (New York: St. Martin's Press, 1996); and Nguyen Van Ky, *La société vietnamienne face à la modernité* (Paris: L'Harmattan, 1995), 261-97.

[45] Two female writers are often cited, Ba Huyen Thanh Quan and Ho Xuan Huong. There are, of course, legions of contemporary female writers.

[46] See Gaudencio Rosales and C. G. Arévalo, eds., *For All Peoples of Asia: Federation of Asian Bishops' Conferences. Documents from 1970 to 1991*, vol. 1 (Maryknoll, N.Y.: Orbis Books, 1991); Franz-Josef Eilers, ed., *For All the Peoples of Asia: Federation of Asian Bishops' Conferences. Documents from 1992 to 1996*, vol. 2 (Quezon City, Philippines: Claretian Publications, 1997); and idem, ed. *For All the Peoples of Asia: Federation of Asian Bishops' Conferences. Documents from 1997-2001*, vol. 3 (Quezon City, Philippines: Claretian Publications, 2002).

Given a number of common traits between Kwan-Yin and Mary, it is natural that Mariology can serve as a fruitful starting point for interreligious dialogue in Vietnam. Of course, a facile identification between the two figures is to be rejected. But it is beyond doubt that both of them allow us to imagine God as a loving, merciful, compassionate, saving, protecting, liberating Father/Mother for all the Vietnamese people, irrespective of their religious traditions, and that all Vietnamese are thereby called to promote a society of love, mercy, compassion, and freedom. An authentic Vietnamese Mariology cannot but be an incentive for this interreligious dialogue.

7

Culture and Liturgy

ANCESTOR VENERATION AS A TEST CASE

There is little doubt that, by any measure, inculturation is taking the lion's share of the efforts of the church and theology, at least in Asia. And one of the areas where inculturation is strongly urged is liturgy and worship. Furthermore, in countries and cultures permeated by Confucianism, such as China, Japan, Korea, and Vietnam, ancestor veneration (or ancestor worship or the cult of ancestors) has been and continues to be a vexing and contentious issue, with immense ramifications for evangelization and church life, as the so-called Chinese Rites Controversy has made painfully clear.

In this chapter I first sketch the history of the Chinese Rites Controversy as the background against which to approach the problem of liturgical inculturation in Asia. The focus is not on the complex and lengthy historical development of the controversy but on the theological issues that underlie it. Second, I outline some of these theological problems. Third, I present a particular case of liturgical inculturation of ancestor veneration, namely, that of Vietnam. In light of the Chinese Rites Controversy and the Vietnamese liturgical experiment, I conclude with some general guidelines on how liturgical inculturation should be implemented today.

THE CHINESE RITES CONTROVERSY: THE HISTORICAL CONTEXT

Early missionaries to China in the sixteenth century, during the Ming dynasty (1368-1643), faced three distinct though related issues: how to translate Christian terms, especially "God," into Chinese;[1] whether the liturgy should be

---

This chapter was written before the issuance of the *Directory on Popular Piety and the Liturgy* by the Congregation for Divine Worship at the Discipline of the Sacraments (2002) and therefore could not take it into account.

[1] The question was which of the three available Chinese terms, namely, *shang-ti* (sovereign on high), *t'ien* (heaven), and *t'ien-ti* (lord of heaven), would be the appropriate equivalent for *Deus*. Matteo Ricci argued that it would be inappropriate to designate God with words such as *T'ai-chi* (supreme ultimate) and *li* (principle), as the Neo-Confucians appeared to him to have done (see *The True Meaning of the Lord of Heaven,*

conducted in the vernacular;[2] and whether to allow certain widely practiced rituals and ceremonies, in particular the veneration of Confucius and the ancestors.[3] While each of these issues had its own complicated history and constitutes a fascinating theme for inculturation by itself, here I focus on the third, and more narrowly, only on its second element, that is, the veneration of ancestors, since it is the only remaining issue that poses serious challenges to liturgical inculturation.[4]

Before examining how Christian missionaries viewed the Chinese practice of the veneration of ancestors, it is useful to review briefly its main rituals,

---

trans., with introduction and notes, Douglas Lancashire and Peter Hu Kuo-chen [Taipei: Ricci Institute, 1985], 99-132). Ricci himself was in favor of using the three words mentioned above, as well as the newly coined *t'ien-chu* (lord of heaven), interchangeably to designate God. The use of *t'ien chu* for God was approved by Pope Clement XI's decree *Ex illa die* (1715) and Pope Benedict XIV's decree *Ex quo singulari* (1742). Today *t'ien-chu* is the official term for God in the Catholic church in China, whereas the Protestant Churches prefer *shang-ti* or *shen* (deity, spirit).

[2] For the use of Chinese in the liturgy, see François Bontinck, *La Lutte autour de la liturgie chinoise aux XVIIè et XVIIIe siècles* (Paris: Béatrice-Nauwelaerts, 1962).

[3] The literature on this theme is immense. It is readily available in the works cited below. For a readable account of the controversy, see George Minamiki, *The Chinese Rites Controversy from Its Beginnings to Modern Times* (Chicago: Loyola University Press, 1985), with a helpful bibliography (325-45). An international symposium was organized in San Francisco in October 1992 by the Ricci Institute on the significance of the Chinese Rites Controversy in the context of the history of the relationship between China and the West. It resulted in two important publications: Ray R. Noll, ed., *100 Roman Documents concerning the Chinese Rites Controversy (1645-1941)* (San Francisco: Ricci Institute for Chinese-Western Cultural History, 1992); and David E. Mungello, ed., *The Chinese Rites Controversy: Its History and Meaning* (Nettetal: Steyler Verlag, 1994). A recent important study is by Roland Jacques, "Le Dossier des rites chinois doit-il être rouvert?" *L'Année canonique* 41 (1999), 363-400. For a brief outline of the controversy, see Noll, *100 Roman Documents*, vi-xviii. On the larger question of how the Jesuits transmitted Christian ideas to the Chinese literati and the latter's reactions, see John D. Young, *Confucianism and Christianity: The First Encounter* (Hong Kong: The University of Hong Kong Press, 1983).

[4] With Vatican II's liturgical reform, the use of vernaculars in liturgical celebrations is no longer an issue. With regard to the cult of Confucius, political changes in China as well as in other countries that had sponsored it have made the practice obsolete. The cult of Confucius probably started out as a practice of his family and clan in the context of ancestor worship. The fact that it became a national practice was due to a fortuitous event. In 213 B.C. during the Ch'in dynasty (221 B.C.-207 B.C.), a decree was issued to burn scholarly books that extolled the traditional ways of the past. The succeeding Western Han dynasty (206 B.C.-A.D. 8) tried to restore the ancient order by recovering classical books which, according to tradition, Confucius had compiled and edited. Thus Confucius became the voice of tradition, and Confucianism was established as the official state orthodoxy. In A.D. 59 Emperor Han Ming Ti made Confucius the patron of scholars and ordered that sacrifice should be offered to him at all government schools. In this way the cult hall became part of the school establishment. During the T'ang dynasty (A.D. 907-60), Emperor T'ai Tsun ordered every district to construct a sanctuary or temple *(wen maio)* to honor Confucius. In this way the cult became a part of the Chinese society, especially when the Confucian classics were made the standard textbooks of Chinese education and later recognized as the canonical books of China.

The ritual for the cult of Confucius was elaborated by the Ministry of Rites and sometimes determined by the emperor himself. The sacrifice takes the form of a solemn

which of course vary widely according to time and place.[5] As soon as a person dies, after the usual acts of preparation of the corpse for burial, a piece of paper or white cloth that bears the name of the deceased is placed in front of the coffin and is carried to the cemetery. After burial, the piece of paper or cloth is brought home and placed on the family altar to receive prayers and acts of piety from family members. Eventually it is replaced by a piece of wood called a spirit tablet. On its front, the name, family status, and societal rank of the deceased are written, and on its back, the date of his or her birth and death. Since this tablet is thought to somehow represent the deceased, or to be something in which the soul of the deceased is believed to reside, characters such as *shen wei* or *ling wei* or *shen zu* (the seat of the spirit) are inscribed on it. Various ceremonies such as the burning of incense and the kowtow (bowing until the forehead touches the ground) are performed in front of this tablet.

On the anniversary of the deceased's death, on the first and fifteenth days of the month of the lunar calendar, and on other solemn festivities such as weddings and New Year, family members gather to perform acts of veneration such as the kowtow, to burn incense and paper money, and to make offerings of food and drink (which will be eaten later in a banquet). At the heart of all these ancestral rites lies *hsiao* (filial piety), the most important virtue in Confucian ethics, by which a person lives out his or her *wu lun* (five relationships)—ruler and subject, parent and child, husband and wife, older and younger siblings, and friend and friend.[6]

The early Jesuit missionaries to China, in accordance with Alessandro Valignano's accommodationist policy,[7] were open to accepting the veneration

---

banquet; strict attention is given to the preparation and offering of selected dishes, including the meat of ox, pig, and sheep, as well as assorted viands and wine. Sacrifice is held twice a year, mid-spring and mid-autumn, and performed by Confucian literati (Confucianism does not have a priestly caste). Another ritual is performed by successful candidates of the national examinations as a sign of gratitude to Confucius. The hall in which the sacrifice is offered contains spirit tablets *(ling-kuei)* of Confucius, his four closest disciples, and additional Confucian scholars (in 1530 Emperor Chia Chung ordered all the images replaced by spirit tablets).

How the cult of Confucius was perceived by missionaries can be gathered from the six questions posed to the Holy Office (see Noll, *101 Roman Documents*, 10-14). The fundamental question for Rome was whether the sacrifice offered and the honors paid to Confucius had a religious character and hence were "tainted with superstition" or were simply a "civil and political rite."

[5] For a fuller description of the funeral rites among Chinese and Vietnamese, see Peter C. Phan, "The Christ of Asia: An Essay on Jesus as the Eldest Son and Ancestor," *Studia Missionalia* 45 (1996), 38-40.

[6] How the missionaries viewed this veneration of ancestors and its rites can be seen from the questions posed to the Holy Office (see Noll, *101 Roman Documents*, 15-18).

[7] Alessandro Valignano (1538-1606) was appointed visitor of the missions to East Asia in 1573. When he came to Japan in 1579, he objected to the Westernizing tendencies of his confreres' missionary methods and recommended instead a gradual inculturation into the Japanese culture and way of life. It was he also who, after arriving in Macao in 1578, decided that the only way for missionaries to have any success in their work was by mastering the local languages. And it was he who assigned Michele Ruggieri and Matteo Ricci the task of studying Chinese. He also made the very important decision

of ancestors as well as the cult of Confucius as legitimate, except when any of these rites seemed to imply superstition. For example, with regard to ancestor worship, Matteo Ricci, who worked in China from 1582 until his death in 1610, wrote in his memoir:

> The most solemn thing among the *literati* and in use from the king down to the very least being is the offering they annually make to the dead at certain times of the year of meat, fruit, perfumes, and pieces of silk cloth— paper among the poorest—and incense. And in this act they make the fulfilment of their duty to their relatives, namely, "to serve them in death as though they were alive." Nor do they think in this matter that the dead will come to eat the things mentioned or that they might need them; but they say they do this because they know of no other way to show their love and grateful spirit toward them [the dead]. And some of them told us that this ceremony was begun more for the living than for the dead, that is, to teach children and the ignorant ones to honor and serve their living relatives, since they [the children] see serious people doing the offices for the relatives after their deaths that they were wont to do to them when they [the relatives] were alive. And since they do not recognize any divinity in these dead ones, nor do they ask or hope for anything from them, all this stands outside of idolatry, and also one can say there is probably no superstition, although it will be better for the souls of these dead ones, if they are Christians, to change this into almsgiving to the poor.[8]

In 1585 Pope Gregory XIII gave the Jesuits the exclusive right to work in China and Japan, but this restriction was later lifted by Popes Paul V and Urban VIII. As a result, the Dominicans and Franciscans from the Philippines entered China in the 1630s.[9] They were joined by the Augustinians in 1680 and the

---

to sever the China mission from the jurisdiction of Macao so that the superior of the China mission could have greater freedom of action. Moreover, it is certain that he issued in 1603 a set of directives regarding the ancestral and Confucian rites, the text of which is now lost but whose contents can safely be derived from Matteo Ricci's writings on the subject. For Valignano's own missionary work through writing catechisms, see Peter C. Phan, *Mission and Catechesis: Alexandre de Rhodes and Inculturation in Seventeenth-Century Vietnam* (Maryknoll, N.Y.: Orbis Books, 1998), 113-14.

[8] Pasquale M. D'Elia, ed., *Fonti Ricciane: Storia dell'introduzione del Cristianesimo in Cina scritta da Matteo Ricci S.I.,* 3 vols. (Rome: La Libreria dello Stato, 1942-1949), 1:177. Translation with emendation from Minamiki, *The Chinese Rites Controversy from Its Beginnings to Modern Times,* 17-18. For the English translation of Ricci's diary, see Matteo Ricci, *China in the Sixteenth Century: Journals of Matthew Ricci 1583-1610,* translated from the Latin of Nicholas Trigault, S.J., by Louis J. Gallagher, S.J. (New York, 1953). Ricci is believed to have issued in 1603 a set of guidelines regarding the cult of Confucius and ancestors. The text is no longer extant, but no doubt the guidelines reflected his understanding of the Chinese rites contained in this passage.

[9] On the work of the Dominicans in the Philippines and China, see John E. Willis Sr., "From Manila to Fuan: Asian Contexts of Dominican Mission Policy," in Mungello, *The Chinese Rites Controversy,* 111-27.

members of the MEP in 1684. These new arrivals, who adopted a missionary method different from that of the Jesuits,[10] found the Jesuits' accommodationist policies objectionable. One of them, Dominican Juan Bautista de Morales, who came in China in 1633 and left in 1638, presented "Seventeen Questions" to the Sacred Congregation for the Propagation of the Faith (Propaganda Fide) in 1643, attacking the Jesuits' practices.[11] In 1645, on the basis of Morales's presentation and with Pope Innocent X's approval, Propaganda Fide condemned the Chinese rites.

Believing that the condemnation was influenced by Morales's inaccurate portrayal of the Chinese rites as having a religious nature, the Jesuits responded by dispatching one of their own, Martino Martini, to Rome in 1651 to plead their case before Propaganda Fide. As a result of Martini's presentation, in 1656 the Holy Office, to which Martini's "Four Questions" had been sent for examination, published, with Pope Alexander VII's approval, a rescript in favor of the Jesuits on the ground that the Chinese rites were "merely civil and political."[12]

Meanwhile, in China persecutions broke out against the Christians, and in 1665 most missionaries were exiled to Canton and put in detention there. Of those detained, nineteen were Jesuits, three were Dominicans, and one was a Franciscan. Taking advantage of their time together, they held a conference (the Canton Conferences) on the missionary strategies to be adopted in China. At the end of these conferences, which lasted for forty days and ended on 26 January 1668, they issued forty-two articles, the forty-first of which recommended that Pope Alexander VII's rescript permitting the practice of the veneration of Confucius and the ancestors be followed unconditionally (omnino).[13] These articles were discussed, amended, and voted upon. Domingo Fernandez Navarette, a Dominican who approved the articles, later changed his mind upon his escape. He returned to Spain and wrote a book attacking the Jesuits' position regarding the rites. Asked by Juan Polanco, O.P., a delegate of the Dominicans from the Philippines, whether its rescript of 1656 had annulled the 1645 decision of Propaganda Fide regarding the Chinese rites, the Holy Office replied in 1669, with Pope Clement IX's approval, that both decrees had to be observed "according to the questions, circumstances, and everything set down in them."[14]

Back in China a momentous and tragic turning point in the Chinese Rites Controversy occurred in 1693 when Monsignor Charles Maigrot, a member of

---

[10] For an explication of these two methods, see James S. Cummings, "Two Missionary Methods in China: Mendicants and Jesuits," *Archivio Ibero-Americano* 37 (1978), 33-108. For a friendly exposition of the Dominican position, see Fidel Villaroel, "The Chinese Rites Controversy: Dominican Viewpoint," *Philippiniana Sacra* 28/82 (1993), 5-61.

[11] For the text of Morales's questions regarding the Chinese Rites, see Noll, *100 Roman Documents*, 1-4.

[12] For the text of Martini's four questions, see Noll, *100 Roman Documents*, 5-6.

[13] For the text of the forty-first article, see Minamiki, *The Chinese Rites Controversy from Its Beginnings to Modern Times*, 33.

[14] See Noll, *100 Roman Documents*, 7.

the MEP and apostolic vicar of Fukien (later bishop of Conon), issued a *mandatum* or *edictum* containing seven points that condemned and forbade, *inter alia,* the cult of Confucius and ancestral rites, which the bishop declared "tarnished with superstition."[15] Maigrot's *mandatum* created a furor of opposition, especially among the Jesuits. Four of them in Peking presented to Emperor K'ang Hsi a statement on the meaning of the cult of Confucius and the ancestors, which they said was only "a means of showing sincere affection for members of the family and thankful devotion to ancestors of the clan" and asked for his authoritative opinion. The emperor confirmed the correctness of their interpretation in a rescript on 30 November 1700.

Meanwhile in Rome Maigrot's *mandatum* reopened the whole question of the Chinese rites because he charged that Pope Alexander VII was misled by Martini's presentation in adopting a favorable stance toward the Chinese rites. In 1704 Pope Clement XI issued a decree confirming Maigrot's condemnation of the Chinese rites but wanted it to be kept secret until its promulgation in China by his newly appointed *legatus a latere,* Carlo Tommaso Maillard de Tournon, after his arrival in the country.[16]

De Tournon's mission was an unmitigated disaster. After three fruitless audiences with Emperor K'ang Hsi in Peking, he left for Nanking.[17] Meanwhile, the emperor examined Maigrot on his knowledge of the Chinese classics and the Chinese language, and finding it woefully inadequate, issued an edict on 21 December 1706 banishing him from the country. Furthermore, he mandated that only those missionaries who had been granted the *p'iao*—the certificate by which they promised to follow the practices of Matteo Ricci and to remain in China all their lives—could remain in China. Apprised of this imperial requirement, de Tournon published in 1707 a decree in which he gave instructions to missionaries about how to answer the emperor's questions and, anticipating Pope Clement XI's still-to-be proclaimed 1704 decree, forbade the veneration of ancestors and Confucius and the use of the spirit tablets.[18]

The strongest condemnation of the Chinese rites came at the hand of the same pope with the apostolic constitution *Ex illa die* (19 March 1715), confirming de Tournon's position.[19] To add force to his rulings, Clement XI attached the penalty of excommunication *latae sententiae* to violations and required missionaries to take an oath on the Bible that they would observe his instructions

---

[15] On Charles Maigrot and his role in the Chinese Rites Controversy, see Claudia von Collani, "Charles Maigrot's Role in the Chinese Rites Controversy," in Mungello, *The Chinese Rites Controversy*, 149-83. For the text of Maigrot's *mandatum,* see Noll, *100 Roman Documents,* 8-10.

[16] For the text of the Holy Office's detailed response to Maigrot's seven articles and of Clement XI's confirmation of Maigrot's *mandatum,* see Noll, *100 Roman Documents,* 8-24.

[17] On the work of de Tournon as papal legate, see Edward J. Malatesta, "A Fatal Clash of Wills: The Condemnation of the Chinese Rites by the Papal Legate Carlo Tommaso Maillard de Tournon," in Mungello, *The Chinese Rites Controversy,* 211-45.

[18] For the text of de Tournon's decree, see Noll, *100 Roman Documents,* 27-29.

[19] For the text of Clement XI's *Ex illa die,* see ibid., 49-54.

"exactly, absolutely and inviolably . . . without any evasion." The new decree, promulgated in Peking on 5 November 1716 by the vicar general, Charles Castorano, met with much opposition. The emperor ordered Castorano to go to Canton, where the decree was circulating, to retrieve all the copies of *Ex illa die* and send them back to the pope.

In another attempt to enforce his decree Pope Clement XI sent Charles Ambrose Mezzabarba as his apostolic legate to China. In his audience with Emperor K'ang Hsi the legate said that he was authorized to grant certain permissions regarding the rites and that he was prepared to relate to the pope the emperor's thinking on the matter. It was in Macao on 4 November 1721 that Mezzabarba issued a pastoral letter in which he granted the infamous "Eight Permissions" regarding the Chinese rites, even though he prefaced his letter by saying that he did not intend to suspend *Ex illa die* or permit what had been prohibited by it.[20] However, despite Mezzabarba's protestations to the contrary, his "permissions" did seem to go against the pope's decree and therefore caused much confusion. Whereas François Saraceni, vicar apostolic of Shansi and Shensi, prohibited the use of the "Eight Permissions," François de la Purification, bishop of Peking, allowed them in his two pastoral letters of 1733. Pope Clement XII had to write a letter in 1735 in which he declared that the two letters of the bishop of Peking "are and forever will be wholly and absolutely null and void and invalid and of utterly no force or importance."

The final and most forceful condemnation of the Chinese rites occurred on 11 July 1742 with Pope Benedict XIV's apostolic constitution *Ex quo singulari*. The document reviewed the history of the Chinese Rites Controversy from its beginning in 1645 and quoted in full the various papal statements against the Chinese rites; reiterated the rejection of Mezzabarba's "Eight Permissions" as "null, void, invalid, and completely futile and ineffective"; ordered *Ex illa die* to be observed "exactly, integrally, absolutely, inviolably, and strictly" under pain of automatic excommunication reserved to the pope; expanded the formula of the oath against the Chinese rites; and continued *Ex illa die*'s prohibition of further discussions of the issue, again under pain of automatic excommunication.[21]

Benedict XIV wanted to settle the Chinese Rites Controversy once and for all with his constitution, which he proclaimed to "remain in force, all of it for all time to come." Unfortunately, political events some two hundred years later, ironically not in China but in Japan, forced the reconsideration of the Chinese rites and led the church to adopt a more flexible stance. On 5 May 1932 some students from the Jesuit Sophia University refused to bow to the famous Yasukuni Shrine where the Japanese war dead were honored. When Jean Alexis Chambon, archbishop of Tokyo, inquired from the Ministry of Education about the meaning of the bow required of visitors to the Shinto shrine, he was informed that the bow "has no other purpose than that of manifesting the sentiment of patriotism

---

[20] For Mezzabarba's text with the "Eight Permissions," see ibid., 55.

[21] For the text of Benedict XIV's constitution, see ibid., 46-61.

and loyalty."[22] A year later Edward Mooney, the apostolic delegate to Japan, issued a statement allowing Japanese Catholics to perform such a bow.

At about the same time, in the state of Manchukuo, which the Japanese Kwantung army had established in Manchuria, an attempt was made to make use of Confucianism, called the *Wangtao* (the way of the benevolent ruler) as a tool to unify the people. As a consequence, Manchurian Catholics were required to render homage to Confucius at the local shrine. Bishop Augustin Ernest Gaspais, in the footsteps of Archbishop Chambon, asked the Manchurian government to clarify the meaning of this act of veneration. He was advised that "the ceremonies in honor of Confucius have as their sole objective the exterior manifestation of the veneration one has for him, but they do not have at all any religious character."[23]

As the result of these governmental declarations on the nonreligious character of the cult of Confucius and the veneration of ancestors, Propaganda Fide issued on 8 December 1939, with Pope Pius XII's approval, the instruction *Plane compertum est,* in which it said that (1) it is lawful for Catholics to participate in public honors paid to Confucius; (2) the image or name tablet of Confucius may be placed in Catholic schools and saluted by a head bow; (3) if Catholics are required to assist at public functions that appear to be superstitious, they should maintain a passive attitude; and (4) bows of heads and other marks of respect in front of the deceased or their images or name tablets are lawful and honorable. In addition, the requirement of the oath was abolished.[24]

With this document, which historian Francis A. Rouleau, S.J., called the "liberating decree" for China, a painful and lengthy chapter of the history of the church in Asia came to an end. The instruction brought immense relief to missionaries to Asia by abolishing the oath and removed a serious obstacle to the conversion of many Asians, in particular the educated class, by permitting, under certain conditions, the cult of Confucius and especially the veneration of ancestors. Nevertheless, in spite of its short-term missionary gains, it left unresolved many theological issues that are of great consequence for the project of liturgical inculturation. It is useful, therefore, to examine the theological issues underlying the Chinese Rites Controversy as well as the doctrinal problems involved in the veneration of ancestors.

THE CHINESE RITES CONTROVERSY: INCULTURATION AND THEOLOGICAL ISSUES

There is no doubt that extra-theological factors, such as rivalries among religious orders (the Jesuits, on the one hand, and the Mendicant Friars and the MEP, on the other), personality conflicts, cultural chauvinism, misguided patriotism, the complications of the *padroado* system (between the Portuguese crown and the Holy See), the misunderstandings between Emperor K'ang Hsi

---

[22] Minamiki, *The Chinese Rites Controversy from Its Beginnings to Modern Times*, 145.

[23] Ibid., 177.

[24] For the text of *Plane compertum est*, see Noll, *100 Roman Documents*, 87-88.

and the Roman representatives, and even the competition between the Holy Office and Propaganda Fide all played a role in the Chinese Rites Controversy. Nevertheless, from the writings of the people involved in the dispute it is clear that theological considerations also loomed large in the decision to accept or condemn the Chinese rites. Indeed, the basic and often repeated argument of those opposed to the Chinese rites was that they were "tainted by superstition," whereas those who argued for their toleration justified their position on the ground that these rites were not religious but "merely civil and political." Even *Plane compertum est*, which allowed Asian Catholics to participate in the cult of Confucius and the veneration of ancestors, did so only because "although in earlier times they [these rituals] were tied in with pagan rites, now that customs and minds have changed with the flow of the centuries, [they] merely preserve civil expression of devotion toward ancestors, or of patriotism, or of respect for fellow countrymen."[25]

Leaving aside for the moment the question of whether ancestor veneration is "merely civil and political," to which I will come back below, clearly the most important theological issue for those opposed to the Chinese Rites was the nature of non-Christian religions. For them ancestor veneration was to be rejected because it formed an essential part of Chinese religions and could not be anything but paganism, superstition, and idolatry, words frequently used in Roman documents to describe the Chinese rites. Even Matteo Ricci, who had a deep respect for the Chinese culture, had reservations about the veneration of ancestors. For Ricci, the cult of ancestors was legitimate only because it was simply a way for the descendants "to show their love and grateful spirit" to their ancestors; because the rite was meant more for the sake of the survivors than for the dead, that is, "to teach the children and the ignorant to honor and serve their relatives"; and because "there is probably no superstition." For Christians, Ricci recommended that the veneration of ancestors be replaced by almsgiving. In other words, despite his acceptance of the veneration of ancestors, Ricci did not recognize its intrinsic value as a religious practice.

My point here is not to find fault with Ricci's or any other seventeenth-century missionary's theology of religions.[26] Indeed, such a theology already represented a commendable openness toward non-Christian religions.[27] Rather, my purpose is to point out that the rejection, total or partial, of the Chinese rites in the seventeenth century was undergirded by a negative view of non-Christian religions and

---

[25] Ibid., 87.

[26] The view that non-Christian, "pagan" religions were infected with superstition and idolatry was almost universal in the seventeenth and subsequent centuries (see Phan, *Mission and Catechesis*, 82-96).

[27] For instance, Ricci maintained that Chinese names for God, *Tian* (heaven) and *Shangdi* (lord on high), which had been used in the Chinese classics (such as the *Book of History* and the *Book of Songs*), correspond with the Christian concept of God. Furthermore, some Jesuits, such as Jean François Foucquet and Joseph de Prémare, known as "figurists," even held that certain Chinese classics (such as the *Book of Changes*) contain figures or types of persons or events in the New Testament, in particular, Jesus. On this theme, see Knud Lundbaek, "Joseph de Prémare and the Name of God in China," in Mungello, *The Chinese Rites Controversy*, 129-24.

to argue that a genuine liturgical inculturation is not possible unless such a theology of religions is abandoned. Undoubtedly there has been a revolution from the seventeenth-century pessimistic theology of religions to Vatican II's *Nostra aetate* and its positive appreciation of and commitment to "acknowledge, preserve, and promote the spiritual and moral goods" found among the "teachings, rules of life, and sacred ceremonies" of other religions (*NA*, no. 2). It was precisely the emergence of this positive theology of religions during the waning years of Pius XI's pontificate and especially at the beginning of Pius XII's that made the reversal of the longstanding rejection of the Chinese rites possible.[28]

Inculturation as a theological and liturgical project was also made possible by a new pneumatology that, in accordance with this positive theology of religions, sees the divine Spirit present and active not only in individuals but also in collective realities such as cultures and religions. John Paul II affirms this kind of presence of the Holy Spirit when he says: "The Spirit's presence and activity affect not only individuals but also society and history, peoples, cultures and religions. Indeed, the Spirit is at the origin of the noble ideals and undertakings which benefit humanity on its journey through history" (*RM*, no. 28). In light of this pneumatology, the primary goal of mission is no longer seen as saving individuals, which was the dominating preoccupation of past missionary efforts. With Vatican II's recognition that salvation is possible outside the visible confines of the church,[29] mission is now focused on the reign of God, which Jesus inaugurated in the power of the Holy Spirit. Mission is carried out in activities such as proclamation, witness, worship, inculturation, liberation, and interreligious dialogue.[30] By means of this complex of activities, what is sought is not merely an external adaptation of Christianity to the local cultures but, in

---

[28] Two encyclicals of Pius XII were of special significance: *Summi pontificatus*, in *Acta Apostolicae Sedis* 31 (1939), 429; and *Evangelii praecones,* in *Acta Apostolicae Sedis* 43 (1951), 521-24.

[29] For a thorough study of the possibility of salvation outside the Church, see Francis Sullivan, *Salvation Outside the Church? Tracing the History of the Catholic Response* (New York: Paulist Press, 1992).

[30] For recent theologies of mission, see David Bosch, *Transforming Mission: Paradigm Shifts in Theology of Mission* (Maryknoll, N.Y.: Orbis Books, 1991); M. Thomas Thangaraj, *The Common Task: A Theology of Mission* (Nashville, Tenn.: Abingdon Press, 1999); James Scherer and Stephen Bevans, eds., *New Directions in Mission and Evangelization*, 3 vols. (Maryknoll, N.Y.: Orbis Books, 1992, 1994, 1999); Robert T. Coote and James M. Phillips, eds., *Toward the Twenty-first Century in Christian Mission* (Grand Rapids, Mich.: Eerdmans, 1993); Leslie Newbigin, *The Gospel in a Pluralist Society* (Grand Rapids, Mich.: Eerdmans, 1990); Wilbert R. Shenk, *Changing Frontiers of Mission* (Maryknoll, N.Y.: Orbis Books, 1999); Andrew F. Walls, *The Missionary Movement in Christian History* (Maryknoll, N.Y.: Orbis Books, 1996); Vinoth Ramachandra, *The Recovery of Mission: Beyond the Pluralist Paradigm* (Grand Rapids, Mich.: Eerdmans, 1996); William Jenkinson and Helene O'Sullivan, eds., *Trends in Mission: Toward the Third Millennium* (Maryknoll, N.Y.: Orbis Books, 1991); Donal Dorr, *Mission in Today's World* (Maryknoll, N.Y.: Orbis Books, 2000); Peter C. Phan, "Christian Mission in Contemporary Theology," *Indian Theological Studies* 31 (1994), 297-347; idem, "Human Development and Evangelization," *Studia Missionalia* 47 (1998), 205-227. There is also the very useful Karl Müller et al., eds., *Dictionary of Mission: Theology, History, Perspectives* (Maryknoll, N.Y.: Orbis Books, 1997).

the words of John Paul II, "the intimate transformation of authentic cultural values through their integration in Christianity and the insertion of Christianity in the various human cultures" (*RM*, no. 52).[31]

In addition to the questions of the salvific value of non-Christian religions and the active presence of the Holy Spirit in cultures, another theological issue underlying the Chinese Rites Controversy is Christology, and, more specifically, the role of Christ as the unique and universal savior, even though it was not framed in these precise terms during the dispute. This issue was indirectly broached by Juan Bautista de Morales when he raised the question of whether the Chinese word *sheng* (holy), which Christian missionaries used to refer to the Trinity, Christ, Mary, and the saints, could be used of Confucius.[32] It was also implied in the question of whether Catholics were permitted to take part in the cult of Confucius. The issue was whether the role of Christ as the unique and universal savior excludes the role of other religious founders as mediators of salvation and other religions as ways to God.

This question has been dealt with in contemporary theology under the rubrics of exclusivism, inclusivism, and pluralism, and of ecclesiocentrism, Christocentrism, theocentrism, and regnocentrism.[33] The challenge here is to find a coherent way to hold together the Christian claim that Jesus is the unique and universal savior and the recognition that various religions "reflect a ray of that Truth which enlightens all human beings" (*NA*, no. 2), between God's particular self-revelation in Jesus and God's general self-revelation in non-Christian religions. The question is whether it is possible to affirm with Jacques Dupuis that there is "a convergence between the religious traditions and the mystery of Jesus Christ, as representing various, though not equal, paths along which, through history, God has sought and continues to seek human beings in his Word and Spirit."[34] Clearly, the possibility of incorporating into Christian liturgy the sacred

[31] Extraordinary Synod of Bishops of 1985, *Final Report*, II, C, 6. Quoted by John Paul II in his encyclical *Redemptoris missio*, no. 52.

[32] See Noll, *100 Roman Documents*, 4.

[33] For these categories, see the works of Paul Knitter, including *No Other Name? A Critical Survey of Christian Attitudes to World Religions* (Maryknoll, N.Y.: Orbis Books, 1985); *One Earth Many Religions: Multifaith Dialogue and Global Responsibility* (Maryknoll, N.Y.: Orbis Books, 1995); and *Jesus and the Other Names: Christian Mission and Global Responsibility* (Maryknoll, N.Y.: Orbis Books, 1996).

[34] Jacques Dupuis, *Toward a Christian Theology of Religious Pluralism* (Maryknoll, N.Y.: Orbis Books, 1997), 328. See also Dupuis's very helpful essay, "Universality of the Word and Particularity of Jesus Christ," in *The Convergence of Theology*, ed. Daniel Kendall and Stephen Davis (New York: Paulist Press, 2001), 320-42; Peter C. Phan, "Are There Other 'Saviors' for Other People? A Discussion of the Problem of the Universal Significance and Uniqueness of Jesus the Christ," in *Christianity and the Wider Ecumenism*, ed. Peter C. Phan (New York: Paragon House, 1990), 163-80; and idem, "The Claim of Uniqueness and Universality in Interreligious Dialogue," *Indian Theological Studies* 31/1 (1994), 44-66. For a different view, see the Congregation of the Doctrine of the Faith, *Dominus Iesus* (6 August 2000). John Paul II emphasizes the subordinate role of other religious founders and religions vis-à-vis Jesus: "Although participated forms of mediation of different kinds and degrees are not excluded, they acquire meaning and value *only* from Christ's own mediation, and they cannot be understood as parallel or complementary to his" (*RM*, no. 5).

texts, prayers, and rituals of non-Christian religions depends on a positive answer to this question.

From the ecclesiastical point of view, during the Chinese Rites Controversy the relationship between Rome and the churches in China was often put to the test, or to put it in terms of contemporary ecclesiology, the nature of the church as *communio ecclesiarum* hung in the balance. This was evident in the activities of the two papal legates Carlo Tommaso Maillard de Tournon and Carlo Ambrogio Mezzabarba and the various decrees by which Pope Clement XII and Benedict XIV annulled the pastoral policies of François de la Purification, bishop of Peking. It was extremely unfortunate that the Roman authorities made decisions regarding the Chinese rites without serious consultation with the Chinese churches and the Chinese Christians themselves.

It is widely admitted today that no real inculturation is possible without a certain autonomy of the local churches. Even Propaganda Fide recognized the wisdom of leaving the matter of giving rules and norms of behavior regarding permitted or forbidden ceremonies in ancestor worship to the local bishops and to the consciences of the priests and the laity.[35] During the special assembly for Asia of the Synod of Bishops in Rome (19 April-14 May 1998), many Asian bishops demanded a legitimate autonomy for the local churches, especially in matters of liturgical inculturation.[36] Pope John Paul II himself has pointed out that "inculturation must involve the whole people of God, and not just a few experts, since the people reflect the authentic *sensus fidei* which must never be lost sight of. . . . It must be an expression of the community's life, one which must mature within the community itself, and not be exclusively the result of erudite research" (*RM*, no. 54). A healthy communion ecclesiology, in which the local churches function in proper autonomy, is a necessary presupposition for inculturation.[37]

For the possibility of the liturgical inculturation of ancestor worship, the question of its nature must be revisited. As has been shown above, the Jesuits considered the practice of ancestor worship theologically acceptable because, in their view, it was not religious but "merely civil and political."[38] It was this

---

[35] See the message of Propaganda Fide, *"Mens,"* addressed to Archbishop Mario Zanin, apostolic delegate to China, on 28 February 1941 (see Noll, *100 Roman Documents*, 88-89).

[36] For example, the Japanese Conference of Catholic Bishops pointed out the absurdity of requiring that translations of liturgical texts, which have been done by the best Japanese experts in Japan and have been approved by the Japanese bishops themselves, be further approved by Rome, whose knowledge of the Japanese language and culture is minimal (see Peter C. Phan, ed., *The Asian Synod, Texts and Commentaries* [Maryknoll, N.Y.: Orbis Books, 2002]).

[37] On communion ecclesiology, see the works of Jean-Marie R. Tillard, *Church of Churches: The Ecclesiology of Communion*, trans. R. C. De Peaux (Collegeville, Minn.: Liturgical Press, 1992), and *Flesh of the Church, Flesh of Christ: At the Sources of the Ecclesiology of Communion*, trans. Madeleine Beaumont (Collegeville, Minn.: Liturgical Press, 2001). See also Dennis Doyle, *Communion Ecclesiology* (Maryknoll, N.Y.: Orbis Books, 2001).

[38] The expression "merely civil and political" was first used in the response of the Congregation of Holy Office to the third question posed by Martino Martini (see Noll, *100 Roman Documents*, 5).

precise understanding, encapsulated in that terse phrase or its equivalents, and officially confirmed by the Japanese Ministry of Education and the government of Manchukuo in 1932 (and already by Emperor K'ang Hsi in 1700!), that allowed Propaganda Fide to reverse the church's three-centuries-long condemnation of the Chinese rites. On the other hand, the Mendicant Friars and the members of the MEP saw in the rituals of ancestor worship nothing but rank superstition; they were to be forbidden because they were, in their view, of a religious nature.[39]

Various explanations have been given for this discrepancy in the evaluations of the Chinese rites, the likely one being that the Jesuits were explaining the veneration of ancestors (and the cult of Confucius) from the perspective of the (mostly rationalistic and atheistic) literati, whereas the Mendicant Friars and the French missionaries were describing the rituals as practiced by the common people among whom they worked. Be that as it may, there is little doubt that ancestor worship, at least, is a deeply religious act, indeed the most religious act in the everyday life of the followers of indigenous religions in Southeast Asia. This point was well understood by Alexandre de Rhodes (1593-1660).[40] It was confirmed by Léopold Cadière (1869-1955), a member of the MEP and a missionary to Vietnam for more fifty years:

> It is impossible to hold that the Vietnamese, at this moment in time, do not believe in the survival and real presence of the ancestors in the tablets, that they do not attribute supernatural powers to these ancestors, and that, therefore, the cult they render to them is not, properly speaking, a religion. Such a theory is in total contradiction with what can be seen every single day in Vietnam. . . . For the immense majority of the Vietnamese, the ancestors continue to be part of the family and the cult rendered to them is clearly religious.[41]

Given the undeniably religious nature of ancestor worship, its liturgical inculturation can no longer be legitimated on the basis of its alleged "merely civil and political" character. Such a view, while making things easier for theologians and liturgists, empties the rituals of ancestor veneration of their deepest meanings and transforming power. Rather, with its religious nature frankly recognized, it is possible to appeal to the doctrine of the communion of saints and enlarge it in such a way that the ancestors can find their appropriate place in this communion and receive due veneration. Of great relevance to this project is Elizabeth Johnson's development of the notion of *communio sanctorum* as composed of *all* people, some of whom are paradigmatic figures, working out of

---

[39] As the Holy Office put it tersely: "They [kowtows in front of the deceased] are intrinsically illicit and superstitious. They are not evil because they are forbidden. They are forbidden because they are evil" (see Noll, *100 Roman Documents*, 65).

[40] See Phan, *Mission and Catechesis*, 92-96.

[41] Léopold Cadière, *Croyances et pratiques religieuses des Vietnamiens* (Hanoi: Imprimerie d'Extrême-Orient, 1944), 1:39, my translation. See also Phan, *Mission and Catechesis*, 26-28.

holiness through creative fidelity in ordinary time, in relation with those who have preceded them into eternal life and are now accessible to them through memory and hope, and in solidarity with the whole community of the natural world.[42]

Finally, of great importance for the liturgical inculturation of the cult of ancestors is a renewed theology of popular devotions (or better popular religiosity or popular Catholicism) that goes beyond the inadequate concept of *pia exercitia* (see *SC*, no. 13). Popular religion is neither mere superstitious practices (the elitist interpretation) nor the false consciousness imposed upon the proletariat by the ruling class (the Marxist interpretation). Nor is popular religion the genuine religion that has been skewed by official religion and now resides in the poor and simple folk (the romanticist interpretation). Nor is it the residue of the previous, pre-Christian religion that now survives in a transformed and purified state in Christianity (the remnant interpretation). Nor, finally, is it an articulation of the social-psychological needs of individuals in their interaction with the cosmic, social, and political patterns of the environment (the social-psychological interpretation).[43]

Rather, it must be recognized that every culture has its own religious symbolization that takes place in two parallel forms—popular religion and organized world religions—each with its own official liturgy and worship. Both popular religion and official religion are distinct symbolizations of the liturgy of life; the one should not be identified with the other, or replaced by the other, or reduced to the other, with the official liturgy deemed superior to popular religiosity. At any rate, without a robust theology of popular religiosity, the veneration of ancestors will be doomed to remain on the margins of liturgical worship.[44]

VENERATION OF ANCESTORS: A VIETNAMESE EXPERIMENT

Vietnam, along with Korea and Japan, has been heavily influenced by China, especially its Confucian culture. This influence is most visible in certain funerary

---

[42] See Elizabeth Johnson, *Friends of God and Prophets: A Feminist Theological Reading of the Communion of Saints* (New York: Continuum, 1999), 219-43.

[43] For a helpful discussion of popular religion, see Robert Schreiter, *Constructing Local Theologies* (Maryknoll, N.Y.: Orbis, 1985), 131-39. See also the various essays in *Liturgical Ministry* 7 (Summer, 1998), 105-46. See also Chapter 5 herein.

[44] On popular religiosity, see Orlando Espín, *The Faith of the People: Theological Reflections on Popular Catholicism* (Maryknoll, N.Y.: Orbis Books, 1997); Anscar Chupungco, *Liturgical Inculturation: Sacramentals, Religiosity, and Catechesis* (Collegeville, Minn.: Liturgical Press, 1992), 95-133; Thomas Bamat and Jean-Paul Wiest, eds., *Popular Catholicism in a World Church: Seven Case Studies in Inculturation* (Maryknoll, N.Y.: Orbis Books, 1999); Peter C. Phan, "The Liturgy of Life as the 'Summit and Source' of the Eucharistic Liturgy: Church Worship as Symbolization of the Liturgy of Life?" in *Incongruities: Who We Are and How We Pray*, ed. Timothy Fitzgerald and David Lysik (Chicago: Liturgy Training Publications, 2000), 25-29; and Robert Brancatelli, "*Religiosidad Popular* in Contemporary Magisterial Documents and Hispanic-American Theology (1974-1997): An Analysis and Critique," Ph.D. dissertation, The Catholic University of America, Washington, D.C., 2001.

rites and especially in the cult of ancestors.[45] Needless to say, the Chinese Rites Controversy and the Roman position regarding ancestor worship affected Vietnamese Catholicism as well, profoundly and extensively, even to today. Indeed, many if not most of the questions brought to Propaganda Fide between 1742 and 1939 about the permissibility of certain rites connected with ancestor worship came from the apostolic vicars of Tonkin and Cochinchina, as Vietnam was known to the West in the seventeenth century.[46]

Curiously, though Propaganda Fide's *Plane compertum est* was issued in 1939, it was not until 1964 that the Vietnamese hierarchy, somewhat unnecessarily, applied for its application to Vietnam. The request was approved on 2 October 1964.[47] On 14 June 1964 the Vietnamese bishops in "The Veneration of Ancestors, National Heroes, and War Dead" spelled out the concrete norms to apply Propaganda Fide's instruction. In general, the bishops distinguished three kinds of acts, attitudes, and rituals: (1) those that are clearly secular, patriotic, and social expressions of piety toward the ancestors, national heroes, and war dead; (2) those that are clearly religious in nature and contrary to Catholic belief, smack of superstition, and are performed in places reserved for worship; and (3) those that are of an ambiguous nature. The first are not only permissible but are to be encouraged and promoted; the second are prohibited. The third need to be examined according to common local opinion; if they are generally thought to be of a nonreligious nature, they are permissible. If doubt concerning their nature persists, one may act according to one's conscience. If possible, explanations of one's intention should be given with due tact, or one can participate in a passive manner.[48]

On 12 April 1974 the Vietnamese bishops issued another communication in which they specified a list of activities, attitudes, and rituals deemed permissible:

---

[45] See Neil L. Jamieson, *Understanding Vietnam* (Berkeley and Los Angeles: University of California Press, 1993), 11-41; Nguyen Huy Lai, *La Tradition religieuse, spirituelle et sociale au Vietnam* (Paris: Beauchesne, 1981), 53-123; and Phan, *Mission and Catechesis*, 20-28.

[46] See Noll, *100 Roman Documents*, 61-82.

[47] In announcing this approval, Nguyen Van Binh, archbishop of Saigon, wrote: "This is a historic day, a new event for the whole Church of Vietnam. . . . It is hoped that the veneration of ancestors and saints and sages, long rooted in the sentiments as well as the customs of the Vietnamese, will henceforth help each Vietnamese increase familial piety. In a world in which many societies are beset by crises, this veneration will help family members to grow in love and unity with each other, religious groups and the general population to grow in deep affection for one another, and especially, everyone to recognize the supreme Origin, the Creator of our ancestors and ourselves and our descendants, that is, God, the common Father in whom all humanity will meet at all times and places" ("Our Father Who Art in Heaven," *Sacerdos* 36 [December 1964], 891-92, my translation). The enthusiastic words with which the archbishop greeted this approval of the veneration of ancestors express well the importance of this practice for Vietnamese Catholics.

[48] See the Vietnamese text in *Sacerdos* 43 (July 1965), 489-92. A French translation is available as "L'Église du Vietnam et la question des rites," *Missions Étrangères de Paris* 145 (May-June 1966), 7-10.

1. An ancestral altar dedicated to the veneration of the ancestors may
   be placed under the altar dedicated to God, provided that nothing
   smacking of superstition such as the "white soul" [the white cloth
   representing the dead] is placed there.
2. Burning incense and lighting candles on the ancestral altar, and pros-
   trating with joined hands in front of the altar or the repository of the
   ancestors are gestures of filial piety and veneration, hence permissible.
3. On death anniversaries it is permissible to present the dead person
   with "offerings of commemorative cult" according to local customs,
   provided that one eliminates things smacking of superstition such
   as burning paper money. It is also recommended that the offerings
   be reduced or changed to express more clearly their true meaning of
   respect and gratitude to the ancestors, for instance, flowers, fruits,
   incense, and lights.
4. During the marriage rites, the bride and groom are permitted to perform the "ceremony of veneration toward the ancestors" in front of
   the ancestral altar or the repository of the ancestors. These rituals
   are expressions of gratitude toward, recognition of, and self-presen-
   tation to the ancestors.
5. During the funerary rites, it is permissible to perform prostrations
   with joined hands before the corpse as well as to hold burning incense sticks in joined hands according to local customs, as a way to
   express veneration for the dead person, just as the Church permits
   the use of candles, incense, and inclination before the corpse.
6. It is permissible to participate in the ceremonies venerating the "lord
   of the place," who is usually called the "titulary genius," in the village community building, to express gratitude toward those who history shows have earned the gratitude of the people, or the benefac-
   tors of the village, and not to express a superstitious belief in evil
   spirits and harmful ghosts.[49]

In addition to permission to practice these rituals of ancestor veneration outside the liturgy, the Vietnamese bishops have introduced two properly *liturgical* innovations.[50] The first is an expansion of the prayer for the dead in the

[49] *Sacerdos* 156 (1974), 878-80, my translation.

[50] The second edition of the *Roman Missal* in Vietnamese was published in 1992 by
the liturgical commission of the Vietnamese episcopal conference. The missal does not
bear the Vietnamese bishops' approval nor the *imprimatur* but only mentions the approval by the Department of Culture and Communication of the Vietnamese government. However, permission for its publication had been given by the Congregation for
Divine Worship and the Discipline of the Sacraments on 21 February 1989 (prot. CD
1375/88; cf. *Notitiae* 29 [1993], 725). The Vietnamese translation was approved by the
same dicastery *ad experimentum* for five years, starting 7 January 1994. It includes the
Vietnamese texts of the Mass for the lunar New Year, the Mass for the feast of Mid-
Autumn for children, and the Mass for the Vietnamese Martyrs (prot. 2444/93/L and

eucharistic prayer of the Mass. In the second eucharistic prayer, instead of the simple formula "Remember our brothers and sisters who have gone to their rest in the hope of rising again," the Vietnamese prayer reads:

> Remember also the faithful, our brothers and sisters, who rest in peace in the expectation of the resurrection, and the dead who can only trust in your mercy. Remember in particular *our ancestors*, our parents, and our friends who have left this world . . . [51]

Obviously, the explicit mention of "ancestors" is an attempt at inculturating ancestor veneration into the liturgy, with significant theological implications that will be detailed below.

The second liturgical innovation is the Masses for the celebration of the lunar New Year or *Tet*. For the Vietnamese, *Tet* is the most important cultural and religious feast, the equivalent of New Year, Independence Day, Thanksgiving, and Christmas rolled into one.[52] It symbolizes the total renewal of all things. All debts should be paid, all bad feelings set aside, and everything should be clean and new. On New Year's Eve, especially at midnight *(giao thua)*, there are various rituals to perform. The main one is to "welcome the ancestors" *(ruoc ong ba)* to the home. Culturally, *Tet* is the celebration of the family. All members of the family are supposed to return to the ancestral home to show gratitude to their ancestors and to renew the family bond. Religiously, it is the occasion for the most solemn celebration of the cult of ancestors. Members of the family gather before the ancestral altar, where pictures of their dead ancestors are displayed, make deep bows, burn incense, make offerings, and pray for their protection. Catholics say their prayers in front of the altar.

Tet is celebrated for at least three days: the first is reserved for the cult of ancestors and the living parents, the second for near relatives, and the third for the dead. Alexandre de Rhodes had already attempted to Christianize *Tet* by suggesting that its three days be dedicated to the Trinity: "The first day in memory of the benefits of creation and conservation, which is dedicated to God the Father; the second in thanksgiving for the inestimable benefit of redemption, which is dedicated to God the Son; and the third in humble gratitude to the Holy Spirit for the grace of being called to be a Christian."[53] In the seventeenth century, and even as recently as the twentieth, as long as the monarchy lasted, on the first day

---

2445/93/L, respectively; cf. *Notitiae* 30 [1994], 324). On the issue of the liturgical inculturation of ancestor worship in Vietnam, see the excellent article by Roland Jacques, "Le Dossier des rites chinois doit-il être rouvert?" and Peter De Ta Vo, "A Cultural and Theological Foundation for Ancestor Veneration among Catholics in Vietnam," Ph.D. dissertation, The Catholic University of America, Washington, D.C., 1999.

[51] My translation. The Vietnamese word for ancestors is *to tien*. Literally, *to* means grandfather, *tien* means go before. A similar addition is found in the third eucharistic prayer.

[52] On the meaning of *Tet*, see Nguyen Huy Lai, *La Tradition religieuse, spirituelle et sociale,* 98-101.

[53] See Phan, *Mission and Catechesis*, 80-81.

of the year the emperor offered in the name of the nation the *Nam Giao* [south gate] sacrifice to heaven, which de Rhodes interpreted as a "sacrifice offered to the heavenly King."[54]

Given the central position of *Tet*, it is not surprising that the Vietnamese bishops have undertaken to solemnize it with eucharistic celebrations. Five Mass formulas have been composed to express the various meanings of *Tet* and are now in use: the first, for the end of the year, to give thanks and ask for forgiveness; the second, for New Year's Eve, to celebrate the passage into the new year *(giao thua)*; the third, for the first day of the new year, to praise God and to ask for peace and prosperity; the fourth, for the second day, to pray for ancestors, grandparents, and parents; and the fifth, for the third day, to pray for the sanctification of labor.[55]

The fourth formula is of special interest. Here are some of its significant prayers:

Collect: Father of mercies, you have commanded us to practice filial piety. Today, on New Year's Day, we have gathered to honor the memory of our ancestors, grandparents, and parents. Deign to reward abundantly those who have brought us into this world, nurtured us, and educated us. Help us live in conformity with our duties toward them . . .

Prayer over the Gifts: Lord, accept our offerings and bestow your graces abundantly upon our ancestors, grandparents, and parents, so that we may in our turn inherit their blessings . . .

Preface: As we look at things in the universe, we clearly see that every being has an origin and principle: birds have their nests, water its source, and the human person coming into this world has a father and mother. Moreover, thanks to your revelation, Father, we recognize that you are the creator of all things that exist and that you are our Father. You have given life to our ancestors, grandparents, and parents so that they may transmit it to us. You have also filled them with good things so we may inherit them by knowing you, adoring you, and serving you . . .

The inclusion of the veneration of ancestors in the Mass, especially the mention of ancestors in the eucharistic prayer, marks a monumental step in liturgical inculturation in Vietnam. We have traveled a long way from the days of the Chinese Rites Controversy. Theologically, it is important for at least two reasons. First, in mentioning the ancestors explicitly in the eucharistic prayer and in praying for them, the Vietnamese text does not distinguish between Christian ancestors and non-Christian ones (among Vietnamese Christians attending Mass there are many whose ancestors were not baptized). In the cult of ancestors, the ancestors are venerated not because they have been saved or were holy but

---

[54] See ibid., 92-93.
[55] See the Vietnamese *Roman Missal*, 1035-1047.

simply because they are ancestors. By virtue of the physical bond with their descendants, the ancestors are bound to protect them and the descendants to honor them. Furthermore, in describing the cult of ancestors, many Vietnamese bishops have used not only the word *to tien* (forebears) but also *thanh hien* (saint and sage) to refer to those who should receive this veneration. They do not mean to say that these are saints in the Christian sense of being officially canonized, but clearly the old objection that the word *saint* should not be used for people like Confucius no longer holds. Of course, there is no suggestion that the non-Christian ancestors have been damned simply because they were not Christian.

Second, there is in the prayers cited above an affirmation that somehow the ancestors act as mediators of the blessings and graces that their descendants receive from God. The descendants are said to "inherit" them from their ancestors. In these prayers the ancestors are not directly asked to "intercede" with God for their descendants, since these prayers are not addressed to them (in contrast to those said in front of the ancestral altar at home). Theologically there can be no objection to asking someone, dead or alive, canonized or not, to intercede for oneself or others before God. The old objection that the cult of ancestors, insofar as they are invoked in prayer, is superstitious is a red herring, because no Asian who practices this cult believes that the ancestors are divine, in the strict sense of this term.[56]

From the liturgical experimentation of the Vietnamese church it is obvious that the church in Southeast Asia has moved a long way from Benedict XIV's *Ex quo singulari* and even from Propaganda Fide's *Plane compertum est*, thanks to the recent theological developments in the six areas mentioned above. However, there is still a long way to go.[57] To guide this further work of liturgical inculturation, I conclude by highlighting certain principles and some of the lessons that can be derived from the Chinese Rites Controversy.[58]

1. Liturgical inculturation is never a simple matter of appropriating rituals, sacred texts, and religious symbols of non-Christian religions for Christian use.

---

[56] The oft-invoked distinction between *veneration* and *cult* of ancestors, accepting the former and condemning the latter, is more for the benefits of Western Christians caught in the issue of iconoclasm and the Protestant reformers' attack on the cult of the saints. In Vietnamese, the word *kinh tho*, literally "venerate-adore," is a compound word; it may be used together, or singly, or in the reverse *(tho kinh)* for living parents, dead ancestors, Christian saints, or God.

[57] One major criticism of the Vietnamese bishops' inculturation of the cult of ancestors is that it has not truly introduced this cult into liturgical and sacramental celebrations, in particular those of Christian initiation, marriage, and funerals. The various rituals that are now permitted are still performed only at home, privately, and have not yet been made an integral part of the liturgy. There is, therefore, still a dichotomy between the liturgy and the most sacred rituals of daily life.

[58] For official guidelines for liturgical inculturation, see the Congregation for Divine Worship and the Discipline of the Sacraments, *The Roman Liturgy and Inculturation: Fourth Instruction for the Right Application of the Conciliar Constitution on the Liturgy* (Rome, 1994), nos. 37-40.

These elements cannot be uprooted from the religious soil in which they grow and by which they are nurtured in order to be grafted onto Christian worship. In so "baptizing" non-Christian religious elements Christians run the risk of committing what Aloysius Pieris calls "theological vandalism," an "irreverent disregard for the soteriological matrix of non-Christian religious symbolism" and "a disguised form of imperialism."[59] Liturgical inculturation must be predicated upon a positive regard for and acceptance of this non-Christian "soteriological matrix."

2. Consequently, an effective liturgical inculturation presupposes a particular brand of theology of religions, the Holy Spirit, Christ, church, communion of saints, and popular religiosity, as outlined above. Without a consistent theology of these aspects of the Christian faith, liturgical inculturation will remain incoherent, piecemeal, fragmented, and limited. Quite often disputes about the acceptability of a particular proposal of liturgical inculturation arise ultimately from fundamental differences in these theologies and not from a superficially different evaluation of the proposal itself.

3. Liturgical inculturation must not be carried out apart from interreligious dialogue and the work for integral liberation, especially in Asia. As Pope John Paul II says in his apostolic exhortation *Ecclesia in Asia*:

> Liturgical inculturation requires more than a focus upon traditional cultural values, symbols and rituals. There is also a need to take account of the shifts in consciousness and attitudes caused by the emerging secularist and consumer cultures that are affecting the Asian sense of worship and prayer. Nor can the specific needs of the poor, migrants, refugees, youth and women be overlooked in any genuine liturgical inculturation in Asia (no. 22).

As the FABC has repeatedly stated, inculturation, interreligious dialogue, and liberation are the three inseparable aspects of Christian mission as well as of liturgical inculturation.

4. In liturgical inculturation a close collaboration between the local churches and the Congregation for Divine Worship and the Discipline of the Sacraments is absolutely necessary. Again, *Ecclesia in Asia* says: "Such cooperation is essential because the sacred liturgy expresses and celebrates the one faith by all and, being the heritage of the whole church, cannot be determined by the local churches in isolation from the universal church" (no. 22).[60]

---

[59] Aloysius Pieris, *An Asian Theology of Liberation* (Maryknoll, N.Y.: Orbis Books, 1988), 53.

[60] Though the apostolic exhortation makes a valid point about the necessity of collaboration between the local churches and the Roman congregation, it is ironic that it stresses the need for the local churches to collaborate with the Roman congregation rather than the other way round (since in fact rules and policies regarding liturgical inculturation have been formulated by the Roman curia without much consultation with the local churches) and that it implicitly identifies the universal church with the church of Rome and its various agencies. Nevertheless, the call for collaboration is a far cry

5. In the liturgical inculturation of the cult of ancestors in particular, it seems that in order for it to be genuine and effective, the simple "adaptation" envisaged by the Congregation for Divine Worship and the Discipline of the Sacraments in *The Roman Liturgy and Inculturation* would not be appropriate. For one thing, its understanding of "popular devotion" is seriously inadequate. Hence, its prohibition of the introduction of devotional practices into liturgical celebrations is not well founded.[61] Furthermore, its view of the veneration of ancestors is prejudicially negative, something, it says, to be "accompanied by purification and, if necessary, a break with the past" (no. 48).[62]

It would seem necessary, therefore, to invoke the possibility of "an even more radical adaptation of the liturgy" (*SC*, no. 40). Indeed, it may be said that the Vietnamese bishops' decision to mention the ancestors in the eucharistic prayer and the composition of a special Mass for the ancestors on New Year's Day—*ad experimentum*—are already significant steps, albeit timid, in this direction. Needless to say, a lot more work remains to be done.[63] But it is encouraging that there is no longer any possibility of going back to the days of Charles Maigrot, Maillard de Tournon, Clement XI, Benedict XIV, and even Propaganda Fide's *Plane compertum est.*

---

from the language of the instruction *The Roman Liturgy and Inculturation*: "Adaptations of the Roman rite, even in the field of inculturation, depend completely on the *authority* of the Church. This authority belongs to the Apostolic See, which exercises it though the Congregation for Divine Worship and the Discipline of the Sacraments; it also belongs, within the limits fixed by law, to the Episcopal Conferences, and to the diocesan bishop" (no. 37). Furthermore, the instruction still speaks of liturgical inculturation as "concessions" (no. 37) granted by the congregation to a particular region.

[61] "Alongside liturgical celebrations and related to them, in some particular Churches there are various manifestations of popular devotion. These were sometimes introduced by missionaries at the time of the initial evangelization, and they often develop according to local custom.

"The introduction of devotional practices into liturgical celebrations under the pretext of inculturation cannot be allowed 'because by its nature, (the liturgy) is superior to them'" (no. 45).

At a minimum, the reason adduced is a non sequitur. The supposed superiority of liturgy over popular devotion is by itself no reason popular devotion cannot be introduced into liturgical celebrations. Indeed, not a few sacramental rituals began their lives as popular devotion. On the presumed superior dignity of the liturgy, see Phan, "The Liturgy of Life as the 'Summit and Source' of the Eucharistic Liturgy," 5-25.

[62] Particularly revealing is the instruction's statement with regard to the veneration of ancestors and other traditional usages: "Obviously the Christian liturgy cannot accept magic rites, superstition, spiritism, vengeance or rites with a sexual connotation" (no. 48).

[63] For example, *liturgical* rituals for baptisms, weddings, anointings, and funerals that incorporate the cult of ancestors should be composed for Vietnam.

8

Crossing the Borders

A SPIRITUALITY FOR MISSION IN OUR TIMES

One of the most enduring images of the missionary in popular imagination is that of someone leaving his or her country for a foreign land to convert the "heathens." But today the concept of what constitutes a "heathen" has changed dramatically, as has the concept of conversion as the goal of mission.[1] Even the borders that used to separate Christians from unbelievers and followers of other faiths have become so porous that they have ceased to be clear and helpful identity markers. Today there is no lack of Christians and non-Christians who claim double or triple religious belongings, and the tribes of "religiously hyphenated people," both inside and outside of Christianity, are on a steady increase.[2]

While the concepts of paganism, conversion, and religious identity have undergone drastic changes in recent years, one aspect has nevertheless remained constant in the job description of the missionary: crossing borders.[3] Not only has this act of crossing remained necessary, but it has also become extremely complex, because the borders between the missionary's native country and foreign lands have grown both porous and multiple. In times past, when borders were mainly geographical, crossing might be hazardous or even deadly. Voyages

---

[1] For reflections on conversion as the goal of mission, see Peter C. Phan, "Conversion and Discipleship as Goals of the Church's Mission," *SEDOS* 34/1 (2002), 19-28. On recent new directions in the theology of mission, see Chapter 3 herein. For a comprehensive theology of mission, see David Bosch, *Transforming Mission: Paradigm Shifts in Theology of Mission* (Maryknoll, N.Y.: Orbis Books, 1991). For reflections on the contemporary situation of mission, see William Jenkinson and Helene O'Sullivan, eds., *Trends in Mission: Toward the Third Millennium* (Maryknoll, N.Y.: Orbis Books, 1991); and James M. Phillips and Robert T. Coote, eds., *Towards the Twenty-first Century in Christian Mission* (Grand Rapids, Mich.: Eerdmans, 1993).

[2] On "hyphenated Christians," see Peter C. Phan, "To Be Catholic or Not to Be: Is It Still the Question? Catholic Identity and Religious Education Today," *Horizons* 25/2 (1998), 159-89.

[3] For a collection of useful essays on the impact of "borders" on theology and the church, see María Pilar Aquino and Roberto S. Goizueta, eds., *Theology: Expanding the Borders* (Mystic, Conn.: Twenty-Third Publications, 1998).

from Lisbon, for instance, from which missionaries under the Portuguese *padroado* had to depart for distant parts of the globe, took years, and not a few missionaries perished during their journey.[4] But at least the borders were visible, and one could be certain of having crossed them. Today, by contrast, crossing geographical boundaries has been made quick, easy, and even comfortable thanks to air travel. But new boundaries have emerged that are invisible and porous. As a result, one may not even be aware that there are boundaries at all and can easily make the mistake of assuming that everything is the same everywhere! Furthermore, borders have become so numerous and diverse that crossing them successfully requires a good deal of skill and effort on the part of the missionary.[5]

This predicament brings new challenges to Christian mission and calls for an appropriate spirituality. Coincidentally, there has been in recent years a strong interest among missionaries in spirituality. Summarizing the presentations and discussions at the mission congress organized by SEDOS in 2000, Robert Schreiter notes, "As missionaries move into the third millennium, it is clear that the issue of spirituality has a high priority."[6] This interest, he suggests, is rooted in the new awareness that Christian mission is primarily *missio Dei*.

In this contribution to a border-crossing mission spirituality, I first describe the new borders that missionaries must cross today. Next, I delineate some of the dispositions and virtues that would help missionaries accomplish and maintain such crossing over. Last, I attempt to ground such border-crossing spirituality theologically in the mystery of the Incarnation itself.

NEW ARENAS OF MISSION AND NEW BORDERS

Perhaps one helpful way to discern the new borders for contemporary mission is to begin with John Paul II's description of three "situations," each with a corresponding activity of the church (*RM*, nos. 33-34).[7] The first situation consists of Christian communities with adequate and solid ecclesial structures, a fervent Christian life, and a commitment to mission. Here the church's activity

---

[4] To cite one example, Jesuit missionary Alexandre de Rhodes's trip from Lisbon to Macao took about five years (October 1618-May 1623), and his return trip from Macao to Rome three years (December 1645-June 1649). Among those who lost their lives during their trips was Bishop Ignatius Cotolendi, who had been appointed the first vicar apostolic of Nankin.

[5] For reflections on the new frontiers of mission, see Wilbert R. Shenk, *Changing Frontiers of Mission* (Maryknoll, N.Y.: Orbis Books, 1999); Philip L. Wickeri, Janice K. Wickeri, and Damayanthi M. A. Niles, eds., *Plurality, Power and Mission: Intercontextual Theological Explorations on the Role of Religion in the New Millennium* (London: The Council for World Mission, 2000); and M. Thomas Thangaraj, *The Common Task: A Theology of Christian Mission* (Nashville, Tenn.: Abingdon Press, 1999).

[6] Robert J. Schreiter, ed., *Mission in the Third Millennium* (Maryknoll, N.Y.: Orbis Books, 2001), 159.

[7] I have changed the order in which the pope listed these three situations to reflect better their logical sequence.

is "pastoral care." The second situation consists of Christian communities, both ancient and young, in which the members have lost a living sense of faith, do not even consider themselves Christian, and live lives contrary to the gospel. Here the church's activity is "new evangelization" or "re-evangelization." The third situation is made of peoples, groups, and socio-cultural contexts in which Christ and his gospel are not known or in which there are no Christians mature enough to proclaim their faith to others. Here the church's activity is "mission *ad gentes*" or "missionary activity proper."

The pope is aware that "the boundaries between *pastoral care of the faithful, new evangelization*, and *specific missionary activity* are not clearly definable" and that there is a " real and growing *interdependence*" among these three activities (*RM*, no. 34). Nevertheless, he maintains these distinctions in order to highlight the continuing necessity and even urgency of the mission *ad gentes,* which has been on the wane and whose validity and relevance have been questioned.[8]

What is of interest to us here is not the usefulness of the pope's distinction of the three situations, each with a corresponding church activity, and the validity of his exclusive reservation of the terms "missionary activity proper" and "mission *ad gentes*" to the third situation.[9] Rather, it is the fact that, having reaffirmed the necessity of the mission to non-Christians, John Paul II goes on to describe the various arenas in which these non-Christians are encountered today and in which a threefold activity of this mission *ad gentes* is carried out, namely, "the work of proclaiming Christ and his Gospel, building up the local Church, and promoting the values of the kingdom" (*RM,* no. 34). The pope specifies that these non-Christian arenas include three distinct categories and hence three possible kinds of borders and border-crossings, namely, "peoples, groups, and socio-cultural contexts" (*RM,* no. 33).

First, "peoples" here may be taken to refer to the followers of other religions as well as persons of no religious affiliation (atheists and agnostics). In the recent past most of these peoples have lived in the so-called mission territories, and John Paul II, who still upholds the criterion of geography, regards certain parts of the world, in particular Asia, as urgently calling for the church's mission *ad gentes*.[10] Today, however, due to frequent and extensive migrations from

---

[8] In a series of rhetorical questions John Paul II presents some of the grounds for questioning the validity and relevance of mission *ad gentes*: "*Is missionary work among non-Christians still relevant?* Has it not been replaced by inter-religious dialogue? Is not human development an adequate goal of the Church's mission? Does not respect for conscience and for freedom exclude all efforts at conversion? Is it not possible to attain salvation in any religion? *Why then should there be missionary activity?*" (*RM,* no. 4).

[9] For a critique of the pope's threefold distinction, see Aylward Shorter, *Evangelization and Culture* (London: Chapman, 1994). Donald Dorr does not agree with Shorter's critique and supports the pope's distinction (see *Mission in Today's World* [Maryknoll, N.Y.: Orbis Books, 2000], 215-17).

[10] "Thus the criterion of geography, although somewhat imprecise and always provisional, is still a valid indicator of the frontiers toward which missionary activity must be directed. . . . Particularly in Asia, toward which the Church's mission *ad gentes* ought to be chiefly directed, Christians are a small minority" (*RM,* no. 37).

East to West, a growing number of non-Christians are settling in the Christianized West, especially in urban centers, where temples, pagodas, and mosques dot the landscape cheek by jowl with churches and synagogues. Even though the population of non-Christians in the West is still relatively small, their active and at times vocal presence makes religious pluralism, to which we will return below, a live and attractive option for many Christians. As a result, religious affiliations, which used to function as identity markers, have been blurred beyond recognition, and the need for missionaries to be able to maintain religious identities and at the same time to negotiate conflicting religious claims has increased dramatically.

In terms of John Paul II's threefold distinction of the situation of the church's mission, it is increasingly a fact—uncomfortable to many Christians—that the presence of non-Christians both in Christian communities with solid ecclesial structures and vibrant faith and in communities that have lost their ancient Christian roots poses more complex and numerous challenges to the mission *ad gentes* than in countries where Christians still form a minority. To cross over to these non-Christians in the West requires a great deal of skill and effort on the part of the missionary, since they are much more cognizant of the problems and even scandals in the Catholic Church (for example, the recent cases of clergy sex abuse and the bishops' misuse of funds and power) than their fellow believers in their native countries and are therefore less likely to "convert" to Christianity than if they had an idealistic picture of the church.

Second, as far as groups are concerned, John Paul II refers to "new worlds and new social phenomena" that widen immeasurably the circle of concerns for mission *ad gentes* (*RM,* no. 37). Among groups that deserve the special attention of missionaries, the pope singles out four categories: dwellers in megalopolises, youth, immigrants and refugees, and the poor. Each group requires specialized forms of ministry. Urbanization creates big cities where a new humanity is emerging and where new models of development are taking shape; it poses a different set of challenges for missionaries, who used to carry out their work in isolated and underdeveloped regions. Youth, who in many countries make up more than half of the population, require associations, institutions, centers, and cultural and social activities that go far beyond ordinary means of evangelization and demand highly specialized skills not possessed by average missionaries. Immigrants and refugees not only raise the awareness of religious pluralism to an unprecedented level but also create fresh opportunities for cultural and religious exchanges between them and Christian missionaries. Finally, the poor and the marginalized demand new forms of evangelization that restore their human dignity and freedom. These four groups create new and pluriform borders, not simply geographical but also social, economic, ethnic, and psychological, that missionaries have to be fully conscious of and marshal the requisite skills to cross over.

Third, with regard to socio-cultural contexts, John Paul II mentions "the modern equivalents of the Areopagus," namely, the worlds of communications and mass media, justice and peace, scientific research, international organizations, and religious revival (*RM,* nos. 37-38). Most if not all of these "worlds" were totally unknown to missionaries *ad gentes* of just a few decades past, the great majority of whom labored in underdeveloped countries and for whom these worlds represented the exclusive concerns of the technologically advanced West. Even today, despite valiant efforts to adapt to a post-industrial society and to an age of information with a heavy emphasis on a service economy and intellectual technology, many missionaries still find themselves incapable of crossing over into these unfamiliar worlds, physical or virtual, whose borders seem to extend everywhere and yet remain elusive and forbidding.

Still, there is no escape from these worlds if one wants to carry out the mission *ad gentes* effectively, even when one retreats to the remotest corners of the globe. This is so because of two other widespread contemporary phenomena: (1) globalization, and (2) postmodernity. Both represent the most salient features of our times. Thanks to easy transportation and communication technologies, not only has our world become a "global village" or better a "global city," but there is also a heightened awareness of our interconnections and interdependencies in all areas of life.[11] As a result of globalization, which extends the effects of modernization to all parts of the globe and at the same time compresses both space and time, there emerges everywhere a popular, homogenizing, deterritorialized "global culture." Of course, local cultures do not passively absorb globalization and its popular culture hook, line, and sinker; they react to it by rejecting it altogether, or by asserting their ethnic differences, or by returning to their premodern roots.[12] Nevertheless, the overwhelming effect of globalization is the removal of boundaries and distinctions with a continuous flow of information, technologies, ideas, tastes, and values throughout the world. As a result, culture is no longer seen as a normative pattern of living characterized by boundedness, distinctiveness, coherence, and stability but much more as a fluid and unbounded social reality marked by openness, variability, inconsistency, and conflict. At the same time, because of globalization, the symbols, ideas, rituals, institutions, artistic representations, and religious traditions of one culture are in constant contact and exchange with those of another, resulting in greater "shared space" than before. In other words, while old borders have disappeared, new and numerous boundaries are constantly being drawn but are much less visible and identifiable than the old ones and thus make missionary crossing over much more complicated.

The other phenomenon, more elusive but no less extensive and influential than globalization, goes under the slippery label of postmodernity. There have been extensive discussions of the historical parameters and nature of postmodernity, especially with reference to modernity and the Enlightenment,

---

[11] For a brief and helpful exposition on globalization and its impact on mission, see María Carmelita de Freitas, "The Mission of Religious Men and Women in Latin America Today," in Schreiter, *Mission in the Third Millennium*, 99-111; and Robert Schreiter, "Globalization and Reconciliation: Challenges to Mission," in ibid., 124-34.

[12] Robert Schreiter describes three ways in which local cultures react to globalization in terms of "antiglobalism," "ethnification," and "primitivism" (*The New Catholicism*: *Theology between the Global and the Local* [Maryknoll, N.Y.: Orbis Books, 1997], 21-25).

and it is not necessary to enter into such a debate here. Suffice it to note, along with Lawrence Cahoone,[13] that, according to some commentators, there are in contemporary social and cultural patterns a number of features pervasive, distinctive, and important enough to warrant the judgment that a new period of history has emerged, markedly different from modernity. For lack of a better term, it may be labeled postmodernity. Epistemologically, postmodernity is characterized by a deep skepticism about our ability to know objective truth, rejection of "universal and unchanging essences" and fixed meanings in human artifacts and language, incredulity toward "metanarratives," preference for local and particular stories, and celebration of diversity and multiplicity.[14] From a theological standpoint, while postmodernism's relativism and skepticism must be rejected, its critique of modernity and the Enlightenment is to be taken seriously. Consequently, some theologians have subjected fundamental concepts such as God, the self, truth, and verification to new scrutiny and reformulation.

From the missiological perspective, the challenges posed by postmodernity are immense. One of the offsprings of postmodernism is religious pluralism, according to which the diversity of religions is not merely a fact but a normative stance that allows no particular religion to make claims to universality and absolute validity. Understood in this way, religious pluralism strikes at the heart of Christology and soteriology and calls into question the very legitimacy of Christian mission as understood and practiced in the past.[15] The question is whether missionaries *ad gentes* can still proclaim the Christian faith effectively and faithfully amid the pluralistic view, widespread in popular culture and in academia, that the Christian faith is but one among many equally legitimate paths to God.[16] How, in other words, can the borders among religions that religious pluralism have erased be rebuilt without being exclusivistic?

In sum, today the many borders that missionaries *ad gentes* of old had to cross have disappeared, but new ones have emerged, more numerous, porous, and even invisible, partly because of the new situations in which the church has

---

[13] Lawrence Cahoone, ed., *From Modernism to Postmodernism: An Anthology* (Oxford: Blackwell, 1996). Cahoone distinguishes three aspects of postmodernism: historical, methodological, and positive.

[14] Proponents of postmodern epistemology include Michel Foucault, Jacques Derrida, Jean-François Lyotard, and Richard Rorty. For a helpful exposition of postmodernism, see Stanley Grenz, *A Primer on Postmodernity* (Grand Rapids, Mich.: Eerdmans, 1996).

[15] See Jacques Dupuis, *Toward a Christian Theology of Religious Pluralism* (Maryknoll, N.Y.: Orbis Books, 1997). An evangelical and more conservative view is proposed by Harold Netland, *Encountering Religious Pluralism: The Challenge to Christian Faith and Mission* (Downers Grove, Ill.: InterVarsity Press, 2002).

[16] Contemporary Christian theologies of religion are usually broken into three categories: exclusivism, inclusivism, and pluralism. These categories, helpful as they are as broad indicators, do not represent clear-cut and mutually exclusive classifications but a continuum of perspectives that a particular author may adopt variously, depending on the issue at hand. See Peter C. Phan, ed., *Christianity and the Wider Ecumenism* (New York: Paragon House, 1990); and Paul F. Knitter, *Introducing Theologies of Religions* (Maryknoll, N.Y.: Orbis Books, 2002). Knitter expands the threefold model and speaks of "replacement," "fulfillment," "mutuality," and "acceptance" models.

to carry out its mission, partly because of new economic, social, cultural, and religious trends such as globalization, postmodernism, and religious pluralism. New peoples, new groups, and new contexts are addressees of evangelization. This fact was brought home by the participants of the SEDOS 2000 congress on the future of mission, who mentioned five new contexts for mission today: globalization, religion-related violence, secularization, the mounting strength of Islam, and ecological destruction.[17] The borders and boundaries that missionaries now have to cross are different, but the act of crossing, which is more subtle, complex, and multiple, still remains. Is there a Christian way of living, a frame of mind, and a set of moral dispositions and virtues, in a word, a spirituality that facilitates and nurtures such crossing over?

BORDER CROSSING: A MISSIONARY WAY OF LIFE

My purpose here is not to speak of missionary spirituality in general, which has been treated at length in recent times by a number of missiologists.[18] John Paul II himself devotes the last chapter of his encyclical *Redemptoris missio* to missionary spirituality and describes it as marked by three basic features: complete docility to the Holy Spirit, intimate communion with Christ the Evangelizer, and apostolic charity for the evangelized and for the church. Emphasizing the priority of spirituality for mission, the pope says:

The renewed impulse to the mission *ad gentes* demands holy missionaries. It is not enough to update pastoral techniques, organize and coordinate ecclesial resources, or delve more deeply into the biblical and theological foundations of faith. What is needed is the encouragement of a new "ardor for holiness" among missionaries and throughout the Christian community, especially among those who work most closely with missionaries (*RM*, no. 90).

Assuming the three features enumerated by the pope as undisputed givens of a missionary spirituality, I would like to single out for reflection some attitudes and practices that appear most appropriate for missionaries in a globalized, postmodern, and religiously plural context with multiple borders and unfamiliar situations. Robert Schreiter, in his assessment of the SEDOS congress on the

---

[17] See Schreiter, *Mission in the Third Millennium*, 151-52.

[18] See, for instance, Anthony Bellagamba, *Mission and Ministry in the Global Church* (Maryknoll, N.Y.: Orbis Books, 1992), esp. 93-114; Robert Schreiter, *Reconciliation: Mission and Ministry in a Changing Social Order* (Maryknoll, N.Y.: Orbis Books, 1992); idem, *The Ministry of Reconciliation: Spirituality and Strategies* (Maryknoll, N.Y.: Orbis Books, 1998); Anthony J. Gittins, *Bread for the Journey: The Mission of Transformation and the Transformation of Mission* (Maryknoll, N.Y.: Orbis Books, 1993); idem, *Reading the Clouds: Mission Spirituality for New Times* (Liguori, Mo.: Liguori Publications, 1999); and idem, *Ministry at the Margins: Strategy and Spirituality for Mission* (Maryknoll, N.Y.: Orbis Books, 2002).

future of mission referred to above, suggests that missionary spirituality in the future will have to develop along four trajectories: spirituality of presence, kenotic spirituality, reconciliation, and holistic anthropology. Taking my cue from the realities of Asia and from the various statements of the FABC and its institutes as well as from the Asian Synod and John Paul II's apostolic exhortation *Ecclesia in Asia*,[19] I elaborate on how these four features form part of a missionary spirituality envisaged as border-crossing spirituality.

Borders or boundaries seem to perform three distinct functions: as markers for one's individual and communal identity, as barriers to fence out other people different from oneself, and as frontiers from which to venture out into new horizons to expand one's knowledge and one's circle of relationships.[20] Corresponding to this triple role of borders, a border-crossing spirituality must first of all help the missionary respect and promote the distinctive identity and "otherness" of those to be evangelized. On the one hand, these differences must not be erased under the pretext of a common human nature; on the other, they should not be absolutized in an ideology of ethnocentrism and nationalism. Such a border-crossing spirituality must also impel the missionary to dismantle the unjust fences that powerful interest groups put up to protect their privileges and to keep the marginalized out, denying them a decent human life. Finally, it must assist the missionary in transcending differences of all kinds and opening up new frontiers in order to build a "civilization of love," which is not merely a confirmation of old identities but a forging of a new, common identity in which the worst of each group is overcome and the best is combined to produce truly intercultural human beings in the image of the triune God.

Spirituality of Presence

To live in Asia is constantly to cross borders separating a dizzying variety of languages, races, ethnicities, cultures, and religions (see *EA*, nos. 5-8). In addition to these traditional boundaries, there are contemporary ones created by the process of globalization, such as the growing gap between the rich and the poor, religious fundamentalism, political and military conflicts among nations, and

---

[19] For a collection of the final statements of FABC's plenary assemblies as well as assorted documents of FABC's various institutes, see Gaudencio Rosales and C. G. Arévalo, eds., *For All the Peoples of Asia: Federation of Asian Bishops' Conferences. Documents from 1970 to 1991*, vol. 1 (Maryknoll, N.Y.: Orbis Books, 1991); Franz-Josef Eilers, ed., *For All the Peoples of Asia: Federation of Asian Bishops' Conferences. Documents from 1992 to 1996*, vol. 2 (Quezon City, Philippines: Claretian Publications, 1997); and idem, ed. *For All the Peoples of Asia: Federation of Asian Bishops' Documents from 1997-2001*, vol. 3 (Quezon City, Philippines: Claretian Publications, 2002). For the Asian Synod and *Ecclesia in Asia,* see *The Asian Synod: Texts and Commentaries*, ed. Peter C. Phan (Maryknoll, N.Y.: Orbis Books, 2002); and James H. Kroeger and Peter C. Phan, eds., *The Future of the Asian Churches: The Asian Synod and Ecclesia in Asia* (Quezon City, Philippines: Claretian Publications, 2002).

[20] See Anne E. Patrick, "Markers, Barriers, and Frontiers: Theology on the Borderlands," in Aquino and Goizueta, *Theology: Expanding the Borders*, 7-16.

communal violence.[21] In Asia, perhaps more than anywhere else on earth, missionaries are called to be present to these multiple realities and to be keenly aware of the borders which are necessary for self-identity but also create many forms of exclusion.

This presence, of course, goes beyond physical accessibility. It demands acceptance of pluralism not as a curse but as a blessing and an opportunity for mutual collaboration and enrichment. Furthermore, it requires an affective and effective solidarity with people on both sides of the borders, especially those who are marginalized and oppressed. To achieve affective solidarity with them, the FABC's Institute for Social Action recommends "exposure" and "immersion," part of a four-stage "pastoral cycle" of exposure-immersion, social analysis, contemplation, and planning. "Exposure brought us closer to the stark reality of poverty, but immersion sought to experience reality from the perspective of the poor themselves. Exposure is like a doctor's visit for diagnosis; immersion is like the visit of a genuine friend entering into a dialogue-of-life."[22]

Thus, a spirituality of presence includes genuine friendship with those living on the other side of the border and a dialogue of life with them. Indeed, this sharing of life is part of a new way of being church in Asia that involves a fourfold presence:

a. The *dialogue of life*, where people strive to live in an open and neighborly spirit, sharing their joys and sorrows, their human problems and preoccupations. b. The *dialogue of action*, in which Christians and others collaborate for the integral development and liberation of people. c. The *dialogue of theological exchange*, where specialists seek to deepen their understanding of their respective religious heritages, and to appreciate each other's spiritual values. d. The *dialogue of religious experience*, where persons, rooted in their own religious traditions, share their spiritual riches, for instance, with regard to prayer and contemplation, faith and ways of searching for God or the Absolute.[23]

In Asia this fourfold dialogue, by which the missionary is truly present to the people who are evangelized, must be carried out, according to the FABC, in three areas: with the Asians themselves, especially the poor and the indigenous peoples (integral development and liberation), with their religions (interreligious dialogue), and with their cultures (inculturation).[24]

---

[21] "While acknowledging its many positive effects, they [the synod fathers] pointed out that globalization has also worked to the detriment of the poor, tending to push poorer countries to the margin of international economic and political relations. Many Asian nations are unable to hold their own in a global market economy. And perhaps more significantly, there is also the aspect of a *cultural* globalization, made possible by the modern communications media, which is quickly drawing Asian societies into a global consumer culture that is both secularist and materialistic" (*EA*, no. 39). In light of this, John Paul calls for "globalization without marginalization."

[22] *For All the Peoples of Asia*, 1:231.

[23] See ibid., 2:21-26, 169. See also *DP*, no. 42; and Chapter 2 herein.

[24] See *For All the Peoples of Asia*, 1:14-16, 22-23.

This spirituality of presence is all the more necessary, and the mission work performed through it all the more effective in those parts of the world, especially in Asia, where an explicit proclamation of Jesus is forbidden and religious freedom is restricted or denied. This presence in the form of "the silent witness of life" is perhaps not always congenial to Western missionaries, in whose training there has been a strong emphasis on a verbal and explicit proclamation of Jesus as the only and universal savior and for whom anything falling short of this would be a failure in mission. Nevertheless, when this silent witness of life, rooted in the experience of God, is accompanied by a lifestyle characterized by "renunciation, detachment, humility, simplicity and silence" and by "the work of justice, charity and compassion," it is perhaps most appropriate for Asia and forms the core of the spirituality of presence which is mission as "*contemplative action and active contemplation*" (*EA,* no. 23).

Since the spirituality of presence is essentially dialogue, it demands all the virtues that make dialogue successful. For this to occur, according to the FABC's Institute of Interreligious Affairs, nothing less than a "spirituality of dialogue" is required, especially in situations of conflict and animosity:

> In a situation of prejudice brought about by fundamentalism and religious revivalism, dialogue means an abiding and genuine search for goodness, beauty, and truth following the beckoning of the Spirit who leads us into all truth. . . . In an atmosphere of animosity brought about by the injustice and violation of human rights, dialogue means powerlessness and vulnerability. From a position of power, one can only negotiate about terms. From a position of weakness, one can truly communicate his or her trust in the other. Trust is most real when there looms the possibility of betrayal. To dialogue then means to open one's heart and to speak one's mind with courage and respect. But, as our experiences have shown, the Spirit has often used powerlessness and vulnerability to effect mutual forgiveness and reconciliation among individuals, families, and communities.[25]

This spirituality of presence from the missionary's position of powerlessness and vulnerability brings us to the next dimension of border-crossing spirituality, namely, kenotic spirituality.

Kenotic Spirituality

What is meant by kenotic spirituality is well explained by the same Institute of Interreligious Affairs:

> To risk being wounded in the act of loving, to seek understanding in a climate of misunderstanding—these are no burdens to bear. Dialogue demands a deep spirituality which enables man, as did Jesus Christ, to hang

---

[25] Ibid., 1:310-11.

on to his faith in God's love, even when everything seems to fall apart. Dialogue, finally, demands a total Christ-like self-emptying so that, led by the Spirit, we may be more effective instruments in building God's kingdom.[26]

Much of Asia is suffering from the legacy of colonialism, widespread poverty, crushing foreign debts, lack of basic health care and adequate educational facilities, and ecological destruction. The missionary who comes from the First World, especially from the United States, which is now the sole superpower wielding absolute military power and enormous wealth, and from the Catholic church, a powerful and rich institution both in the West and in Asia, is often perceived by Asians as having unlimited resources to alleviate their pain and suffering. Furthermore, from the religious point of view, the Catholic Church is often presented as possessing the fullness of truth and all the means of sanctification and as charged with the mission of sharing these divine gifts with others. As a consequence, the missionary is presented with unrealistic expectations and is tempted to think that part of the missionary's mission is to meet them.

It is here that kenotic spirituality will play a key role. As Antonio M. Perna, the Filipino superior general of the Society of the Divine Word (SVD), echoing the voice of the FABC, puts it: "Much of Asia, as we know, is characterized by the historical experience of colonization, a socio-economic condition of poverty, and a religious situation where Christianity is a minority. So, the Asian missionary cannot, or ought not, evangelize from a position of power or superiority. He or she must approach mission from a position of powerlessness and humility."[27] This means that the good news is not something owned by the missionary but rather given into his or her stewardship: "Thus, the Asian missionary will not, or ought not, share the faith as if he or she owned it, dictating thereby the terms by which it must be understood, lived and celebrated. His or her approach to mission will be to share the faith as a gift received from God through others, conscious of himself or herself as merely its steward or servant and never its owner or master."[28]

The necessity of this kenotic spirituality is even more pressing in the case of Asians going as missionaries to the First World, as happens frequently these days as the First World imports Asian priests and religious to remedy its shortage of clergy. As Leo Kleden, an Indonesian SVD, has shrewdly observed, these missionaries cannot expect to do what missionaries from the First World have done in Asia in terms of health care, education, and social development. Asian missionaries, originating mostly from premodern cultures and moving into the modern and postmodern cultures of the West, come literally empty handed. But this situation need not be simply weakness but also strength, says Kleden:

---

[26] Ibid., 1:311.

[27] Stephen Bevans and Roger Schroeder, eds., *Mission for the Twenty-First Century* (Chicago: The Chicago Center for Global Ministries, 2001), 19.

[28] Ibid.

This kind of weakness can and should be the strength of the new missionaries. Here is a golden opportunity to follow the example of the first disciples of Jesus who were sent empty handed but who were inspired by the Spirit of the Crucified and Risen Lord. The empty handed approach is therefore possible if their heart is full of faith, with the willingness to serve others as the Lord Jesus. Through the Spirit of the Lord human weakness (in the socio-political sense) is transformed into evangelical *kenosis*.[29]

In terms of evangelization, with kenotic spirituality missionaries cross over borders less with the attitude of givers than of receivers. They do not go into the mission lands with an advanced technology to modernize the underdeveloped, with a superior culture to civilize the "barbarians," with a true religion to wipe out superstitions, with a set of revealed truths to teach the "unenlightened." As Anthony Gittins has pointed out, they come primarily as strangers and as guests. As strangers, they will be perceived by the hosts as "foreign," "abnormal," "alien," "odd," "strange." As guests, they must depend on the generosity and kindness of the hosts, respect and follow the rules and customs of the new environment, and change the ways of life of the place only if asked or allowed. Furthermore, in many cases missionaries are *not* invited guests, they invite themselves or even force their way into the hosts' countries. This makes their condition of stranger and guest even more pronounced and precarious.

In light of these two existential predicaments of the missionary, Gittins suggests that part of kenotic spirituality is for the missionary to "*accept our marginal and ambiguous status*. We are no longer—if we ever truly were—primary movers, but collaborators and assistants, servants."[30] He goes on to say:

> To allow oneself to be a stranger is to allow oneself to be placed at the disposition of the God who calls. To embrace the status of a stranger is to empower other people and to dare to infuse some trust into a world where self-interest and suspicion seem to walk unimpeded. To choose to be a stranger is, it might be argued, to be a willing disciple of Jesus.[31]

Kenotic spirituality also requires that, as guest, the missionary learn to be a gracious and grateful receiver, not only in matters of room and board, but above all in the areas of culture, moral behavior, and religious insights and practices. In this respect, perhaps, the virtues that were extolled in the past as requisites of a successful missionary, such as independence, self-reliance, risk-taking, and creativity, might no longer be appropriate, at least during the phase of incorporation into the local community, and must be replaced by vulnerability, interdependence, deference, conformity, and willingness to give up self-control. Of

---

[29] Leo Kleden, "*Missio ad gentes*: An Asian Way of Mission Today," in Bevans and Schroeder, *Mission for the Twenty-first Century*, 188.

[30] Anthony Gittins, *Gifts and Strangers: Meeting the Challenge of Inculturation* (New York: Paulist Press, 1989), 132. See also Gittins, *Ministry at the Margins*, 151.

[31] Gittins, *Gifts and Strangers*, 133-34.

course, as etiquette demands, the missionary as guest must also bring some gifts of his or her own, not to "repay" the host but to "return" the host's graciousness. Consequently, the missionary must bear witness to Jesus Christ and present God's gift of faith. But gifts are offered in gratitude and humility; they should never be imposed on the host.[32]

Spirituality of Reconciliation and Harmony

It is a fact of life that borders do not serve simply to define and affirm identity. Good fences do *not* always make good neighbors. It all depends on who puts up the fence and where and for what. It may happen that a more powerful neighbor puts up the fence as a barrier to keep others out. Perhaps it is placed beyond his or her properties, thus encroaching upon other people's lands, or maybe it is intended to protect ill-gotten wealth and unjust privileges. It is also a fact of life that the guest and the host are not always in a friendly relationship; hospitality may turn into hostility. Then there arises the need to restore harmony and make peace.

Given the increase of violence not only among nations but also within nations, not only in secular society but also in the church since the end of communism in Eastern European countries in 1989, the need for reconciliation has grown more acute. Among contemporary missiologists Robert Schreiter has devoted a lot of attention to reconciliation.[33] Schreiter warns that reconciliation must not be undertaken as "a hasty peace" by suppressing the memory of past violence; as an "alternative to liberation," which is a precondition for reconciliation; or as a "managed process" to be conducted with technical rationality.[34] Rather reconciliation must be seen as part of Christian mission (2 Cor 5:18-19) based on the Christian redeeming narrative of violence (sin), death, cross, and blood in the life of Jesus of Nazareth.

Following José Comblin, Schreiter suggests that this reconciliation, which is initiated and brought about by God, is accomplished on three levels: "a christological level, in which Christ is the mediator through whom God reconciles the world to God's self; an ecclesiological level, in which Christ reconciles Jew and Gentile; and a cosmic level, in which Christ reconciles all the powers in heaven and on earth."[35] To fulfill this ministry of reconciliation, missionaries, according to Schreiter, must develop a "spirituality of reconciliation." This spirituality consists in cultivating an attitude of "listening and waiting," of "attention and compassion," and of "post-exilic existence." By listening and waiting, one learns to retrieve the memory of suffering and violence and to wait patiently for God's gift of peace and forgiveness; by attention and compassion,

---

[32] For helpful reflections on the dynamics of gift-giving and gift-receiving as a model of mission, see ibid., 84-109, and Gittins, *Ministry at the Margins*, 107-20.

[33] See Schreiter's works cited above. For a brief exposition, see his "Globalization and Reconciliation: Challenge to Mission," 121-43, esp. 135-43.

[34] See Schreiter, *Reconciliation*, 18-27.

[35] Ibid., 42.

one enters into solidarity with those who suffer violence; and by post-exilic existence one begins to construct a new society with chastened optimism and hope.[36]

Reconciliation as restoration of harmony is also a pervasive theme in Asian theologies as embodied in the the FABC's documents.[37] There is no doubt that harmony is central to Asian cultures and religions. It is said to constitute "the intellectual and affective, religious and artistic, personal and social soul of both persons and institutions in Asia."[38] After expounding the concept of harmony as espoused by Asian philosophies, primal religions, and religious traditions (including Hinduism, Buddhism, Confucianism, Taoism, Christianity, and Islam), the FABC's Theological Advisory Committee concludes: "It is clear there is an Asian approach to reality, an Asian understanding of reality that is profoundly organic, i.e., a world view wherein the whole, the unity, is the sum-total of the web of relations, and interaction of the various parts with each other."[39]

Thus, harmony is not simply "the absence of strife" but lies in "acceptance of diversity and richness." Nor is it merely a pragmatic strategy for successful living amid differences. Fundamentally, it is an Asian *spirituality* involving all the four dimensions of human existence: the individual self, his or her relationships with other human beings, the material universe, and God. This is clear from the teachings of various Asian religious traditions. The Hindu way is marked by a quest for a harmonious integration of the whole and the parts at all levels: individual, social, and cosmic. The cosmos is sustained by a harmonious order; society is held together by the order of *dharma* (law); and the individual achieves harmony by observing the cosmic order and society's moral and religious code.

In Buddhism, harmony in the individual, which leads to liberation from suffering, is achieved by following the so-called Eightfold Path: right speech, action, and livelihood (morality); right effort, mindfulness, and concentration (mental discipline); and right understanding and thought (wisdom). According to Zen Buddhism, harmony in the individual is the unity of body and mind in all the person's activities and produces enlightenment and a deep sense of peace. Because of the unity between body and soul, physical practices such as proper sitting position, regulating the breath, and composing the mind are necessary conduits to spiritual enlightenment.

Harmony in the individual leads to harmony with other human beings, which, according to Confucius, include the family, the nation, and the world. According to the Chinese sage, one cannot pacify the world without governing one's nation well; one cannot govern one's nation well without ordering one's family rightly; and one cannot order one's family rightly without achieving mastery over oneself. And self-mastery is achieved by living out five relationships correctly:

---

[36] See ibid., 71-73.

[37] See in particular the lengthy document of the FABC's Theological Advisory Commission entitled *Asian Christian Perspectives on Harmony*, in *For All the Peoples of Asia*, 2:229-98.

[38] Ibid., 2:232.

[39] Ibid., 2:276.

between ruler and subject, between husband and wife, between parent and child, between elder sibling and younger sibling, and between friend and friend. Each of these five relationships implies a set of obligations and duties, and if one fulfills them rightly, one lives in harmony with oneself and with others.

Furthermore, because the human person is a microcosm reflecting the macrocosm, the person must also be in harmony with nature or the cosmos. This harmony is particularly emphasized in Taoism. Chuang Tzu, the greatest Taoist after Lao Tzu, declares: "The cosmos and I were born together; all things and I are one." In practical terms, cosmic harmony demands that humans maintain a healthy and sustainable ecosystem, avoid the pollution of the environment, reduce the consumption of energy resources, and in general develop an attitude of reverence for, a contemplative posture toward, and a sense of oneness with the Earth and nonhuman creation.

Finally, harmony in oneself, harmony with one's fellow human beings, and harmony with the cosmos are rooted in and strengthened by harmony with God. This harmony with the Divine is the fundamental teaching of Islam, an Arabic term meaning "surrender." To be in harmony with God we must in all things submit to God's holy will in mind, heart, and action. We must, to use a Confucian expression, learn to know and fulfill the mandate of heaven.

When this view of harmony of Asian non-Christian religions is integrated with the Christian understanding of God's reconciliation of the world to himself in Jesus and by the power of the Spirit, what emerges, in the view of the Theological Advisory Commission, is a new spirituality of harmony as a web of peaceful relationships, a new theology of harmony as communion, and a deeper commitment to harmony as reconciliation. The spirituality of harmony will shape human life as an unfolding of right relationships:

> Starting from consciousness of the God-given harmony within oneself, one moves into harmonious relationship with one's fellow humans; then one spreads out to be in harmony with nature and the wider universe. This unfolding and realization of right relationship within oneself, with the neighbors and the cosmos leads to the summit experience of harmony with God.[40]

On the basis of this spirituality, a theology of harmony is developed, not as conclusions deduced from Christian texts but as a contextual reflection on the realities of conflict in Asia, in dialogue and collaboration with followers of other religions, and in solidarity with the victims of discrimination and violence. In this theology of harmony there is an emphasis on ethics as "the ethic and aesthetic of right relationships in the original harmony," on Christ as "the sacrament of the new harmony," and on the church as "the sacrament of unity." Finally, this new spirituality and theology of harmony call for an active commitment to peacemaking and reconciliation as individuals, as church, and in collaboration with others.

---

[40] *For All the Peoples of Asia*, 2:286-87.

For the missionaries, this spirituality of reconciliation and harmony implies that in their border crossing they be aware that borders as markers can be made to function as barriers, especially by those who have vested economic and political interests to maintain and protect. Here the role of prophecy is indispensable. The missionaries will be in solidarity with those who are marginalized and discriminated against by these borders/barriers and with courage denounce the injustices committed against them. Harmony, says the Theological Advisory Commission, "is neither a compromising with conflictual realities, nor a complacency about the existing order. Harmony demands a transformative attitude and action, to bring about a change in contemporary society. This can be provided only by a prophetic spirituality which exercises charitable but courageous criticism of the situation."[41]

Another aspect of mission to which the spirituality of harmony applies is interreligious dialogue and the religious boundaries that have often been manipulated to pit one religious group against another. Religions should not be barriers separating people but rather different paths leading to God. As Michael Amaladoss has pointed out, a new approach to religions is needed, in which all religions are seen as players and collaborators in humanity's movement toward God's kingdom: "In promoting the kingdom, then, our enemies are Satan and Mammon, not other religions."[42] This spirit of complementarity and harmony is strongly insisted upon by the Asian bishops at the Asian Synod when speaking of the Asian cultural and religious values as forming the basis of the Asianness of the church:

> All of this indicates an innate spiritual insight and moral wisdom in the Asian soul, and it is the core around which a growing sense of "being Asian" is built. This "being Asian" is best discovered and affirmed not in confrontation and opposition, but in the spirit of complementarity and harmony. In this framework of complementarity and harmony, the Church can communicate the Gospel in a way which is faithful to her own Tradition and to the Asian soul (*EA, no. 6*).[43]

Holistic Spirituality

The last dimension of border-crossing spirituality, intimately connected with the spirituality of harmony and reconciliation, is holistic spirituality. Central to this spirituality is a holistic anthropology, which is already intimated above, when harmony is said to embrace four dimensions: the self, fellow human beings, the cosmos, and God. Arguing for "a more cosmic and holistic anthropology," María Carmelita de Freitas suggests that it will make possible "a more

---

[41] Ibid., 1:290.

[42] Michael Amaladoss, "Identity and Harmony: Challenges to Mission in South Asia," in Schreiter, *Mission in the Third Millennium*, 32.

[43] See also the final statement of the FABC's seventh plenary assembly in *For All the Peoples of Asia*, 3:8-9.

integrated and open religious life, one with wider horizons, more in harmony with what is beautiful, simple, human, joyful, cheerful, with nature, and with everything."[44] Only in this way, de Freitas believes, can the evils of globalization with its "neo-liberal creed" of monetary and economic stability, its "ethics of efficiency," its "gospel of competition," and its "logic of exclusion" be counteracted.[45]

From our reflections on harmony it is obvious that holistic spirituality is a central concern of not only various Asian religious traditions but also the FABC. The fifth plenary assembly in 1990 insisted that a spirituality for the new millennium must "integrate every aspect of Christian life: liturgy, prayer, community living, solidarity with all and especially the poor, evangelization, catechesis, dialogue, social commitment, etc. There has to be no dichotomy between faith and life, or between love and action."[46]

In holistic spirituality as part of border crossing, boundaries cease to be barriers and become frontiers from which the missionary ventures forth with people on both sides of the borders to create new realities out of their common assets. Among Hispanic/Latino theologians, Virgilio P. Elizondo has developed the concept of *mestizaje*, that is, a blending of two or more races, ethnicities, cultures, and religions into a "new race," as the early Christians were called. In this new race, as Elizondo points out,

> borders will not disappear, differences will not fade away, but they need not divide and keep peoples apart. . . . Rather than seeing them as the ultimate dividing line between you and me, between us and them, we can see borders as the privileged meeting places where different persons and peoples will come together to form a new and most inclusive humanity.[47]

The spirituality of missionary border crossing that we have elaborated in terms of presence, *kenosis*, harmony, and holistic integration is well expressed by Anthony Bellagamba in his description of the identity of the missionaries as "persons of the present" and "persons of the beyond." As "persons of the present," missionaries must live in contact with the realities of the people they seek to evangelize: "The struggle of the people, their hopes and concerns, their vision of life, their experience of death, their cosmological theories, their methods of being community, their understanding of authority, their use of authority, their sexual drives, and their whole system of values are, or should be, of great interest to cross-cultural personnel."[48] As "persons of the beyond," they must go

---

[44] María Carmelita de Freitas, "The Mission of Religious Men and Women in Latin America Today: A Liberating Mission in a Neoliberal World," in Schreiter, *Mission in the Third Millennium*, 111-12.

[45] See ibid., 100-101.

[46] *For All the Peoples of Asia*, 1:288.

[47] Virgil Elizondo, "Transformation of Borders: Border Separation or New Identity," in Aquino and Goizueta, *Theology*, 34.

[48] Bellagamba, *Mission and Ministry in the Global Church*, 95.

beyond their own cultures, histories, values, mother tongues, native symbols, even their religions, not in the sense of rejecting them, but in the sense of "emptying" themselves of them in order to be guests and strangers among the people they evangelize and to receive and adopt as far as possible their hosts' cultures and ways of life.

JESUS, THE BORDER CROSSER

Border-crossing spirituality, a necessity for missionaries in a culture with multiple and porous boundaries created by globalization, postmodernity, and religious pluralism, is not simply a practical strategy for successful evangelization but a theological imperative of Christian life as *imitatio Christi*. Christian evangelization in any period of history and in any culture worthy of the name must be modeled after the way Jesus proclaimed God's kingdom to the people of his time. There are, of course, many different ways to represent Jesus' life and ministry. For example, it is possible to explain the significance of Jesus by the various titles the New Testament and Christian tradition have attributed to him. Needless to say, no one title can ever exhaust the significance of Jesus' words and deeds and the multifaceted method of his ministry. For our present purposes it would be useful to explore Jesus' life and ministry in terms of border crossing. In this way the missionary spirituality that has been proposed here will be seen to be rooted in the mystery of Christ the Border Crosser himself. For reasons of space, I will limit our consideration to the incarnation, some aspects of Jesus' ministry, and his death and resurrection.[49]

The Incarnation as Border Crossing

The mystery of the Word of God made flesh in Jesus can certainly be viewed as an act of border crossing. Essentially, it is the culmination of that primordial border crossing by which the triune God steps out of self and eternity and crosses into the *other*, namely, the world of space and time, which God brings into existence by this very act of crossing. In the Incarnation, the border that was crossed is not only that which separates the eternal and the temporal, the invisible and the visible, spirit and matter, but more specifically, the divine and the human, with the latter's reality of soul and body.

In this divine crossing over to the human, the border between the divine nature and the human nature of Jesus functions as the marker constituting the distinct identity of each. One is not transmuted into the other or confused with it; rather, the two natures are "without confusion, without change." As the Council of Chalcedon teaches: "The distinction between the natures was never abolished

---

[49] One theologian who has reflected at length on Jesus as the marginal person par excellence (and by implication as a border crosser) and on Christian life as a mode of marginalization is Jung Young Lee (see *Marginality: The Key to Multicultural Theology* [Minneapolis: Fortress, 1995]).

by their union, but rather the character proper to each of the two natures was preserved as they came together in one person *(prosopon)* and one hypostasis."

On the other hand, the same border is no longer a barrier preventing God and the human from joining together. Indeed, by crossing the divine-human border, the Logos transforms the barrier into a frontier and creates a new reality, Jesus of Nazareth, whose humanity the Logos assumes and makes his own, so that, as the Council of Chalcedon teaches, his two natures—divine and human—are united with each other "without division, without separation." In this humanity the Logos now exists in a new way, not available to him before the Incarnation, and this historical mode of existence, in time and space, and above all, as we will see, in suffering and death, now belongs to God's eternal and trinitarian life itself.

Thus, in the Incarnation as border crossing, the boundaries are preserved as identity markers, but at the same time they are overcome as barriers and transformed into frontiers from which a totally new reality, a *mestizaje*, emerges: the divine and human reconciled and harmonized with each other into one single reality. Like Jesus, missionaries are constantly challenged to cross all kinds of borders and, out of the best of each group of people these borders divide and separate, to create a new human family characterized by harmony and reconciliation.

Jesus' Ministry as Dwelling at the Margins

A border crosser at the very roots of his being, Jesus performed his ministry of announcing and ushering in the kingdom of God always at the places where borders meet and hence at the margins of the two worlds separated by their borders. He was a "marginal Jew," to use the title of John Meier's multi-volume work on the historical Jesus. He crossed these borders back and forth, repeatedly and freely, whether geographical, racial, sexual, social, economic, political, cultural, or religious. What is new about his message about the kingdom of God, which is good news to some and a scandal to others, is that for him it removes all borders, both natural and manmade, as barriers and is absolutely all-inclusive. Jews and non-Jews, men and women, the old and the young, the rich and the poor, the powerful and the weak, the healthy and the sick, the clean and the impure, the righteous and the sinners, and any other imaginable categories of peoples and groups—Jesus invited them all to enter into the house of his merciful and forgiving Father. Even in his "preferential option for the poor" Jesus did not abandon and exclude the rich and the powerful. These too are called to conversion and to live a just, all-inclusive life.

Standing between the two worlds, excluding neither but embracing both, Jesus was able to be fully inclusive of both. But this also means that he is the marginal person par excellence. People at the center of any society or group as a rule possess wealth, power, and influence. As the threefold temptation shows, Jesus, the border crosser and the dweller at the margins, renounced precisely these three things. Because he was at the margins, in his teaching and miracle working, Jesus creates a new and different center, the center constituted by the meeting of the borders of the many and diverse worlds, often in conflict with one another, each with its own center that relegates the "other" to the margins. It is here that marginal people meet one another. In Jesus, the margin where he lived became the center of a new society without borders and barriers, reconciling all peoples, "Jew or Greek, slave or free, male or female" (Gal 3:28). Missionaries are invited to become marginal people, to dwell at the margins of societies with marginalized people, like Jesus, in order to create with them new all-inclusive centers of reconciliation and harmony.

Dying "Outside the City Gate and Outside the Camp" (Heb 13:12-13)

Jesus' violent death on the cross was a direct result of his border crossing and ministry at the margins, which posed a serious threat to the interests of those occupying the economic, political, and religious center.[50] Even the form of his death, crucifixion, indicates that Jesus was an outcast. He died, as the Letter to Hebrews says, "outside the city gate and out side the camp." Symbolically, however, hung between heaven and earth, at the margins of both worlds, Jesus acted as the mediator and intercessor between God and humanity.

Even in death Jesus did not remain within the boundaries of what death means: failure, defeat, destruction. By his resurrection he crossed the borders of death into a new life, thus bringing hope where there was despair, victory where there was vanquishment, freedom where there was slavery, and life where there was death. In this way the borders of death become frontiers to life in abundance. Like Jesus, missionaries have to live out the dynamics of death and resurrection, or, to use the words of Philippians 2:6-11, of self-emptying and exaltation.

Samuel Escobar's beautiful rendering of this christological hymn, which portrays Jesus as the border crosser par excellence and summarizes well the missionary border-crossing spirituality, serves as a fitting conclusion to our reflections:

> Let there be in us the same feeling and mind that was
>   also in Christ Jesus,
> Who in order to reach us crossed the border between
>   heaven and earth.
> He crossed the border of poverty to be born in a stable
>   and live without knowing where he was going to
>   rest his head at night.
> He crossed the border of marginalization to befriend
>   women and embrace publicans and Samaritans.
> He crossed the border of spiritual power to free those
>   afflicted by legions of devils.

---

[50] For reflections on Jesus' death in these terms, see Choan-Seng Song, *Jesus, the Crucified People* (New York: Crossroad, 1990), 89-100.

He crossed the border of social protest to sing truths to
the Pharisees, scribes, and traffickers of the
temple.
He crossed the border of the cross and death to help us
all pass over to the other side.
Risen Lord, who therefore awaits us there, at every
border that we have to cross with his gospel.[51]

---

[51] Samuel Escobar, *Changing Tides: Latin America and World Mission Today* (Maryknoll, N.Y.: Orbis Books, 2002), 176.

PART THREE

Doing Theology in Asia Today

9

Doing Theology in the Context of Mission

LESSONS FROM ALEXANDRE DE RHODES
FOR COMPARATIVE THEOLOGY

Perhaps at no time does a Christian theologian feel more challenged to do theology in a novel way and to renew the received tradition than when communicating the good news of Jesus to those who have never heard it, in a foreign land, in an unfamiliar culture, in a different language; in short, when doing theology in view of or in the context of mission.[1] Of course, no theologian, whether fundamental, systematic, or practical, can eschew the task of reformulating the contents of Christian revelation in terms understandable to the audience, whether academy, church, or society, to use David Tracy's categories.[2] To fulfill the task of making the word of God meaningful for their contemporaries, theologians must bring into a critical correlation the two poles of theology, whether these are termed "question" and "answer" (Tillich), "*oratio obliqua*" and "*oratio recta*" (Lonergan), or "common human experience and language" and "the Christian texts" (Tracy). In carrying out this task of mutual correlation, a certain amount of adapting the Christian message to the linguistic, cultural, politico-economic, and religious conditions of the hearers (as well as confronting the contemporary world with the revealed word) is both necessary and desirable.[3]

---

[1] This is true not only of Western theologians but also of the so-called third-world theologians, who have to "unlearn" Western theologies once they come home and begin teaching theology to their own people. Kosuke Koyama has spoken about his need to "reconstruct my theological knowledge in terms of my experience in Thailand" (*Water Buffalo Theology*, rev. and exp. ed. [Maryknoll, N.Y.: Orbis Books, 1999], 174). Koyoma, a Japanese, obtained his doctorate in theology from Princeton Theological Seminary and later was a missionary in Thailand. He spoke of "a triple accommodation process with Tokyo, New Jersey, and Chengmai" (ibid.).

[2] See David Tracy, *The Analogical Imagination* (New York: Crossroad, 1981), 3-46.

[3] David Tracy argues that because of the pervasive religious pluralism in contemporary society "any theology in any tradition that takes religious pluralism seriously must eventually become comparative theology" (see David Tracy, "Comparative Theology," in *Encyclopedia of Religion* [New York: Macmillan, 1987], 14:454; see also idem, *Dialogue with the Other: The Inter-Religious Dialogue* [Grand Rapids, Mich.: Eerdmans, 1990]).

For most theologians who live and work in the West, this "adaptation," to use a somewhat neutral term, might not seem a formidable task. Linguistically, it is relatively easy to translate most philosophical and theological French or German or Spanish words into English and the other way round, because they share the same roots (for example, "substance" and "hypostatic union"). In cases of idiosyncratic coinages (such as Heidegger's "*existential*" and "*existentiell*"), the difficulty could be obviated by simply transliterating the words without thereby sounding too exotic (and with the added benefit of appearing learned and profound to boot!). Even theological terms that had been objects of long and bitter controversies (e.g., *hypostasis/ousia*) before their admission into the realm of the Christian discourse have become so much part of the lingua franca of the academy that knowledge of their meaning is considered a condition for cultural literacy.

Furthermore, in spite of the much-trumpeted pluralism, there remains in the West a two-thousand-year common (implicitly Christian) cultural heritage that offers a shared language with which ideological opponents can at least make themselves understood to one another.[4] Moreover, with the demise of socialism and communism, democracy and capitalism are gaining ground as the only viable political and economic systems, creating a relatively homogeneous and free ambiance, at least in the West, in which theology as an academic discipline can be cultivated. Here, more than anywhere else, theologians can organize themselves into professional guilds, with their own associations, journals, and conferences, so that theology has become, to use Thomas Kuhn's expression, a "normal science."[5] Finally, as far as Christianity is concerned, it is true that it has long lost its hegemony, but numerically Christians, who still exercise a powerful influence on Western society, constitute by far the majority of believers. All these commonalities—linguistic, cultural, politico-economic, and religious—simplify somewhat the task of adapting the Christian faith to the contemporary society in the West.

That no such common terrain exists in countries, especially in Asia, where Christians form but the tiniest part of the population, hardly needs a lengthy elaboration. Even such fundamental words as *God, sin,* and *salvation,* let alone the theological contents they carry, do not have exact equivalents in some Asian languages,[6] which makes translation, even by way of dynamic equivalence,

---

[4] David Walsh has convincingly shown that Western culture has been and remains deeply Christian in spite of the repeated attempts by modernity and postmodernity to deny its Christian roots (see David Walsh, *The Third Millennium: Reflections on Faith and Reason* [Washington, D.C.: Georgetown University Press, 1999]).

[5] See Thomas S. Kuhn, *The Structure of Scientific Revolutions,* 2d ed. enl. (Chicago: The University of Chicago Press, 1970), 10. Of course, in the postmodern era, with its foundation and its fundamental methodological presuppositions questioned and deconstructed, theology has lost this status of "normal science."

[6] David Ng was reminded that there is no word in Chinese for *community* when he went to the Chinese University of Hong Kong to study the Chinese and Confucian understandings of community. There is, however, *tuen kai* for *koinonia* (see Peter Phan and Jung Young Lee, eds., *Journeys at the Margin: Toward an Autobiographical Theology in American-Asian Perspective* [Collegeville, Minn.: Liturgical Press, 1999], 102).

extremely difficult.[7] Nor can recourse be had to simple transliteration, which would make the words sound unbearably foreign.[8] Moreover, differences among world views are so deep that the same verbal expression, gesture, ritual, and material object present in both Christianity and non-Christian religions generally have different functions and meanings.[9] Finally, in many Third-World (or Two-Thirds-World) countries, especially those under the communist regime, conditions are generally hostile to the development of theology as an academic discipline, not only in the academy but also in the church. Needless to say, under these circumstances, the "adaptation" of the Christian faith to the local cultures is an extremely complex affair.

This chapter will examine some of the challenges confronting Christian theology as it goes about the task of expressing the contents of the Christian faith in various cultural forms, especially the non-Western ones, a task that is now known under the neologism of inculturation. The results now emerging from this work will contribute to the construction of the theological discipline called comparative theology.[10] As has been noted above, this task is incumbent upon

---

[7] The debate about the use of the Chinese words *t'ien, shang-ti, t'ien-chu,* and *t'ien-ti* to translate *God* is widely known. Of the four only *t'ien-chu* was ratified by Clement XI *(Ex illa die)* in 1715 and by Benedict XIV *(Ex quo singulari)* in 1742 (see Peter C. Phan, *Mission and Catechesis: Alexandre de Rhodes and Inculturation in Seventeenth-Century Vietnam* [Maryknoll, N.Y.: Orbis Books, 1998], 135). Note that the word "inappropriate" on the last line of this page should read "appropriate." For Alexandre de Rhodes's translation of the term *God* into Vietnamese, see below.

[8] For example, the word *Christ* has not been translated in all Asian languages but transliterated (of course, in all other languages as well). However, while *Christ* does not sound strange in European languages (students sometimes think that it is Jesus' last name), to Asian ears it is a foreign product, just as Christianity is. To make matters worse, in many Asian countries Catholics and Protestants have insisted on using two different sets of biblical and theological terms to translate or transliterate European terms.

[9] One typical example is the dragon. In the Bible the dragon stands for the devil (see Revelation), but in Vietnam it is the symbol of divinity. According to the Vietnamese legend, the Vietnamese are descended from the dragon (the sea god) and a mountain goddess. For more examples of cultural differences, see Charles Kraft, *Anthropology for Christian Witness* (Maryknoll, N.Y.: Orbis Books, 1996); and Louis J. Luzbetak, *The Church and Cultures: New Perspectives in Missiological Anthropology* (Maryknoll, N.Y.: Orbis Books, 1988).

[10] On the nature and tasks of comparative (or cross-cultural or intercultural) theology, see Francis X. Clooney, *Theology after Vedanta: An Experiment in Comparative Theology* (Albany, N.Y.: State University of New York Press, 1993); idem, *Seeing Through Texts: Doing Theology among the Srivaisnavas of South India* (Albany, N.Y.: State University of New York Press, 1996); idem, "Comparative Theology: A Review of Recent Books (1989-1995)," *Theological Studies* 56 (1995): 521-50; James Fredericks, *Faith among Faiths: Christian Theology and non-Christian Religions* (New York: Paulist Press, 1999). Clooney distinguishes three moments of comparative theology: comparison of the theologies of different religions (a discipline within the history of religions), comparisons tested by the posing of theological questions (a part of theology), and construction of theologies generated after and from comparative practice (the ultimate goal of comparative theology). Comparative theology is intimately connected, though not identical, with the elaboration of local theologies, inculturation, and missiology.

all types of theology, but it is of special urgency for the kind of theology done in the context of mission. To limit the scope of the discussion and to make it concrete, I refer here to the work of Alexander de Rhodes, a seventeenth-century Jesuit missionary to Vietnam.[11]

Before broaching the subject, a word about mission is in order. By mission or evangelization is meant here the church's task of continuing the *missio Dei,* the work of the triune God as Creator, Redeemer, and Sanctifier, for the sake of the world.[12] Pope John Paul II distinguishes three "situations" for contemporary mission. The first is that in which the church addresses peoples, groups and socio-cultural contexts "in which Christ and his Gospel are not known, or which lack Christian communities sufficiently mature to be able to incarnate the faith in their environment and proclaim it to other groups" (mission *ad gentes*). The second is that in which there are Christian communities "with adequate and solid ecclesial structures," able to "bear witness to the Gospel in their surroundings" and committed to the "universal mission" (pastoral care). The third is that in which the ancient, and occasionally, younger churches have "lost their living sense of faith" or have moved away from Christ and the church (new evangelization or reevangelization) (see *RM,* no. 33).[13] Finally, missionary activities include but cannot be reduced to any of the following: proclamation, witness, worship, inculturation, liberation, or interreligious dialogue.

In this chapter, though not excluding the other situations of mission and its manifold activities, I focus on the mission *ad gentes* as well as on inculturation and interreligious dialogue (especially theological dialogue), because it is here that theologians are most strongly challenged to do theology in a new way. I preface my discussion with a brief outline of Alexandre de Rhodes's life and work as a missionary in Vietnam. After this overview, I reflect on some aspects of doing theology in view of mission by examining the relevant missionary strategies of de Rhodes. Finally, I conclude with suggestions as to how this missionary and comparative theology could be done today.

ALEXANDRE DE RHODES AND HIS MISSION IN VIETNAM

Though not the first to arrive in Vietnam, de Rhodes is often proclaimed the founder of Vietnamese Christianity. No doubt he deserves this accolade. First, he carried out a highly successful mission in both parts of Vietnam, Tonkin and Cochinchina. Second, besides two priceless memoirs on the Vietnamese society in the seventeenth century and on the beginnings of Vietnamese

---

[11] This chapter is not as such a discussion of de Rhodes's missionary and theological achievements. For a study of de Rhodes, see Phan, *Mission and Catechesis.*

[12] See David Bosch, *Transforming Mission: Paradigm Shifts in Theology of Mission* (Maryknoll, N.Y.: Orbis Books, 1991), 389-93. See also Chapters 2 and 3 herein.

[13] This triple division, though helpful, is not without difficulties of its own. For one thing, it gratuitously assumes that lacking "adequate and solid ecclesial structures" Christian communities are unable to "incarnate the faith in their own environment and proclaim it to other groups." For a discussion of these three situations, see Chapter 8 herein.

Christianity,[14] he published the first books, including a dictionary and a catechism, in Vietnamese in the Romanized script.[15] Third, he successfully lobbied for the establishment of a hierarchy in Vietnam. Thanks to his persistent efforts, in 1659 two bishops were appointed apostolic vicars of Tonkin and Cochinchina, respectively.

Born in Avignon on 15 March 1593, Alexandre de Rhodes joined the Jesuit novitiate in Rome to pursue his missionary vocation.[16] Shortly after his priestly ordination in 1618, de Rhodes was granted permission by Superior General Mutio Vitelleschi to go to the mission in Japan. On 20 July 1619 de Rhodes left Lisbon, and after six months and ten days arrived in Goa. After a lengthy delay in Goa, on 22 April 1622, de Rhodes resumed his journey to Macao, where he

---

[14] The first work is entitled *Histoire du Royaume de Tunquin, et des grands progrez que la predication de l'Evangile y a faits en la conversion des infideles. Depuis l'année 1627 jusques à l'Année 1646. Composée en latin par le R. P. Alexandre de Rhodes, de la Compagnie de Jesus. Et traduite en françois par le R. P. Henry Albi, de la mesme Compagnie*, 2 vols. (Lyon, 1651), in *ARSI JS* 83 and 84, f. 1-62v. It was composed in 1639 when de Rhodes was in Macao, teaching theology at the Madre de Deus College. It was published first in Italian in Rome in 1650 under the title *Relazione De' felici successi della Santa Fede Predicata da Padri della Compagnia di Giesu nel regno di Tunchino, alla santita di N.S.PP. Innocenzio decimo. Di Alessandro de Rhodes avignonese* in 326 pages. The Latin original was last published in Lyon in 1652 under the title *Tunchinensis historiae libri duo, quorum altero status temporalis hujus Regni, altero mirabiles evangelicae praedicationsi progressus referuntur. Coeptas per Patres Societatis Jesu, ab anno 1627, ad Annum 1646. Authore P. Alexandro de Rhodes, Avenionensi, eiusdem Societatis Presbytero, Eorum quae hic narrantur teste oculato.* Volume 1 has eighty-nine pages, and Volume 2 two hundred pages. The last part of this work (chapters 37-51) describes the situation of the church in Tonkin until 1646, which means that it was not written in Macao in 1636 but possibly after the author had come back to Rome (27 June 1649). The second work is entitled *Divers voyages et missions du P. Alexandre de Rhodes en la Chine, et autres Royaumes de l'Orient. Avec son retour en Europe par la Perse et l'Arménie. Le tout divisé en trois parties.* It was first published in Paris in 1653 and republished in 1666, 1681, 1683, 1854, and 1884. The book is composed of three parts. The first two parts are paginated continuously and have 276 pages. The third part begins with a new pagination. The book has been translated into English by Solange Hertz (Westminster, Md.: The Newman Press, 1966). A Latin manuscript, written in Macassar and dated 4 June 1647, entitled *Alexandri Rhodes è Societate Jesu terra marique decem annorum itinerarium* is located in *ARSI JS*, 69, f. 95r-140v. It contains 61 chapters, with chapters 50-58 and the last part of chapter 61 missing. This Latin manuscript forms the second part of *Divers voyages*, though the French printed text differs considerably from the Latin manuscript.

[15] On this dictionary and catechism, see note 14 of Chapter 6 herein. With regard to the alphabetization of the Vietnamese language, de Rhodes was not its inventor but perfecter and popularizer. In this work he derived much help from the unpublished dictionaries of Gaspar do Amaral and António Barbosa, both now lost. After being confined to Roman Catholics for two centuries, the Romanized script became the national script *(quoc ngu)* at the beginning of the twentieth century, replacing both Chinese and *chu nom* (the demotic script).

[16] For a detailed biography of de Rhodes, see the excellent dissertation of Do Quang Chinh, "La mission au Viet-Nam 1624-30 et 1640-45 d'Alexandre de Rhodes, S.J. avignonnais," Sorbonne, 1969.

arrived on 29 May 1623. De Rhodes stayed at the Jesuit college Madre de Deus, preparing himself for his mission in Japan by learning the Japanese language.

De Rhodes's First Mission in Cochinchina (1624-26)

De Rhodes's dream of being a missionary in Japan was not to be realized. Because of persecutions in Japan, de Rhodes's superiors dispatched him to Cochinchina.[17]

There were three Jesuit residences in Cochinchina when de Rhodes arrived. He was assigned to Thanh Chiem to study the language under the guidance of Francisco de Pina.[18] Meanwhile, Andrea Palmiero, the Jesuit visitor, was planning to send missionaries to Tonkin. In July 1626 de Rhodes and Pêro Marques were recalled to Macao to prepare for their mission in Tonkin.

De Rhodes's Mission in Tonkin (1627-30)

In March 1627 the two missionaries embarked on a Portuguese merchant ship for Tonkin; they arrived at Cua Bang (today Ba Lang) on 19 March 1627. Shortly afterward, they met Lord Trinh Trang, who was on his way to wage war against Cochinchina. When Lord Trinh Trang returned in defeat from his military expedition, the missionaries accompanied him to Thang Long, the capital, and there began their mission in earnest. The great number of conversions aroused the opposition of eunuchs, Buddhist monks, and concubines dismissed by husbands who decided to become Christian. One of the monks accused the missionaries of joining in a plot against Lord Trinh Trang. As a result, on 28 May 1628 Lord Trinh Trang issued a decree forbidding his subjects, under pain of death, to meet with the missionaries and to embrace the religion they preached.

However, the lord tolerated the presence of de Rhodes and Marques in the hope that they would attract Portuguese traders. However, when the Portuguese ships did not come during the sailing season, he expelled the missionaries. In March 1629 they left for the south, planning to return to Macao. However, in November, when two Jesuits, Gaspar do Amaral and Paul Saito, arrived, de Rhodes and Marques returned to the capital in their company. At first Lord Trinh Trang tolerated their presence, but after six months, when the Portuguese ship returned to Macao, he ordered them to leave the country.

---

[17] For a full description of de Rhodes's mission in Vietnam, see ibid. With regard to the political situation of Vietnam in the seventeenth century, it is to be briefly noted that though there was a king of the Le dynasty, he was in fact nothing more than a puppet. The real power lay in the hands of two clans. The north, known to the West as Tonkin, was under the Trinh clan, and the center, known then as Cochinchina, was under the Nguyen clan. Continuous warfare was conducted between the two rival clans for total control of the country with no definitive results. De Rhodes's entire ministry in Vietnam was carried out during this struggle for power between Tonkin and Cochinchina.

[18] The other two residences were located at Hoi An and Nuoc Man (Qui Nhon).

In May 1630 de Rhodes left Tonkin, never to return. He had worked there for more than three years. When he left, there were 5,602 Christians.[19]

Banished from Tonkin, de Rhodes returned to Macao and stayed there for ten years, during which he taught theology at the Madre de Deus College and took care of Chinese Christians. However, in 1639 events in Cochinchina once again made de Rhodes's missionary experience highly desirable. There were then some fifteen thousand Christians and twenty churches in central Vietnam.[20] In 1639 the lord of Cochinchina, Nguyen Phuoc Lan, who suspected that the missionaries had assisted his brother's rebellion against him, ordered the seven Jesuits to leave the country.

De Rhodes's Second Mission to Cochinchina (1640-45)

Eager to continue the mission in Cochinchina, the new visitor Antonio Rubino canvassed for someone to send there. De Rhodes volunteered and was accepted. Thus began de Rhodes's second mission to Cochinchina. It was divided into four trips and lasted a total of fifty months. As a whole, it was far more difficult and eventful than his mission in Tonkin. Four times he was exiled from the country.

During the time de Rhodes spent in Cochinchina between 1640 and 1645, he baptized some 3,400 people, without counting the baptisms administered by his catechists. Compared with his mission in Tonkin, which produced 5,602 conversions, de Rhodes's second mission in Cochinchina produced significantly fewer converts, though it was much longer and much more strenuous (fifty versus thirty-eight months). On 3 July 1645, sentenced to perpetual exile from Cochinchina, de Rhodes left Vietnam for Macao.

Return to Rome and the Establishment of the Hierarchy in Vietnam

De Rhodes's superiors in Macao decided that a man of his experience could render a vast service to the missions by going back to Europe to fetch spiritual and temporal help. In December 1645 de Rhodes began his return journey to Rome. Immediately after his arrival, on 27 June 1649, he set out to realize his plan of having a hierarchy established in Vietnam.

On 11 September 1652 de Rhodes left for Paris, where he found three priests of the Société des Bons Amis who were judged worthy candidates for the episcopacy, among whom was François Pallu. Upon learning that Rome was about

---

[19] António Francisco Cardim, *Relation de ce qui s'est passé depuis quelque années, jusques à l'An 1644 au Japon, à la Cochinchine, au Malabar, en l'Isle de Ceilan, et en plusieurs autres Isles et Royaumes de l'Orient compris le nom des Provinces du Japon & du Malabar, de la Compagnie de Jésus. Divisée en deux Parties selon ces deux Provinces* (Paris, 1646), 85.

[20] This number is given by B. Roboredo in his report "Relaçao das perseguiçoes da Missam de Cochinchina desde Dezembro de 1640 ate Abril de 1641," *ARSI JS* 70, f. 1r. According to de Rhodes, the number is twelve thousand (*Divers voyages*, 117).

to send French bishops to Vietnam, Portugal voiced fierce opposition. Meanwhile, the Jesuit general, believing that de Rhodes's presence in the project of establishing a hierarchy in Vietnam would prevent it from being realized, decided to make him superior of the Jesuit mission in Persia. On 16 November 1654 de Rhodes left Marseilles for his new mission, where he died on 5 November 1660. But his dream of having a hierarchy for Vietnam was fulfilled a year before his death when, on 9 September 1659, Propaganda Fide published a decree, confirmed by Pope Alexander VII, establishing two apostolic vicariates with two bishops, François Pallu and Pierre Lambert de la Motte.[21]

DOING THEOLOGY IN THE CONTEXT OF MISSION

As one of the first missionaries to Vietnam, sometimes working alone for long stretches of time, de Rhodes faced a plethora of diverse challenges. Besides having to adapt his personal lifestyle to the local way of life,[22] he had to deal with Vietnamese cultural practices that appeared to be at odds with Christian faith and ethics.[23] In addition, and more important, there were issues arising from the differences between Christianity, on the one hand, and the four religions of Vietnam—Buddhism, Confucianism, Taoism, and the indigenous religion—on the other. Finally, there were ecclesial concerns such as sacramental and liturgical celebrations and the organization of the nascent church.[24]

However, the most urgent task for de Rhodes in the seventeenth century, as well as for theologians working today in view of the mission *ad gentes*, was no

---

[21] For a history of Vietnamese Christianity in the seventeenth century, see Henri Chappoulie, *Aux origines d'une Eglise. Rome et les Missions d'Indochine au XVIIe siècle,* 2 vols. (Paris: Blou et Gay, 1943); and Nguyen Huu Trong, *Les origines du clergé vietnamien* (Saigon: Tinh Viet, 1959).

[22] In contrast to his colleagues Matteo Ricci in China and Roberto di Nobili in India, de Rhodes did not adopt the costumes of mandarins or the upper class. Furthermore, like Vietnamese men he wore long hair, letting it fall in long braids on his shoulders, which he noted was the way the Vietnamese expressed their independence from the Chinese *(Histoire du Royaume)*. Like most enthusiastic missionaries, de Rhodes took great pleasure in indigenous foods and cuisine. With genuine delight he described the taste of various Vietnamese fruits *(Histoire du Royaume,* 50) and native delicacies, such as fish sauce and bird-nest soup *(Histoire du Royaume,* 48; and *Divers voyages,* 66). He enthusiastically endorsed tea as a remedy for headache, stomach troubles, and kidney complaints *(Divers voyages,* 45-53). He strongly recommended eating fish that had been swallowed by other fish (cooked with pepper) before sea travel—a native folk medicine—as an effective antidote against seasickness *(Divers voyages,* 124). He also praised Vietnamese traditional medicine *(Divers voyages,* 189-91).

[23] Among the Vietnamese cultural practices that de Rhodes wanted to abolish was polygamy *(Cathechismus,* 77-78). Other practices he tried to modify, giving them a Christian meaning, such as swearing loyalty to the lord *(Histoire du Royaume,* 35-37) and the celebrations of the New Year *(Histoire du Royaume,* 105).

[24] De Rhodes had to adapt various Christian liturgical celebrations (such as Christmas, the feast of the Purification of the Mary, and Palm Sunday) to the Vietnamese situation and to direct the organization of the Christian communities with the help of lay catechists. For an account of how de Rhodes dealt with all the issues mentioned so far, see Phan, *Mission and Catechesis,* 69-106.

doubt how to translate Christian theological terms into the language of the people to whom the gospel is preached. Most often this task is undertaken in the process of translating the Bible (which obtains priority with Protestant missionaries) or the catechism (which usually receives the immediate attention of Catholics) into the vernacular. But whether it is the Bible or the catechism, the task of finding the equivalent expressions in the vernacular for Christian terms remains an indispensable first step of the process of constructing a Christian theology in view of mission.

Translating Christian Texts into the Vernacular

Translating texts from one language to another belonging to a different linguistic family is much more difficult than from one language to another belonging to the same linguistic group or family. In the former case, which obtains in most missionary situations, the formal-equivalence approach to translation, matching the vocabulary, structure, and even the word order of the original as closely as possible in the receptor language, is rarely achievable. Indeed, any striving for fidelity by means of formal equivalence will lead very quickly, as Eugene Nida has shown with abundant examples, to infidelity if not absurdity.[25] The dynamic-equivalence approach, which attempts to respect the individuality of each receptor language by expressing the meaning of the original in a linguistic structure peculiar to that language, with a watchful and sharp eye for its cultural context, is the only appropriate one.[26]

Without the benefit of linguistics and the science of translation, de Rhodes instinctively gravitated toward the dynamic-equivalence approach when he composed his *Cathechismus* and in the process, had to find Vietnamese equivalents for Christian terms.[27] That he had at his disposal the resources of his colleagues, in particular Francisco de Pina (1585-1625) and the handwritten (now lost) dictionaries by Gaspar do Amaral (1592-1645) and António Barbosa (1594-1647)[28] does not lessen his merits and the importance of his work.

While space does not allow a detailed consideration of how de Rhodes translated Christian theological terms into Vietnamese, one example will show how he was extremely careful in translating the most important word, *God.* When Christian missionaries arrived in China, they were faced with the problem of deciding which of the three available terms, *t'ien* (heaven), *shang ti* (sovereign

---

[25] See Eugene Nida, *God's Word in Man's Language* (New York: Harper and Brothers, 1952).

[26] See Eugene Nida, *Towards a Science of Translating: With Special Reference to Principles and Procedures Involved in Bible Translating* (Leiden: E. J. Brill, 1964).

[27] De Rhodes did not translate the Bible, but in his catechism he made use of the Gospel according to John (almost exclusively) and so indirectly contributed to the translation of the Bible.

[28] We are informed by de Rhodes that do Amaral composed a *Diccionário anamita-português-latim* and that Barbosa composed *Diccionário português-anamita.* De Rhodes acknowledged he relied on both dictionaries to compose his own. See *Dictionarium*, ad lectorem.

on high), and *t'ien chu* or *t'ien ti* (lord of heaven), to use. Ricci's proposal to use all four terms interchangeably for God was, as mentioned above, rejected by Benedict XIV, who decreed that only *t'ien chu* should be used. In seventeenth-century Vietnam there were two modes of written communication. One was the Chinese language and its script, the knowledge of which was the mark of education; it was used in official documents and was known as *chu nho* (learned script). The other was the *chu nom* (demotic or popular script), which combined various Chinese characters to convey the meaning and to represent the sound of Vietnamese words.[29]

Due to the millennium-long domination of the Chinese over Vietnam, there developed in the Vietnamese language a set of vocabularies parallel to the native language. These words, called Sino-Vietnamese in distinction from the pure Vietnamese ones, originate from Chinese and are used mostly in literary, philosophical, and scientific disciplines (a parallel case is found in English, in which words of Germanic origin are paired with those of Greek or Latin derivation, for example, *all-knowing* and *omniscient*). With regard to God, there were in de Rhodes's time Sino-Vietnamese words corresponding to the Chinese ones: *thien (t'ien)*, *thuong de (shang ti)*, *thien chua (t'ien chu)*, and *thien de (t'ien ti)*.

Interestingly, the earliest missionaries did not make use of any of these terms but rather transliterated the Latin *Deus* into *Chua Deu* (Lord Deus). While the expression may be "faithful" to the original, it suffers an enormous disadvantage in that it fails to convey to the Vietnamese the meaning of who God is and runs the risk of suggesting to them that the Christian God is some other god than the one of the Vietnamese religions. More important, it does not attempt to inculturate the Christian notion of God into the Vietnamese culture.

De Rhodes's own practice in translating the word *God* is extremely instructive and has important implications for constructing a comparative theology. He himself explained how he arrived at a suitable translation for *God.* On 19 March 1627 he and his companion Pêro Marques arrived at Cua Bang in Tonkin. As the Portuguese ship came ashore, a crowd of Vietnamese rushed out to see who the newcomers were, where they came from, and what merchandise they were bringing in. De Rhodes took advantage of the people's curiosity to explain in fluent Vietnamese (to their surprise and delight) the purpose of his mission. He explained that while most of the people who had just arrived were Portuguese merchants seeking to trade goods and arms, he had a precious pearl to sell so cheaply that even the poorest among them could afford. When the people wanted to see the pearl, he told that it could not be seen with bodily eyes but

---

[29] For a brief explanation of the *chu nho* and *chu nom*, see Phan, *Mission and Catechesis*, 29-31. It is significant that the first missionaries made use of *chu nom* rather than the Chinese characters in composing catechisms and prayer books. One of them, Gerolamo Maiorica, an Italian Jesuit, wrote some forty books in this script. One reason for its use was that *chu nom*, being more widely known, would permit a more extensive communication with the Vietnamese. More significantly, the missionaries' preference for *chu nom* signaled their decision, in line with the Jesuits' (for example, Alessandro Valignano) policy of inculturation, to keep the nascent Vietnamese Christian church rooted in the native culture rather than in the foreign culture of which the Chinese characters were a potent symbol and instrument of expansion.

only with spiritual eyes. The pearl, he said, was the true way (*dao*, which also means "religion" in Vietnamese) that leads to the happy and everlasting life. In an illuminating passage de Rhodes records this momentous exchange:

> Having heard of the Law which they call *dao* in scholarly language and *dang* in popular tongue, which means *way*, they became all the more curious to know from me the true law, the true way that I wanted to show them. Thereupon I talked to them about the sovereign Principle of all created beings. I decided to announce it to them under the name of the Lord of heaven and earth, finding no proper word in their language to refer to God. Indeed, what they commonly call *Phat* or *But* designates nothing but an idol. And knowing that the cult of idols was held in high esteem by the leaders and doctors of the kingdom, I do not think proper to designate God with these words. Rather I decided to employ the name used by the apostle Saint Paul when he preached to the Athenians who had set up an altar to an unknown God. This God, he said, whom they adored without knowing him, is the Lord of heaven and earth. It was therefore under this name, full of majesty even in the hearts of the pagans, that I first announced to them that the true way consisted first and foremost in fulfilling our legitimate duties to the Lord of heaven and earth by the means he has revealed to us.[30]

In contrast to Athens, there were no altars dedicated to the Unknown God at Cua Bang, though there were no doubt pagodas and temples in honor of the Buddha and the spirits. However, like the Athenians, who were said by Paul to be "deisidaimonesterous" (not superstitious, as the King James Version would have it), the Vietnamese were no less religious since the name the Lord of heaven and earth was said to be "full of majesty, even in the hearts of the pagans." There is therefore an explicit recognition of the presence of God among those who have not yet accepted the gospel (the "pagans"). Nevertheless, in trying to translate *God* into Vietnamese, de Rhodes faced a quandary. He found, he said, "no proper word in their language to refer to God." The two words *Phat* and *But*, which presumably most of his audience knew, do not refer to God. The former refers to the Buddha; the latter also refers to the Buddha, but in popular language. There was another word, widely used by the Vietnamese to refer to God but not mentioned by de Rhodes, Ong Troi, literally, "Mr. Heaven."[31] De

---

[30] *Histoire du Royaume*, 129-30. All the translations of de Rhodes's works in this chapter are mine.

[31] The belief in Ong Troi is the basic element of the Vietnamese indigenous religion that consists essentially in the cult of "heaven," the spirits, and the ancestors. At the head of the hierarchy of spirits, the Vietnamese place Ong Troi above all deities, immortals, spirits, and genies. In this "Mr. Heaven" the Vietnamese see the personal, transcendent, benevolent, and just God, creator of the universe, source of life, and supreme judge. There is no cult of heaven at the popular level; the rendering of cult to this God was reserved to the emperor who once a year (since the nineteenth century once every three years) offered a solemn sacrifice, known as *Te Nam Giao*, in the name of the entire people. For the Vietnamese people's understanding of heaven and their native religion, see Phan, *Mission and Catechesis*, 24-28.

Rhodes objected to the use of *Phat* and *But* because they designate "nothing but an idol." The reason he did not mention Ong Troi might be that, as we read later in *Cathechismus*, he was afraid that it might suggest that the material heaven is divine, which he believed to be a common misconception among the Chinese and the Vietnamese.[32]

There were, of course, the four Sino-Vietnamese terms for God mentioned above. But de Rhodes declined to use them, probably because being part of the learned language, they would not be readily understandable to the common people who were gathering around him. Instead, on the basis of the Pauline terminology, he coined a new expression: *duc Chua troi dat* (the honorable Lord of heaven and earth). *Duc* is an honorific title; *Chua* means "lord" and was used as the title of the heads of the states of Tonkin and Cochinchina; *troi* means "heaven" or "firmament"; and *dat* means "earth."

In his translation de Rhodes achieved several significant things that should be kept in mind as useful guidelines as we embark upon our task of constructing a comparative theology. First, he did not have recourse to transliteration but attempted to find a dynamic equivalent in Vietnamese for *God;* in so doing he was beginning the first step of the process that today goes under the name of inculturation. Second, he paid careful attention to the religious context and the various meanings and functions a word has in it. This context, it must be noted, consists not only of classic texts but also of the concrete practice of the common people. In this way he could avoid the misunderstandings caused by the use of words in the receptor language that seem to be similar to the Christian vocabulary in written texts but have acquired a different connotation in popular religious practice. Third, he opted for the popular but pure Vietnamese language over the learned but foreign language; in this way he kept close to the "soul" of the culture and indirectly contributed to the emergence of cultural and national identity. Fourth, in devising linguistic equivalents he derived his inspiration as far as possible from biblical terminologies and expressions, in this case Paul's "*ouranou kai gēs kurios*" (Acts 17:24). Finally, though perhaps unintentionally, de Rhodes invoked one of the fundamental principles of Vietnamese philosophy, which may be termed cosmotheandric or theanthropocosmic,[33] according to which heaven (the divine), earth (the cosmos), and humanity *(troi, dat, nguoi)* must always be viewed in strict unity with one another. At the same time, thanks to the Christian doctrine of creation, he could highlight God's transcendence in his immanence as creator.[34]

---

[32] De Rhodes went to great lengths to show that "heaven" is not divine but created (see *Cathechismus*, 12-16).

[33] For an explanation of this principle as a unified vision of reality, see Raimon Panikkar, *The Cosmotheandric Experience: Emerging Religious Consciousness* (Maryknoll, N.Y.: Orbis Books, 1993).

[34] For de Rhodes's translation of other Christian terms, see Phan, *Mission and Catechesis*, 137-40. At times de Rhodes combined different Vietnamese words into new ones; at other times, he used circumlocutions for technical terms such as *hypostatic union;* sometimes (though rarely), he left the foreign words untranslated. Most significant among the latter is *Spiritus Sanctus* in the baptismal formula. The reason he did not translate *Spiritus Sanctus* might be that the word *spiritus (than)* is associated in

Encounter with Non-Christian Religions

Inevitable for any Christian missionary and theologian working in Southeast Asia, both in de Rhodes's time and in our own, is an encounter with Buddhism, Confucianism, Taoism, and the indigenous religions of each country. Developments in Catholic theology since the seventeenth century, especially after the Second Vatican Council, have created a paradigm shift in the Catholic church's attitude toward and evaluation of non-Christian religions.[35] It has abandoned the "exclusivistic" theology of religions embodied in the axiom *extra ecclesiam nulla salus,* and most of its theologians have embraced "inclusivism," with a few proposing even "pluralism."[36]

It would be altogether anachronistic to expect de Rhodes to have entertained the possibility that non-Christians could be saved without baptism or to have regarded non-Christian religions as alternative ways of salvation. Indeed, it is not difficult to show how his expositions of the doctrines and beliefs of the "Three Religions" *(tam giao)* as well as the indigenous religion of Vietnam are riddled with inaccuracies and misunderstandings.[37] Unlike Matteo Ricci, de Rhodes did not know enough Chinese to read and study the Chinese classics firsthand; whatever information he had on Confucianism, Buddhism, and Taoism as systems of beliefs were secondhand or thirdhand. Moreover, his interest was predominantly apologetic and missionary. Viewing these religions mainly as "superstition," de Rhodes was concerned with helping the catechumens reject them in favor of Christianity.[38] Needless to say, no one today would and

---

Vietnamese with angel or devil (see *Dictionarium,* col. 740-41, 763),, and the word *Sanctus (thanh* or *thanh hien)* is given in Vietnamese to Confucius (see *Dictionarium,* col. 747-48) to whom de Rhodes refused the title of saint (see *Histoire du Royaume,* 63-64; *Cathechismus,* 113).

[35] For a magisterial study of the development of contemporary theology of religions, see Jacques Dupuis, *Toward a Christian Theology of Religious Pluralism* (Maryknoll, N.Y.: Orbis Books, 1997); see also Peter C. Phan, ed., *Christianity and the Wider Ecumenism* (New York: Paragon House, 1990).

[36] Among Catholic theologians, inclusivism is associated with Karl Rahner, whereas pluralism is associated with Paul Knitter. Most contemporary theologians of religion are rightly dissatisfied with the usefulness of these categories as ways to describe possible Christian attitudes toward non-Christian religions. For a discussion of these three positions, see Peter C. Phan, "Are There Other 'Saviors' for Other Peoples? A Discussion of the Problem of the Universal Significance and Uniqueness of Jesus the Christ," in Phan, *Christianity and the Wider Ecumenism,* 163-80; idem, "The Claim of Uniqueness and Universality in Interreligious Dialogue," *Indian Theological Studies* 31 (1994), 44-66.

[37] For de Rhodes's exposition of the Three Religions in China, see *Divers voyages,* 53-55. He discussed the Vietnamese religions mainly in *Histoire du Royaume,* 61-92; *Divers voyages,* 86-89; and *Cathechismus,* 104-24.

[38] For a presentation of de Rhodes's attitudes toward the Three Religions and the Vietnamese indigenous religion, see Phan, *Mission and Catechesis,* 82-96. In general, of the three religions de Rhodes considered Taoism the crassest and the most pernicious because "it is the most widespread and the most devoted to the service of the devil" (*Histoire du Royaume,* 72). With regard to Buddhism, he followed the practice of his times summarized in the expression "Ch'in ju p'ai fo," that is, draw close to Confucianism and repudiate Buddhism. For him, the basic error of Buddhism is its atheism. Finally, de

should take de Rhodes as a reliable guide on the *beliefs* of Vietnamese Confucianism, Buddhism, Taoism, and indigenous religion.

This necessary caveat said, it must be acknowledged that there are things in de Rhodes's dealing with non-Christian religions that can furnish useful suggestions as to how a comparative or missionary theology can be constructed. First, in spite of his vigorous attacks against the doctrines of the non-Christian religions, de Rhodes was firm in rejecting the method that he noted was adopted by other missionaries according to which "it is necessary first to destroy the errors of paganism and disabuse the minds of pagans of these erroneous views before establishing and teaching the doctrines and principles of the Christian religion."[39] Instead, de Rhodes recommended that one not attack the errors of the non-Christian religions "before establishing the truths knowable by the light of natural reason. . . . The goal is to build in the hearers' minds a sort of firm foundation on which the rest of their faith can be supported and not turn them off, which often happens, by our rebutting and ridiculing their devotions, false though they are, and their superstitious observances."[40] In other words, it is necessary in interreligious dialogue as well as in comparative theology to search out first the common doctrines shared by Christianity and the other religions. This method should not be construed as false irenicism, which would ignore the real doctrinal differences among various religions. For the sake of the truth, a critique of the errors of the other religions is necessary, but it should be done only *after* a sympathetic study of the commonalities that bring all the religions together. Thus, de Rhodes was convinced that there were elements of truth and goodness in non-Christian religions.[41]

Second, and perhaps more important, in trying to understand non-Christian religions, de Rhodes focused more on how people actually *lived* their religions in their daily lives than on the classical texts of these religions. Partly because he did not know the Chinese classics well, partly because he was primarily a "hands-on" missionary,[42] de Rhodes rarely referred to texts in describing the

---

Rhodes held Confucianism in highest esteem because of its moral teachings: "Confucius, in the books we have received from him, gives proper instructions to form good morals" (*Histoire du Royaume*, 62). He acknowledged that there is harmony between certain Confucian and Christian teachings on law, politics, and the administration of justice. In these matters, "there is nothing contrary to the principles of the Christian religion that should be rejected or condemned by those who follow them" (*Histoire du Royaume*, 63).

[39] *Histoire du Royaume*, 175.

[40] Ibid., 175-76.

[41] Among the common truths that can be established by reason, de Rhodes cited the belief in the creation of the world, the purpose of human life, and the moral obligation to know and serve God (*Histoire du Royaume*, 175-76). Elsewhere he confessed: "My favorite method was to propose to them [the non-Christians] the immortality of the soul and the afterlife. From thence I went on to prove God's existence and providence" (*Divers voyages*, 96).

[42] In his debates with Vietnamese Confucian scholars and Buddhist monks, de Rhodes often sought the help of those converts of his who had obtained the doctoral degree or had functioned as mandarins.

Three Religions and the Vietnamese indigenous religion.[43] But whatever lack of theoretical knowledge he might have had of the *beliefs* of non-Christian religions, he made up for, superbly and abundantly, with his firsthand and extensive knowledge of the religious *practices* of seventeenth-century Vietnamese. Almost all of his descriptions of the prayers, devotions, rituals, and customs of the Vietnamese religions are eyewitness reports. In a true sense de Rhodes was an anthropologist engaged in field work *avant la lettre*. Given the scarcity of Vietnamese historical documents, were it not for his memoirs, we would be very much in the dark about the religious practices of seventeenth-century Vietnam.

For the purpose of comparative theology, de Rhodes's practice serves as an important reminder that methodological comparisons among various religions should not be limited to the analysis of classic texts nor to that of rituals and practices as *prescribed* in liturgical and ethical manuals (the metier of academic theologians). Rather, religious beliefs, moral code, and rituals as well as texts that describe or prescribe them can be fully understood only when attention is paid to the context of the actual practicing of these beliefs and moral code, and celebration of these rituals. The text and the context are intimately intertwined, the one illuminating, modifying, and correcting the other. Thus, a comparative theology constructed on the basis of texts alone is necessarily incomplete and even skewed.

An example of extreme importance for the Catholic church in Asia, not only in the seventeenth century but also today, will drive home this point. The question of the veneration of ancestors was hotly debated among missionaries in China, with (generally) Jesuits taking a favorable position, and (generally) Franciscans, Dominicans, and other religious taking the opposing side.[44] Prescinding from ecclesiastical politics and differences in missionary methods, it is clear that Matteo Ricci and his fellow Jesuits could defend the legitimacy of ancestor veneration (in particular, the cult of Confucius) on the ground that it is "political and civic in nature" and not religious only by appealing to texts and perhaps the practice of the elite.

However, de Rhodes, a Jesuit himself, was deeply convinced otherwise and was adamantly and vigorously opposed to the practice of ancestor worship because it was considered religious and therefore "superstitious." His arguments were not derived from an analysis of texts but from his firsthand observation of how the Vietnamese people "worshiped" Confucius and how they celebrated funerals and death anniversaries. He gave detailed, vivid, and surprisingly accurate descriptions of these rituals and prayers and severely proscribed them.[45]

---

[43] The Vietnamese do not possess philosophical and religious classics. Instead, the main source of Vietnamese philosophy is constituted by Vietnamese mythologies, legends, works of literature, and, especially, proverbs and sayings.

[44] For a history of this issue, see Chapter 7 herein.

[45] For de Rhodes's description of the cult of Confucius in Tonkin, see *Histoire du Royaume*, 64-65; for his description of funerals and celebrations of death anniversaries, see *Histoire du Royaume*, 84-89. It is interesting to note that Léopold Cadière (1869-1955), a missionary to Vietnam and probably the greatest anthropologist on matters Vietnamese, agreed with de Rhodes on the basis of over fifty years of living with and

A contemporary comparative theology of the cult of ancestors would thus be severely lopsided were it limited only to an analysis of classical texts. It must take into account popular understanding and practices of this cult and recognize its deeply religious character. Of course, with this recognition it need not conclude that this cult is a superstition and therefore to be proscribed. The precise challenge for such comparative theology is to understand how such religious practice can legitimately be incorporated into Christian theology and liturgy.

The Ordering of Christian Doctrines

Another issue for comparative theology on which de Rhodes's practice may shed useful light is the ordering of Christian doctrines. Which Christian doctrines should be given priority, both methodologically and substantively, in the dialogue with non-Christian religions, especially in Asia? De Rhodes was aware that for many missionaries the mystery of the Trinity "should be expounded to catechumens only after they have been disposed to receive baptism in order to avoid troubling their minds with doubts which this sublime and ineffable mystery might induce."[46] Experience, de Rhodes claimed, taught him otherwise:

> I do not believe that we should wait until the time of baptism to propose to the catechumens the faith in the Trinity of the divine persons. On the contrary, we must begin with an exposition of this mystery, and then it will be easier to go from there to the incarnation of the Son of God. . . . For myself, during the many years I have been engaged in teaching the pagans, I have not found anyone who objected to our faith with regard to the exposition of the incomprehensible mystery of the Trinity.[47]

In line with this method, de Rhodes divided his catechesis for baptism into eight days, the first four devoted to an exposition of the truths that can be known by reason, followed by a critique of the errors of non-Christian religions, and the second four to the exposition of the Christian truths, beginning with the Trinity, and not postponing it toward the end, shortly before baptism, as was done by his colleagues.[48]

De Rhodes's exposition of the Trinity was deeply informed by the Thomistic synthesis,[49] and insofar as this system has been shown to suffer from certain

---

observing the Vietnamese: "Such a theory [that the veneration of ancestors is not religious] is in total contradiction with what can be seen every single day in Vietnam. . . . For the immense majority of the Vietnamese, the ancestors continue to be part of the family and the cult rendered them is clearly religious" (see Léopold Cadière, *Croyances et pratiques religieuses des Vietnamiens* [Hanoi: Imprimerie d'Extrême Orient, 1944], 1:39. my translation).

[46] *Histoire du Royaume*, 129.

[47] Ibid., 130.

[48] For an explanation of *Cathechismus*, see Phan, *Mission and Catechesis*, 131-35.

[49] For an exposition of de Rhodes's trinitarian theology, especially his contributions to the Vietnamese theological language, see Phan, *Mission and Catechesis*, 175-78.

weaknesses, de Rhodes's trinitarian theology is liable to the same criticism.[50] Whatever the merits of his trinitarian theology, however, de Rhodes's methodology serves as a useful reminder that the doctrine of the Trinity must be given a central position in any comparative theology and must not be relegated to an appendix, as was done in liberal theology.[51]

AN INTERCULTURAL THEOLOGY IN VIEW OF MISSION

It is well known that Christian mission has been undergoing a crisis, in the sense of both danger and opportunity, since the end of the Second World War. David Bosch opens his magisterial work on mission with reflections on the various factors that have brought about a call for a moratorium in Christian mission.[52] On the other hand, thanks especially to the Second Vatican Council, a new theology of mission has emerged in which the church is said to be missionary by its very nature, and hence each and every member of the people of God is deemed to have personal missionary responsibility. Furthermore, in this new theology of mission, the missionary task of the church is understood not primarily as church planting but holistically, comprising the proclamation of the word *(kerygma)*, witness *(martyria)*, worship *(leiturgia)*, fellowship *(koinonia)*, and service *(diakonia)*.

Yet, despite notable achievements in the theologies of liberation, inculturation, and interreligious dialogue in the intervening years, a lot of work remains to be done. The question is whether a kind of "comparative theology"—or theology in view of mission or intercultural theology, in the context of this chapter— should be attempted, and if so, how.

In a review of works in comparative theology from 1989 to 1995, Francis Clooney describes comparative theology as a constructive theology

distinguished by its sources and ways of proceeding, by its foundation in more than one tradition (although the comparativist remains rooted in one

---

[50] For a critique of the Thomistic trinitarian synthesis, see Catherine LaCugna, *God for Us: The Trinity and Christian Life* (San Francisco: HarperSanFrancisco, 1991), 143-69. For a feminist critique, see Elizabeth Johnson, *She Who Is: The Mystery of God in Feminist Theological Discourse* (New York: Crossroad, 1993).

[51] For a discussion of how the doctrine of the Trinity must occupy a central position in systematics and impart unity to the exposition of the Christian faith, see Peter Phan, "Now That I Know How to Teach, What Do I Teach? In Search of the Unity of Faith in Religious Education," *Salesianum* 60 (1998), 125-45.

[52] Bosch, *Transforming Mission*, 3-4. Bosch mentions the worldwide process of secularization, the dechristianization of the West, religious pluralism, the sense of guilt among Western missionaries, the growing gap between the rich and the poor, and the maturity of the churches in the Third World. Louis Luzbetak mentions the rapid rise and growth of independent and Pentecostal churches, the development of liberation and other local theologies, the spread of base communities, the rise of new ministries, the continuing strength of popular religiosity, theological pluralism, and ecumenical and interreligious understanding and collaboration (see Luzbetak, *The Church and Cultures*, 106-9).

tradition) and by reflection which builds on that foundation, rather than simply on themes or by methods already articulated prior to the comparative practice. Comparative theology . . . is a theology deeply changed by its attention to the details of multiple religious and theological traditions; it is a theology that occurs truly only *after* comparison.[53]

At the end of his review, Clooney highlights two facts: "comparative theologians are still finding out how to do their work properly, they have not agreed on a specific thematic agenda; and the fruits of comparative work pertain to every area of theology, they are not comfortably apportioned to one corner of theological discourse."[54]

In the light of de Rhodes's missionary practice, the following suggestions are put forward with the hope of advancing the discussion of both the nature and tasks of comparative theology and the two issues mentioned by Clooney.

1. The importance and necessity of comparative theology are rooted in the very nature of the Christian faith as a *translatable* phenomenon. As Lamin Sanneh has argued, Christianity's need to translate out of Aramaic and Hebrew—what Andrew Walls calls the "translation principle"[55]—brought about a double result: relativization of its Judaic roots and destigmatization of Gentile culture, now adopted as a natural extension of the life of the new religion.[56] The implicit theological principle behind the translation of the Bible into the vernacular is the recognition that all cultures, and the languages in which they are embodied, are equally worthy in God's eyes and therefore capable of bearing the divine message. Hence, translatability functions as an antidote to cultural absolutism, whether Hebrew, Greek, or Latin. Translatability is rooted in and at the same time expands the radical pluralism inherent in Christianity. Because of the translation principle, Christianity, unlike Judaism, does not require incorporation into an ethnic community as a condition for conversion to its faith; and unlike Islam, it does not make becoming a Christian equivalent to being identified with a particular culture (as Islamicization means Arabization). Also, thanks to this "infinite translatability of the Christian faith"[57] Christianity has been able to develop a fruitful dialogue with different cultures.

A comparative theology will therefore begin with the task of translation from Western languages to other languages and vice versa. Such a work by itself

---

[53] Clooney, "Comparative Theology," 522.

[54] Ibid., 550. What Clooney said about comparative theology in this essay must be complemented by what he wrote in *Theology after Vedanta*, esp. chap. 5, entitled "Theology after Advaita Vedānta: The Text, The Truth, and the Theologian" (153-208).

[55] Andrew Walls, *The Missionary Movement in Christian History* (Maryknoll, N.Y.: Orbis Books, 1996), 26. Walls sees translation into the vernacular as the linguistic consequence of the Incarnation.

[56] See Lamin Sanneh, *Translating the Message* (Maryknoll, N.Y.: Orbis Books, 1989), 1. He goes on to say: "Missionary adoption of the vernacular, therefore, was tantamount to adopting indigenous cultural criteria for the message, a piece of radical indigenization far greater than the standard portrayal of mission as Western cultural imperialism" (3).

[57] Walls, *The Missionary Movement in Christian History*, 22.

already enriches our understanding of other religions because it forces us to distinguish between the message and its linguistic vehicle, between meaning and form, and makes us compare the terms and concepts of the text to be translated with those (perhaps non-existing) of the receptor language. In the process we may, as de Rhodes and many other missionaries did, enrich the receptor language by introducing ancillary linguistic tools such as alphabetization of these vernaculars, grammars, dictionaries, and histories.

2. The translation and the subsequent comparison among religions to construct a comparative theology must not be limited to religious texts, however influential they may be in a particular culture. The methods of textual comparison that Clooney expounds—setting the comparison, finding similarities and differences, and reading by means of "coordination," "superimposition," "conversation," "tension," and "collage"—are very helpful indeed.[58] However, texts should be enlarged beyond the classics (for example, the Five Classics and Four Books of Confucianism) to include folktale, stories, legends, dance, proverbs (especially for the Vietnamese).[59] Morever, it is important and necessary, as de Rhodes has shown, to go beyond texts to religions as actually lived at the popular level to understand what these texts mean to people today. In so doing, in addition to gaining a better understanding of classical texts, comparative theology can avoid the charge of archeologism, that is, creating systems of thought of interest only to historians and antiquarians.

There is a further reason why one must go beyond the classical texts. These texts almost invariably represent certain interests, quite often those of the dominant social and religious classes (such as the caste system in India and the bias against women in Confucianism). Voices from the margins—economic, gender, racial, and cultural—have been silenced. To redress this injustice, attempts have been made to listen to the voices of indigenous minority people (such as the Ainu, Okinawans, Korean residents, and the Burakumin people in Japan), the *Dalits* and the tribal people in India, the oppressed mass *(minjung)* in Korea, and women in general.[60] A comparative theology that neglects these voices not only is incomplete but also runs the risk of perpetuating the injustices committed against these marginalized people.

Connected with the suppressed voices are the alternative methods of doing theology and canons of scholarship. Of course, the methods of rational and

---

[58] See Clooney, *Theology after Vedanta*, 159-75.

[59] See, among Choan-Seng Song's many works, *Third-Eye Theology*, rev. ed. (Maryknoll, N.Y.: Orbis Books, 1990); idem, *Tell Us Our Names: Story Theology from an Asian Perspective* (Maryknoll, N.Y.: Orbis Books, 1964); idem, *The Tears of Lady Meng: A Parable of People's Political Theology* (Geneva: The World Council of Churches, 1982); idem, *The Believing Heart: An Invitation to Story Theology* (Minneapolis: Fortress Press, 1999); and Peter C. Phan, "Method in Liberation Theologies," *Theological Studies* 61 (2000), 40-63.

[60] See R. S. Sugirtharajah, ed., *Voices from the Margin: Interpreting the Bible in the Third World* (Maryknoll, N.Y.: Orbis Books, 1991); idem, *Asian Faces of Jesus* (Maryknoll, N.Y.: Orbis Books, 1993); and idem, *Frontiers in Asian Christian Theology: Emerging Trends* (Maryknoll, N.Y.: Orbis Books, 1994).

analytical sciences developed in the West should not be abandoned in doing intercultural theology, but they must be complemented by the more intuitive and less academy-oriented methods of research and communication such as poetry, dance, art, meditation, oral transmission, and social action.

3. The question of truth, as Clooney has rightly argued, must be broached in comparative theology. Because comparative theology is *theology*, the truth of its theological proposals must be evaluated. However, their truths cannot be quickly and easily determined, and Clooney's counsel for patience is well taken: "Only through a long and patient process of reading and rereading does a particular reader approach the point where even one of the contested theological truths is apprehended as superseding its texts and as becoming simply 'the truth.'"[61] The difficulty of deciding the truth of a text is further heightened when it is seen in relation to the practical effects it has produced on the moral and spiritual lives of the believers (the pragmatic criterion of truth). In this respect de Rhodes's (as well as past missionaries') certitude about the superstitions of non-Christian religions appears rash and presumptuous. Against their negative attitude toward non-Christian religions, we may subscribe to the recent hypothesis that there is "a convergence between the religious traditions and the mystery of Jesus Christ, as representing various, though not equal, paths along which, through history, God has sought and continues to seek human beings in his Word and his Spirit."[62]

Furthermore, truth in comparative theology must be seen, as Clooney acknowledges, in correlation with the issues such as the uniqueness and universality of Christ that are the subject matter of the newly developed theological specialty known as "theology of religions."[63] The theology of religions and comparative theology must not be seen as mutually exclusive; nor should there be a moratorium on the theology of religions until a satisfactory comparative theology has been achieved. On the contrary, the two theologies must be seen as adopting two mutually complementary approaches to the study of religion—the theology of religions as the a priori, and comparative theology as the a posteriori—and therefore should be performed in tandem, as Stephen Duffy has rightly argued.[64]

4. Finally, there is the question of the order of theological doctrines in comparative theology. While it is legitimate to let the thematic agenda of comparative theology be determined by the texts and practices of a particular religious tradition under examination, it is necessary to ask how in an eventual systematic re-elaboration of Christian theology *after* comparison, which is the ultimate goal

---

[61] Clooney, *Theology after Vedanta*, 192.

[62] Jacques Dupuis, *Toward a Christian Theology of Religious Pluralism*, 328. See also The International Theological Commission, "Christianity and the World Religions," *Origins* 27 (1997), 149-66 and its evaluation by Terrence Tilley, "'Christianity and the World Religions,' A Recent Vatican Document," *Theological Studies* 60 (1999), 318-37.

[63] Clooney, *Theology after Vedanta*, 193-96.

[64] See Stephen Duffy, "A Theology of the Religions and/or a Comparative Theology," *Horizons* 26/1 (1999),105-15.

of comparative theology, the various doctrines are to be related to one another. As we have seen, de Rhodes proposed the doctrine of the Trinity as a possible unifying theme. Given the centrality of the Trinity in Christian faith, the recent emergence of the trinitarian doctrine into preeminence in contemporary theology,[65] and above all, given the tripartite structure present in the belief systems of many Asian religions, it seems likely that it will be taken up as the unifying doctrine of a future intercultural or cross-cultural theology. Meanwhile, of course, comparativists should pursue, according to his or her expertise and preference, the examination of any Christian doctrine and practice in the light of non-Christian religions and, on the basis of this comparison, elaborate a new understanding of it.

The purpose of this chapter is not to make de Rhodes into a comparativist theologian. He would be shocked to learn that he is one. Indeed, he would not even understand what the expression *comparative theology* means, and, were he to understand it, he would no doubt strenuously object to some of its goals and theological principles. More than three hundred years separated his world and ours, and the distance between him and us is unbridgeable in places.

In the age such as ours, in which the world is becoming more and more a global village and in which the survival of the human race and even of the planet depends on the collaboration of the followers of all religions, comparative theology (or intercultural theology, cross-cultural theology, contextual theology, ethnotheology, global theology, theology in the context of mission, or any other nomenclature) has become an urgent necessity. As theologians grope for the contours of this theology and attempt to construct it by trial and error, it would behoove them to recognize that they are not pioneers embarking upon an utterly new adventure in a terra incognita. Humbly and gratefully, they should set out to learn from the wisdom and achievements of their predecessors—Matteo Ricci, Roberto di Nobili, Alexandre de Rhodes—all the while courageously pointing out the shortcomings of these giants, just as their own successors will do to them.

---

[65] For a survey of recent trinitarian theology, see Ted Peters, *God as Trinity: Relationality and Temporality in Divine Life* (Louisville, Ky.: Westminster/John Knox Press, 1993); Anne Hunt, *The Trinity and the Paschal Mystery: A Development in Recent Catholic Theology* (Collegeville, Minn.: Liturgical Press, 1997); and idem, *What Are They Saying about the Trinity?* (New York: Paulist Press, 1998).

10

Doing Theology, Asian Style

One of the many signs of the times in our days is no doubt what has been called religious pluralism, or more precisely, a widespread and vigorous revival of religions in their multiple forms. Modernity's confident prediction of the eventual disappearance of religion as a social institution under the assault of technical rationality as well as Christian missionaries' rosy prognostication in the nineteenth century about the imminent triumph of Christianity over non-Christian religions by virtue of its radiant truth proved in hindsight to be little more than wishful thinking.[1]

Not only have religions such as Hinduism, Buddhism, Islam, and tribal religions experienced a powerful resurgence in Asia in the last few decades, at times in virulent forms of fundamentalism, but their proselytizing efforts have also spread far and wide into the West. Now temples, pagodas, and mosques adorn the landscape of almost all European and North American metropolises along with churches and synagogues. Furthermore, since religion is inextricably connected with culture and ethnicity, a society that is religiously pluralistic is multicultural and multi-ethnic as well. It is in this multicultural, multi-ethnic, and multi-religious context that the church has to carry out its evangelizing mission and ministry today in almost all corners of the world, and it is also in this context that theology is practiced as a scholarly discipline.

The burden of this chapter is to reflect on the challenges posed by cultural and religious pluralism to the church's mission and theology and to outline, from the resources and perspectives of Asia, a theological method, in particular a cross-cultural hermeneutics, that can meet these challenges. Insights will be drawn from FABC documents and the writings of selected Asian theologians. The chapter concludes with a few suggestions on how this new way of being church and of theologizing should shape the theological training of future ministers.

---

[1] For Voltaire and modern philosophers, religion represents prejudice, obscurantism, superstition, and despotism, which must be crushed (consider Voltaire's famous battle-cry, *Écrasez l'infâme!* [Crush the infamy!]). On the other hand, the missionary movement's optimism was reflected in the 1910 Edinburgh World Missionary Conference at which John R. Mott's slogan "The Evangelization of the World in This Generation" by means of preaching combined with the progress of modern science was taken as a fully realizable goal.

THE CHALLENGES OF CULTURAL AND RELIGIOUS PLURALISM
TO CHRISTIAN THEOLOGY

Karl Rahner has remarked that with Vatican II the Roman Catholic Church began an epochal shift by transforming itself from a predominantly Hellenistic-Latin (Eurocentric) institution into a "world church" characterized by cultural and religious pluralism and facing as a result a host of theological and pastoral challenges and problems unprecedented in Christian history.[2] Many factors, both within and without the church, contributed to this radical transmutation that dismantled the hegemony of Europe and North America and their churches and created, in the words of Johann Baptist Metz, a "polycentric" world and church.[3] Foremost among these factors are the constitutional separation of church and state, the decolonization of African and Asian countries in the 1950s, widespread international migration in recent decades, the maturity of so-called mission churches, the renewal of pre–Vatican II theology (in particular, the emergence of communion ecclesiology), the revival of non-Christian religions, the emergence of so-called postmodernity, and the process of globalization.[4] These elements and others have brought about a vibrant and potentially enriching yet deeply conflictive encounter of diverse peoples, cultures, and religions, resulting in widespread cultural and religious pluralism.

Challenges to Christian Doctrines

By religious pluralism is meant here not only the mere fact of the co-existence of different religions in most societies (de facto pluralism) but also, and more importantly, pluralism de jure or "in principle," to use Jacques Dupuis's expressions.[5] The issue at stake is whether the plurality of religions is to be regarded as a merely historical accident or as belonging to God's intention and purpose for humankind itself. If the former, then religious pluralism may be viewed as a curse to be overcome in order to achieve religious uniformity; if the latter, such pluralism is a blessing to be joyously and gratefully accepted, and efforts should be undertaken to promote the mutual enrichment and cross-fertilization of religions. In this way, to be religious is, as the Indian Theologi-

---

[2] Karl Rahner, "Toward a Fundamental Interpretation of Vatican II," *Theological Studies* 40 (1979), 716-27.

[3] See Johann Baptist Metz, "Unity and Diversity: Problems and Prospects for Inculturation," *Concilium* 204 (1989),79-87. For Metz, the conditions for a successful polycentrism are (1) the church must be committed to seeking freedom and justice for all; and (2) the church must acknowledge others in their otherness. It must renounce the "hermeneutics of domination" and practice the "hermeneutics of acknowledgment."

[4] For a discussion of these factors in relation to the church's mission, see David J. Bosch, *Transforming Mission: Paradigm Shifts in Theology of Mission* (Maryknoll, N.Y.: Orbis Books, 1991), 1-4.

[5] Jacques Dupuis, *Toward a Theology of Religious Pluralism* (Maryknoll, N.Y.: Orbis Books, 1997), 11. These expressions are also used in the Congregation for the Doctrine of the Faith, *Dominus Iesus* (6 August 2000), no. 4.

cal Association contends, necessarily to be interreligious,[6] and consequently a theology of religions as an interreligious theology is a "universal imperative."[7]

Religious pluralism understood in this latter sense no doubt poses serious challenges to certain traditional Christian doctrines and ultimately to the traditional way of doing theology itself. Indeed, the Congregation for the Doctrine of the Faith has alleged that religious pluralism contradicts certain Christian doctrines:

> The Church's constant missionary proclamation is endangered today by relativistic theories which seek to justify religious pluralism, not only *de facto* but also *de iure* (or *in principle*). As a consequence, it is held that certain truths have been superseded; for example, the definitive and complete character of the revelation of Jesus Christ, the nature of Christian faith as compared with that of belief in other religions, the inspired nature of the books of Sacred Scripture, the personal unity between the Eternal Word and Jesus of Nazareth, the unity of the economy of the Incarnate Word and the Holy Spirit, the unicity and salvific universality of the mystery of Jesus Christ, the universal salvific mediation of the Church, the inseparability—while recognizing the distinction—of the kingdom of God, the kingdom of Christ, and the Church, and the subsistence of the one Church of Christ in the Catholic Church.[8]

My interest here is not to evaluate the accuracy of the Congregation for the Doctrine of the Faith's claim that these central Christian doctrines are denied by de jure religious pluralism but only to note that religious pluralism, if regarded as forming part of God's plan of salvation for humanity, will entail a reinterpretation of three types of fundamental Christian beliefs, that is, those regarding God, Christ, and the church. Such reinterpretation would raise at least the following questions concerning each of them:

1. *The unity of God's plan of salvation:* Does God have one or several plans of salvation, one for Christians, and others for the adherents of other faiths? Religious pluralism would find a ready justification were the second alternative true. But would not the truth that Jesus died for all and is the savior of all be jeopardized by this hypothesis? However, granted that God has only one plan of salvation for the whole of humanity, how does God's trinitarian reality affect the unity of this one plan? Is this plan carried out only in one way? Should not

---

[6] See Kuncheria Pathil, ed., *Religious Pluralism: An Indian Christian Perspective* (Delhi: ISPCK, 1991), 338-49.

[7] See Joseph S. O'Leary, *La vérité chrétienne à l'âge du pluralisme religieux* (Paris: Cerf, 1994), 291.

[8] *Dominus Iesus*, no. 4. For an analysis and critique of *Dominus Iesus*, see "*Dominus Jesus*: A Panel Discussion," in *The Catholic Theological Society of America: Proceedings of the Fifty-Sixth Annual Convention*, ed. Richard Sparks (Macon, Ga.: Mercer University Press, 2001), 97-116; and Stephen J. Pope and Charles Helfling, eds., *Sic et Non: Encountering* Dominus Jesus (Maryknoll, N.Y.: Orbis Books, 2002).

the economy of the Son be distinguished, though not separated from, the economy of the Spirit? Is there not then a plurality in the unity of God's single plan? Even in this one plan, can one not speak of several covenants, distinct but related, not parallel but complementary, as Irenaeus does, referring to four covenants, that is, with Adam before the flood, with Noah after the flood, with Moses in the Law, and in Jesus?[9]

2. *The salvific significance of the Christ-event:* Is Jesus the unique savior? How is this uniqueness to be understood? Does it exclude any other form of mediatorship, distinct but participating in and dependent upon, Jesus' mediation?[10] Is Jesus the universal savior? How is this universality to be understood in reference to the particularity and the temporal and spatial limitations of the Incarnation? Even granted, as it must, according to the Christian faith, the personal identity between Jesus and the Logos, still it may be asked whether and how it is possible to see the economy of the Incarnate Word as the sacrament of the wider and, spatially and temporally, more universal economy of the unincarnate Logos *(Logos asarkos)?* In this context is it impossible to regard the Buddha and other founders of non-Christian religions as "salvation figures" mediating "salvation" to their adherents?

3. *The Church as a necessary instrument of salvation:* The Christian faith professes the church to be the sacrament, that is, the sign and instrument of the union between humanity and God and among human being themselves. But this truth of the church as a necessary instrument of salvation does not exclude but rather includes the possibility that non-Christians and nonbelievers may be saved, as Vatican II teaches.[11] The question is whether these individuals are saved in spite of or thanks to their religions by believing the truths they teach and by practicing the commandments they enjoin. If it is theologically possible and even necessary to affirm the second alternative, may not these religions be said

---

[9] See Irenaeus, *Adversus haereses* III, 11, 8.

[10] *Dominus Iesus*, following John Paul II's *Redemptoris missio*, no. 5, admits the possibility of "participated mediation" and says: "The Second Vatican Council, in fact, has stated that: 'the unique mediation of the Redeemer does not exclude, but rather gives rise to a manifold cooperation which is but a participation in this one source.' The content of this participated mediation should be explored more deeply, but must remain always consistent with the principle of Christ's unique mediation" (no. 14). In light of this participated mediation, it is curious to read further that "in this sense, one can and must say that Jesus Christ has a significance and a value for the human race and its history, which are unique and singular, proper to him alone, *exclusive*, universal, and absolute" (no. 15, italics added). If a mediation is "exclusive," how can it be "participated" at the same time?

[11] "Those who, through no fault of their own, do not know the Gospel of Christ or his Church, but who nevertheless seek God with a sincere heart, and, moved by grace, try in their actions to do his will as they know it through the dictates of their conscience—those too may achieve eternal salvation. Nor shall divine providence deny the assistance necessary to those who, without any fault of theirs, have not yet arrived at an explicit knowledge of God, and who, not without grace, strive to lead a good life" (*LG*, no. 16).

to be "ways," or "channels," or "means" of salvation for their adherents? Are these religions in their own ways "sacraments" of God's salvation?[12]

Challenges to Theological Method

As important and interesting as these three themes and issues are, my goal in this chapter is not to develop a doctrinal basis for a theology of de jure religious pluralism that remains within the bounds of orthodoxy.[13] Rather, my intent is to outline a theological methodology that is both appropriate for the normative expressions of the Christian faith and adequate to the contemporary context of religious pluralism. Indeed, as Dupuis has rightly pointed out,

> the theology of religions is not a new theme added to traditional theological discourse, but a new *way* of theologizing—like a new *method* of theologizing in a situation of religious pluralism. Such an "interreligious hermeneutics" invites us to broaden the whole discourse; it should also enable us to discover at a new depth the cosmic dimensions of the divine plan and of the gifts God has lavished and continues to lavish throughout history.[14]

Interestingly enough, *Dominus Iesus* too argues that the alleged errors of religious pluralism are rooted in methodological approaches:

> The roots of these problems are to be found in certain presuppositions of both a philosophical and theological nature, which hinder the understanding and acceptance of the revealed truth. Some of these can be mentioned: the conviction of the elusiveness and inexpressibility of divine truth, even

---

[12] *DP* seems to favor this position: "From the mystery of unity it follows that all men and women who are saved share, though differently, in the same mystery of salvation in Jesus Christ through his Spirit. Christians know this through their faith, while others remain unaware that Jesus Christ is the source of their salvation. The mystery reaches out to them, in a way known to God, through the invisible action of the Spirit of Christ. Concretely, it will be in the sincere practice of what is good in their own religious traditions and by following the dictates of their conscience that the members of other religions respond positively to God's invitation and receive salvation in Jesus Christ, even while they do not recognize or acknowledge him as their savior (cf. *Ad Gentes* 3, 9, 11)." For the English text of *DP* as well as an insightful commentary by Jacques Dupuis on this document, see William Burrows, ed., *Redemption and Dialogue: Reading* Redemptoris Missio *and* Dialogue and Proclamation (Maryknoll, N.Y.: Orbis Books, 1993), 93-118 (text), 119-58 (commentary).

[13] I am persuaded that Jacques Dupuis's "trinitarian Christology" as developed in his *Toward a Christian Theology of Religious Pluralism* succeeds in both maintaining the traditional teaching on Jesus as the universal savior and responding to the challenges of religious pluralism. See my review of this work in *Dialogue and Alliance* 14/1 (2000), 121-22.

[14] J. Dupuis, "One God, One Christ, Convergent Ways," *Theology Digest* 47/3 (2000), 211. See his fuller text, "Le pluralism religieux dans le plan divin de salut," *Revue théologique de Louvain* 29 (1998), 484-505.

by Christian revelation; relativistic attitudes toward truth itself, according to which what is true for some would not be true for others; the radical opposition posited between the logical mentality of the West and the symbolic mentality of the East; the subjectivism which, by regarding reason as the only source of knowledge, becomes incapable of raising its "gaze to the heights, not daring to rise to the truth of being"; the difficulty in understanding and accepting the presence of definitive and eschatological events in history; the metaphysical emptying of the historical incarnation of the Eternal Logos, reduced to a mere appearing of God in history; the eclecticism of those who, in theological research, uncritically absorb ideas from a variety of philosophical and theological contexts without regard for consistency, systematic connection, or compatibility with Christian truth; finally, the tendency to read and to interpret Sacred Scripture outside the Tradition and Magisterium of the Church (no. 4).

Once again, my interest here is not to evaluate the validity of these charges.[15] Rather, it is to note that both *Dominus Iesus* and Jacques Dupuis, a putative target of its censures, are agreed that de jure religious pluralism, whatever its theological merits, operates on (according to the Congregation for the Doctrine of the Faith) or requires (according to J. Dupuis) a methodology different from that of traditional theology.

Before expounding on the method of Asian theologies, it would be helpful to spell out, albeit cursorily, the major features of some the theological methods that have been widely in use in the West. These methods will provide a foil for highlighting the distinctive characteristics and procedures of Asian theologies. Christian theology as *fides quaerens intellectum* is by definition an attempt to mediate the Christian creed, cult, code, and community as embodied in scripture and tradition to the changing local cultures. To put it in David Tracy's language, the task of theology is to correlate critically the two principal sources of Christian discourse, namely, the "Christian texts" and "common human experience and language."[16] Variety in the ways this correlation is carried out as well as the different kinds of resources *(loci)* that are pressed into service in this endeavor give rise to different types of theology.[17] While all theologies are necessarily contextual, there is a whole spectrum in which they can be located, from the most conservative to the most progressive, depending on the emphasis each of them places on either fidelity to scripture and tradition or on identification with

---

[15] In general terms each of the eight criticisms against the philosophical and theological presuppositions of religious pluralism given in *Dominus Iesus* can be countered by anyone tolerably familiar with various theologies of religious pluralism, especially of the "pluralistic" stamp (as proposed, for example, by John Hick, Wilfred Cantwell Smith, and Paul Knitter), with a *sic et non*.

[16] See David Tracy, *Blessed Rage for Order* (New York: The Seabury Press, 1975), 43.

[17] Tracy himself presents five models of contemporary theology on the basis of this correlation: orthodox, liberal, neo-orthodox, radical, and revisionist (see *Blessed Rage for Order*, 24-34).

the changing local cultures.[18] Needless to say, traditional or classical theology, while not inattentive to the changing cultural contexts, lays a greater if not exclusive stress on fidelity to the scripture, regarded as the *norma normans non normata* of theology, and to the authoritative teachings of the tradition (in particular the magisterium) and claims to be a universally valid *theologia perennis*. The overriding concern of classical theology is a total appropriateness of its expressions to the "Christian texts."[19]

It is this priority given to the scripture and tradition that distinguishes classical theology or Christian doctrine, whether it is conceived as *sapientia* (Augustine), *sacra doctrina* (Thomas Aquinas), or *scientia conclusionum* (neo-Scholasticism). The dialogue partner of choice between Christian faith and culture is philosophy, whether Platonic or Aristotelean or Stoic. The starting point of classical theology is either the scripture (in Augustine and Thomas) or church teachings (in neo-Scholasticism), and its preferred genres are exegetical, homiletical, and commentarial.[20] Little attention is given to the socio-political and economic contexts of the authoritative sources to be explicated, the theologians who interpret them, and the readers who are targeted, and to how these situations have acted as powerful forces in the formation, transmission, interpretation, and reception of these sources. No question is asked about the process whereby these sources and not others became authoritative (for example, the canonization of the Bible) and about what and whose vested interests have been served by the acts of knowledge implicated in interpretation.[21]

---

[18] On the basis of these various emphases, Stephen Bevans discerns five models of contextual theologies, which he terms "translation, anthropological, praxis, synthetic, and transcendental models." To these Bevans adds the "countercultural" model (see Stephen Bevans, *Models of Contextual Theology*, rev. and exp. ed. [Maryknoll, N.Y.: Orbis Books, 2002]).

[19] Tracy distinguishes between criteria of "appropriateness" to the Christian texts and criteria of "adequacy" to the human experience and language (see *Blessed Rage for Order*, 64-73).

[20] This is true most of all of Augustine, who develops elaborate principles for biblical hermeneutics (e.g., in *De Doctrina Christiana*), but also of Thomas Aquinas, for whom theology is mainly *sacra scriptura* or *sacra pagina* and Sacred Scripture is used as an authority, *proprie* and *ex necessitate*. For a typical treatment of the sources of neo-Scholastic theology, see Melchior Cano (1509-60), *De locis theologicis* (Salamanca, 1563). As is well known, Cano's posthumous work argues that there are ten authoritative sources from which theological arguments may be derived: seven properly theological sources (i.e., scripture, oral tradition, the Catholic church, the general councils, the Roman church, the fathers of the church, and the Scholastic theologians), and three extrinsic sources (i.e., human reason, philosophers, and history). For a brief and lucid discussion of Augustinian, Thomistic, and neo-Scholastic theological methods, see Francis Schüssler Fiorenza, "Systematic Theology: Task and Methods," in *Systematic Theology: Roman Catholic Perspectives*, ed. F. S. Fiorenza and John P. Galvin (Minneapolis: Fortress Press, 1989), 10-35.

[21] For a helpful presentation of postmodern epistemology, see John Phillips, *Contested Knowledge: A Guide to Critical Theory* (New York: Zed Books, 2000). For reflections on how critical theory affects theology, see Graham Ward, *Theology and Contemporary Critical Theory*, 2d ed. (New York: St. Martin's Press, 2000).

Of course, it would be anachronistic to expect Augustine, or Thomas, or neo-Scholastic theologians to approach the *loci theologici* with this critical sociology of knowledge in mind before the dawn of historical consciousness and the "turn to the subject" that are the hallmarks of modernity. But it is precisely this anthropological turn, at first in the subjective and personal, and subsequently in the collective and socio-political dimensions of human existence, that separates the classical theologies and their methods from the contemporary, both modern and postmodern, approaches to theology, including the transcendental, hermeneutical, analytical, correlation, and liberation theologies.[22]

It is within this turn to the subject in its socio-political and economic contexts and its attendant constructivist epistemology that emphasizes the cultural conditioning and the historicity of all knowledge that pluralism is seen not as an accidental fact of history but as a constitutive and intrinsic dimension of human knowing. This epistemological pluralism, which is vigorously propounded by postmodern philosophers, in opposition to the modern ideal of universal and instrumental rationality, is extended to the field of religion and highlights religious pluralism not just as de facto but also as de jure.[23] The dangers of such a postmodern sociology of knowledge are, as has been pointed out by its critics, relativism, skepticism, and nihilism. In the words of Jean-François Lyotard, there has been a death of "metanarratives."[24]

As will be shown below, Asian theologies stand in continuity with various modern and postmodern theologies in their emphasis on the unavoidable embeddedness of the Christian faith in socio-political and economic contexts and in privileging the criterion of adequacy to the contemporary "human experience and language." In this sense they constitute a departure from, though by no means a total rejection of, the methodology of the classical theologies of Augustine, Thomas, and neo-Scholasticism. Like Latin American liberation theology, to which they are very much indebted, Asian theologies understand themselves as, in the words of Gustavo Gutiérrez, "critical reflection on praxis." Thus, they are differentiated from, though not opposed to, theologies practiced as "wisdom" and "rational knowledge."[25]

---

[22] For an exposition and critique of these five methods, see Fiorenza, "Systematic Theology," 35-65.

[23] For a helpful introduction to postmodern philosophies and their impact on theology, see Stanley J. Grenz, *A Primer on Postmodernism* (Grand Rapids, Mich.: Eerdmans, 1996); Paul Lakeland, *Theology and Critical Theory: The Discourse of the Church* (Nashville, Tenn.: Abingdon Press, 199); idem, *Postmodernity: Christian Identity in a Fragmented Age* (Minneapolis: Fortress Press, 1997); and John E. Thiel, *Nonfoundationalism* (Minneapolis: Fortress Press, 1994).

[24] See Jean-François Lyotard, *The Postmodern Condition: A Report on Knowledge*, trans. Geoff Bennington and Brian Massumi (Minneapolis: University of Minnesota Press, 1984).

[25] See Gustavo Gutiérrez, *A Theology of Liberation*, trans. Sister Caridad Inda and John Eagleson, rev. ed. with a new intro. (Maryknoll, N.Y.: Orbis Books, 1988), 4-11. Gutiérrez says: "Theology as a critical reflection on Christian praxis in the light of the Word does not replace the other functions of theology, such as wisdom and rational knowledge; rather it presupposes and needs them" (11).

The crucial question is whether in defending epistemological and religious pluralism, Asian theologies will run aground on the shoals of relativism, indifferentism, and syncretism, and consequently be forced to deny the basic Christian beliefs, as *Dominus Iesus* alleges religious pluralism to do. To answer this question and to understand the method of Asian theologies in general, we now turn to the ways in which Asian theologians understand the task of theology, their notion of context, the resources they employ, and their hermeneutical procedure.[26]

DOING THEOLOGY IN ASIA IN THE CONTEXT
OF CULTURAL AND RELIGIOUS PLURALISM

As thinkers usually come to reflect on their methods only after long practice and not at the beginning of their careers, so too the FABC and its various offices as well Asian theologians did not set out with a detailed elaboration of their theological approaches and methods, like Athena sprung full-grown from the head of Zeus. Rather, they reflected on them only gradually, over time, as they became more and more conscious of the need to do theology in Asia in ways different from those of Western theologies.

At first, Asian theologians, both in Asia and the United States, began with a trenchant critique of Western theologies. Tissa Balasuriya, a Sri Lankan Oblate of Mary Immaculate, decries Western theologies as largely irrelevant to Asians, tribalistic, church-centered, clericalist, patriarchal, pro-capitalistic, devoid of socio-economic analysis, and lacking orientation toward praxis.[27] Aloysius Pieris, a Sri Lankan Jesuit, regards Western theologies as unfit for the Asian situation of crushing poverty and deep religiousness.[28] Choan-Seng Song, a Presbyterian Taiwanese, faults Western theologies for being overly rationalistic and lacking theological imagination. Jung Young Lee, a Korean Methodist, criticizes Western theologies for their exclusivism based on the Aristotelean logic of the excluded middle.[29] Many Asian women theologians reject Western theologies' patriarchal

---

[26] For a collection of the final statements of FABC's plenary assemblies as well as assorted documents of FABC's various institutes, see Gaudencio Rosales and C. G. Arévalo, eds., *For All Peoples of Asia: Federation of Asian Bishops' Conferences. Documents from 1970 to 1991*, vol. 1 (Maryknoll, N.Y.: Orbis Books, 1991); Franz-Josef Eilers, ed., *For All the Peoples of Asia: Federation of Asian Bishops' Conferences. Documents from 1992 to 1996*, vol. 2 (Quezon City, Philippines: Claretian Publications, 1997); and idem, ed. *For All the Peoples of Asia: Federation of Asian Bishops' Documents from 1997 to 2001*, vol. 3 (Quezon City, Philippines: Claretian Publications, 2002). Of special interest to our theme is the document of the Office of Theological Concerns of the FABC, no. 96, entitled *Methodology: Asian Christian Theology. Doing Theology in Asia Today* (January 2000). The paper is available from the FABC, 16 Caine Road, Hong Kong. E-mail: hkdavc@hk.super.net.

[27] See Tissa Balasuriya, "Towards the Liberation of Theology in Asia," in *Asia's Struggle for Full Humanity: Towards a Relevant Theology*, ed. Virginia Fabella (Maryknoll, N.Y.: Orbis Books, 1980), 26; and idem, *Planetary Theology* (Maryknoll, N.Y.: Orbis Books, 1984), 2-10.

[28] See Aloysius Pieris, *An Asian Theology of Liberation* (Maryknoll, N.Y.: Orbis Books, 1988), 81-83.

[29] See Jung Young Lee, *Marginality: The Key to Multicultural Theology* (Minneapolis: Fortress Press, 1995), 64-70.

image of God, predominantly male interpretation of the Bible, overemphasis on the maleness of Christ, and propagation of an anti-woman Mary cult.[30]

To some, these criticisms may sound too harsh or unjustified. But the point here is not whether they are accurate or undeserved; rather, it is that there is a widespread perception that Euro-American theologies are not meaningful or relevant to Asian peoples. A significant group of Asian theologians, most of whom belong to the Ecumenical Association of Third World Theologians (EATWOT), have recently attempted to construct an alternative theology based on Asian methods and resources.

Prior to these theologians, there have been others, mostly Indian, who have undertaken the task of formulating a Christian theology on the basis of their own cultures. For example, attempts have been made to understand the Trinity in terms of the *trimurti* of Brahma, Vishnu, and Shiva. Other theologians have sought to present Christ in terms of Hindu theology, for example, Jesus as Prajapati (Lord of creatures), as Cit (consciousness), as Avatara (incarnation), as Isvara (the cosmic Christ), as Guru (teacher), as Adi Purasha (the first person), as Shakti (power), as eternal Om (logos), as Avalokiteśuara (the bodhisattva who postpones enlightenment in order to help others achieve nirvana).[31]

Since the 1970s, a younger generation of Asian theologians, including several women, mostly influenced by Latin American liberation theologies, have applied new methods and brought new insights to enrich the older, more culture-based approaches. The result is a new and more holistic way of doing theology not only *in* but also *of* and *for* Asia. Of course, no Christian theology can be entirely new, but there are undeniably novel features in this emerging Asian theology that need to be highlighted as important contributions to the way of doing theology in the context of cultural and religious pluralism.[32]

---

[30] See Virginia Fabella and Sun Ai Lee Park, eds., *We Dare to Dream: Doing Theology as Asian Women* (Hong Kong: Asian Women's Resource Centre for Culture and Theology, 1989), 149.

[31] For a collection of recent essays on Asian Christology, see R. S. Sugirtharajah, ed., *Asian Faces of Jesus* (Maryknoll, N.Y.: Orbis Books, 1993); A. Alangaram, *Christ of the Asian Peoples: Towards an Asian Contextual Christology Based on the Documents of the FABC* (Bangalore, India: Asian Trading Corporation, 1999). For a discussion of Asian Christologies, see Peter C. Phan, "Jesus the Christ with an Asian Face," *Theological Studies* 57 (1996), 399-430.

[32] For a general discussion of recent Asian theology, see Peter C. Phan, "Experience and Theology: An Asian Liberation Perspective," *Zeitschrift für Missionswissenschaft und Religionswissenschaft* 77/2 (1993), 99-121. See also Barbara and Leon Howell, *Southeast Asians Speak Out: Hope and Despair in Many Lands* (New York: Friendship Press, 1975); Gerald H. Anderson, eds., *Asian Voices in Christian Theology* (Maryknoll, N.Y.: Orbis Books, 1976); Douglas Elwood, ed., *What Asian Christians Are Thinking: A Theological Source Book* (Quezon City, The Philippines: Newday Publishers, 1976); Douglas Elwood, *Asian Christian Theology: Emerging Themes* (Philadelphia: The Westminster Press, 1980); Dayanandan T. Francis and F. J. Balsudaram, eds., *Asian Expressions of Christian Commitment* (Madras: The Christian Literature Society, 1992); and R. S. Sugirtharajah, ed., *Frontiers in Asian Christian Theology: Emerging Trends* (Maryknoll, N.Y.: Orbis Books, 1994).

Pluralism, Not Relativism, in Theological Method

The first important point made by the FABC's Office of Theological Concerns is that while pluralism is intrinsic to the multidimensionality of human experience, by which "a variety of viewpoints, explanations or perspectives are offered to account for the same reality," it is not relativism and indeed is opposed to it: "Relativism holds that there are many truths which vary according to the subjects who hold different opinions of reality. Such relativism destroys the rich meaning of pluralism."[33] It goes on to say:

> Pluralism need not always entail a radical subjectivism or relativism, in the sense of claiming that all points are equally valid. . . . Today there are persons and groups who hold all reality to be relative. For such persons and groups, pluralism means relativism, in the sense that they claim all points of view are equally valid. Such philosophical or theological claims are to be rejected; and, in fact, all major Asian religions condemn such relativizing of reality, especially the relativizing of basic human values.[34]

Invoking Vatican II's encouragement to promote a "legitimate variety" in theology as well as in all other expressions of church life, FABC's various offices or institutes have sought to foster diversity in unity and unity in diversity as both condition and effect of harmony, a fundamental value in Asian thinking and way of life. They have consistently and repeatedly emphasized the need to promote what they called "a stance of *receptive pluralism*,"[35] that is, an attitude of openness to and acceptance of the working of the Spirit beyond the boundaries of the church. They see that the Asian churches have the "key challenge and urgent task of building up a pluralist community where peoples of diverse faiths, cultures, and classes live together in love and justice."[36] The Bishops' Institute for Interreligious Affairs pointed out in 1988 that pluralism is not "something to be regretted and abolished, but to be rejoiced [in] and promoted, since it represents richness and strength" and is essential to harmony:

> One of the obstacles to harmony is the attitude of exclusivity, not willing to open oneself and see the beauty and truth in the other. . . . For the promotion of harmony, it is important to cultivate an all-embracing and complementary way of thinking. This is something very characteristic of Asian traditions which consider the various dimensions of reality not as contradictory, but as complementary (yin yang).[37]

The Office of Theological Concerns notes, however, that in recognizing the value of pluralism in theology, the church cannot allow doctrinal irresponsibility or indifferentism. It offers the following criteria:

---

[33] FABC, *Methodology*, 5.
[34] Ibid., 6.
[35] *For All the Peoples of Asia,* 1:261.
[36] Ibid., 1:300.
[37] Ibid., 1:322.

Legitimate theological pluralism ought to meet the basic standards of revelation (as conveyed through Scripture and Tradition), of the sensus fidelium (as contained in the faith of the People of God as a whole), and of the Magisterium of the Church. We need to emphasize three basic criteria: Revelation, the sensus fidelium, and the Magisterium. They help us differentiate a legitimate pluralism of theological expression from a pluralism which would destroy the doctrinal unity of the Church.[38]

Asian Integral Pastoral Approach: A New Way of Being Church in Asia

The crucial question is therefore how to develop this legitimate theological pluralism. In 1993, at a consultation on integral formation in Petaling Jaya, Malaysia, a fundamental approach was articulated under the name of Asian Integral Pastoral Approach (ASIPA), which aims at promoting a "new way of being church" in Asia.[39] This new ecclesiology consists mainly in making the church, in the words of the fifth plenary assembly of the FABC in 1990,

> a *communion of communities*, where laity, Religious and clergy recognize and accept each other as sisters and brothers . . . a *participatory* Church where the gifts that the Holy Spirit gives to all the faithful—lay, Religious and clerics alike—are recognized and activated . . . a Church that faithfully and lovingly *witnesses* to the Risen Lord Jesus and reaches out to people of other faiths and persuasions in a dialogue of life towards the integral liberation of all . . . a leaven of transformation in this world and . . . a *prophetic sign* daring to point beyond this world to the ineffable Kingdom that is yet fully to come.[40]

"Asian" in this approach means a deep sensitivity to the peculiar situation of Asian countries: socio-political and economic conditions of oppression, exploitation and poverty; religious pluralism; and rich cultural traditions. Hence, the necessity of Christian mission conducted in the mode of a triple, intrinsically connected dialogue: with the poor and the marginalized people of Asia, in particular women and youth (liberation and integral development); with Asian religions (interreligious dialogue); and with Asian cultures (inculturation). "Integral" means wholeness in communicating the contents of the Christian faith, collaboration among all members of the church, and coordination of church structures at different levels. "Pastoral" emphasizes the primary goal of being church in Asia in a new way, that is, by becoming a participatory church. "Approach" refers to a pastoral process made up of various but related programs to realize this new way of being church in all the local churches.

---

[38] FABC, *Methodology*, 10.
[39] On ASIPA, see *For All the Peoples of Asia*, 2:107-11, 137-39. The ASIPA was developed along the lines of the Lumko Approach, a pastoral training program, that Bishop Fritz Lobinger and Fr. Oswald Hirmer originated to promote lay participation through Basic Christian Communities in South Africa. See also Chapter 2 herein.
[40] *For All the Peoples of Asia*, 1:287-88.

It is important to note that it is in this context of ASIPA and its proposed new way of being church that Asian theologies conceive their task and their methodology. Like their Latin American colleagues, Asian theologians insist that theology is only a second act critically reflecting on the first act, which is commitment to and solidarity with those who struggle for full humanity. Since this praxis is inspired by God's preferential love for the poor and the oppressed realized in and by Jesus Christ, it may be called *theopraxis*. Theology is not "God-talk" based on some canonical texts in search of a practical application. Rather, it originates from Christian praxis, moves to critical reflection, and returns to praxis, and the circle of praxis-critical theory-praxis repeats itself again and again in ever new contexts. Furthermore, in light of the peculiar context of Asia as described above, which is not only economic poverty but also religious and cultural pluralism, Asian theologies will have to include, besides liberation, interreligious dialogue and inculturation as their essential tasks and develop an appropriate methodology for such a triple dialogue.

Contextual Realities as Resources and Sources of Theology

Traditionally, *context* has been used as merely the background against which theology was done. It was understood as the religious and cultural situation to which the Christian message was to be adapted or applied in the process of accommodation—Vatican II's *aptatio*. A particular theology—most often the Western-European kind—claimed universal validity for itself and was imposed, through translation and the use of manuals in seminary training, on all parts of the church as the guarantee of the unity of the Christian creed, code, cult, and community. Such a theology's claim to universal normativity, besides being invalidated by the irremediable particularity of its social location, effectively prevents the formation of genuinely local theologies, since the context is treated as something extrinsic to theology itself.[41]

In contrast, the FABC's Office of Theological Concerns holds that "context, or contextual realities, are considered resources for theology *(loci theologici)* together with the Christian sources of Scripture and Tradition. Contextual realities become resources of theology insofar as they embody and manifest the presence and action of God and his Spirit."[42] It spells out the use of these resources in some detail:

> As Asian Christians, we do theology together with Asian realities as resources, insofar as we discern in them God's presence, action and the work of the Spirit. We use these resources in correlation with the Bible

---

[41] The following is the frank assessment of European/Western theology by the Office of Theological Concerns: "The impressive unity in the theological enterprise could only be achieved at the expense of theological pluralism. It is striking how Eurocentric, and even parochial, this theological enterprise now appears. The claim of being *the* universal way of doing theology is negated by the obvious limitation that it really is restricted to the particular context in which it originated" (see FABC, *Methodology*, 28).

[42] Ibid., 30.

and the Tradition of the Church. Use of these resources implies a tremendous change in theological methodology. The cultures of peoples, the history of their struggles, their religions, their religious scriptures, oral traditions, popular religiosity, economic and political realities and world events, historical personages, stories of oppressed people crying for justice, freedom, dignity, life, and solidarity become resources of theology, and assume methodological importance in our context. The totality of life is the raw material of theology. God is redemptively present in the totality of human life. This implies theologically that one is using "context" (or contextual realities) in a new way.[43]

Asian Resources for Theology

These Asian contextual realities, which are the *loci theologici* of Asian theologies and are to be correlated with the specifically Christian sources of scripture and tradition, can be classified according to their provenance: (1) culture with its manifold expressions; (2) religions with their scriptures, oral traditions, rituals, and popular religiosity; (3) social movements, in particular women's, tribal, ecological, the poor's, and popular movements.[44] In what follows, I highlight some of these resources, bearing in mind what Choan-Seng Song has said about them: "Resources in Asia for doing theology are unlimited. What is limited is our theological imagination. Powerful is the voice crying out of the abyss of the Asian heart, but powerless is the power of our theological imaging."[45]

The first resource is the billions of Asian peoples themselves, with their stories of joy and suffering, hope and despair, love and hatred, freedom and oppression, stories not recorded in history books written by victors but kept alive in the "dangerous memory" (Johann Baptist Metz) of the "underside of history" (Gustavo Gutiérrez). Preferential love is reserved for "the migrants, refugees, the displaced ethnic and indigenous peoples . . . exploited workers, especially the child laborers."[46] In recent years, people as doers of theology have assumed a special role in Asian theology.[47] Korean theologians have developed a distinctive theology called *minjung* theology as a faith reflection of, by, and for the masses in their struggle against oppression.[48] In India, there is *Dalit* theology, a

---

[43] Ibid., 29.

[44] See ibid., 30-37.

[45] Choan-Seng Song, *Theology from the Womb of Asia* (Maryknoll, N.Y.: Orbis Books, 1986), 16.

[46] FABC, *Christian Discipleship in Asia Today: Service to Life,* final statement of the FABC's sixth plenary assembly (1995), in *For All the Peoples of Asia,* 2:4.

[47] For reflections on "theology by the people," see S. Amirtham and John S. Pobee, eds., *Theology by the People* (Geneva: WCC, 1986); F. Castillo, *Theologie aus der Praxis des Folkes* (Munich: Kaiser, 1978); and Ernesto Cardenal, *The Gospel in Solentiname* (Maryknoll, N.Y.: Orbis Books, 1976).

[48] *Minjung,* a Korean word, is often left untranslated. By *minjung* are meant "the oppressed, exploited, dominated, discriminated against, alienated and suppressed politically, economically, socially, culturally, and intellectually, like women, ethnic groups, the poor, workers and farmers, including intellectuals themselves." See Chung Hyun

liberation theology that incorporates the sufferings of the people known as the "casteless," the "fifth caste," the "scheduled caste," who form the majority of Indian Christians.[49] In addition, there is also in many Asian countries tribal theology, which calls attention to the oppression of the indigenous peoples.[50]

The second resource is a subset of the first, namely, the stories of Asian women and girls. Given the pervasive patriarchalism of Asian society, the stories of oppression and poverty of Asian women occupy a special place in Asian theology. As Chung Hyun Kyung has said, "Women's truth was generated by their *epistemology from the broken body*."[51] First, the women's stories (Korean *minjung* theologian Kim Young Bok calls them "socio-biography") are carefully listened to; a critical social analysis is then carried out to discern the complex interconnections in the evil structures that produce women's oppression; and finally, theological reflection is done on them from the relevant teachings of the Bible.[52]

The third resource is the sacred texts and practices of Asian religions that have nourished the life of Asian peoples for thousands of years before the coming of Christianity into their lands and since: the Hindu *prasthanatraya* (triple

---

Kyung, "'Han-pu-ri': Doing Theology from Korean Women's Perspective," in Fabella and Lee Park, *We Dare to Dream*, 138-39. For a discussion of *minjung* theology, see Jung Young Lee, ed., *An Emerging Theology in World Perspective: Commentary on Korean Minjung Theology* (Mystic, Conn.: Twenty-Third Publications, 1988); and David Kwang-sun Suh, *The Korean Minjung in Christ* (Hong Kong: Christian Conference of Asia, 1991).

[49] The *Dalits* are considered too polluted to participate in the social life of Indian society; they are untouchable. Between two-thirds and three-quarters of the Indian Christian community are *Dalits*. On *Dalit* theology, see Sathianathan Clarke, *Dalit and Christianity: Subaltern Religion and Liberation Theology in India* (New Delhi: Oxford University Press, 1998); James Massey, *Towards Dalit Hermeneutics: Re-reading the Text, the History, and the Literature* (Delhi: ISPCK, 1994); idem, *Dalits in India: Religion as a Source of Bondage or Liberation with Special Reference to Christians* (New Delhi: Mahohar, 1995); and M. E. Prabhakar, *Towards a Dalit Theology* (Madras: Gurukul, 1989).

[50] On tribal theology, see Nirmal Minz, *Rise Up, My People, and Claim the Promise: The Gospel among the Tribes of India* (Delhi: ISPCK, 1997); and K. Thanzauva, *Theology of Community: Tribal Theology in the Making* (Aizawl, Mizoram: Mizo Theological Conference, 1997). See also Sugirtharajah, *Frontiers in Asian Christian Theology*, 11-62. The FABC's seventh plenary assembly (3-12 January 2000) draws attention to the plight of the indigenous people: "Today, in many countries of Asia, their right to land is threatened and their fields are laid bare; they themselves are subjected to economic exploitation, excluded from political participation and reduced to the status of second-class citizens. Detribalization, a process of imposed alienation from their social and cultural roots, is even a hidden policy in several places. Their cultures are under pressure by dominant cultures and 'Great Traditions.' Mighty projects for the exploitation of mineral, forest and water resources, often in areas which have been the home of the tribal population, have generally worked to the disadvantage of the tribals" (see *A Renewed Church in Asia: A Mission of Love and Service*, FABC Papers, no. 93 [Hong Kong: FABC, 2000], 11).

[51] Chung Hyun Kyung, *Struggle to Be the Sun Again: Introducing Asian Women's Theology* (Maryknoll, N.Y.: Orbis Books, 1990), 104.

[52] See ibid., 103-9.

canon) of the *Upanishads, Brahma Sutra,* and the *Bhagavadgita*; the Buddhist *tripitaka* (the three baskets) of the *vinaya pitaka,* the *sutta pitaka,* and the *abhidhama*; the Confucian *Analects* and the Five Classics; and the Taoist *Tao Te Ching* and *Chuang Tzu,* just to mention the most widely known Asian classics. These writings, together with their innumerable commentaries, serve as an inexhaustible fountain of wisdom for Christian theology.

Intimately connected with these religious texts is the fourth resource known as philosophy since in Asia religion and philosophy are inextricably conjoined. Philosophy is a way of life and religion is a world view, each being both *darsana* (view of life) and *pratipada* (way of life). To explicate Christian beliefs, Asian theology makes use of, for instance, the metaphysics of *yin* and *yang* rather than Greek metaphysics or process philosophy.[53]

The fifth resource is Asian monastic traditions, with their rituals, ascetic practices, and social commitment. This last element, namely, social commitment, needs emphasizing. Pieris has consistently argued that the most appropriate form of inculturation of Christianity in Asia is not the Latin model of incarnation in a non-Christian *culture,* nor the Greek model of assimilation of a non-Christian *philosophy,* nor the North European model of accommodation to a non-Christian *religiousness.* What is required of Asian Christians is the monastic model of participation in a non-Christian *spirituality.* However, this monastic spirituality is not to be understood as a withdrawal from the world into leisurely prayer centers or ashrams. Asian monks have always been involved in socio-political struggles through their *voluntary* poverty and their participation in social and cultural activities.[54] At any rate, interreligious dialogue in all its multiple forms is an essential element of an Asian theology.[55]

The sixth resource is Asian cultures in general, with their immense treasures of stories, myths, folklore, symbols, poetry, songs, visual art, and dance. The use of these cultural artifacts adds a very distinctive voice to Christian theology coming from the deepest yearnings of the peoples of Asia. For example, *minjung* theology has made a creative use of real-life stories and folktales. These stories are narrated and sung at Korean mask dances *(talch'um),* opera *(pansori),* or shamanistic rituals *(kut).*

Asian theologies can make full use of these and other contextual realities of Asia because of two theological convictions. As the Office of Theological Concerns has pointed out, "First, Christian faith considers the whole universe, all of creation, as a manifestation of God's glory and goodness," and "secondly, Christian faith affirms that God is the Lord of history . . . that God, who created the universe and humankind, is present and active in and through

---

[53] See, for instance, Jung Young Lee, *A Theology of Change: A Christian Concept of God from an Eastern Perspective* (Maryknoll, N.Y.: Orbis Books, 1979); and idem, *The Trinity in Asian Perspective* (Nashville, Tenn.: Abingdon Press, 1996).

[54] See Aloysius Pieris, *An Asian Theology of Liberation* (Maryknoll, N.Y.: Orbis Books, 1988), 51-58; and idem, *Love Meets Wisdom* (Maryknoll, N.Y.: Orbis Books, 1988), 61-72; 89-96.

[55] See Chapter 2 herein.

his Spirit in the whole gamut of human history, leading all to the eschaton of God's kingdom."[56]

TOWARD AN ASIAN BIBLICAL HERMENEUTICS

The "Pastoral Cycle"

These contextual realities are not transparent by themselves. Because of their ambiguity and their sinfulness, they require discernment and interpretation. On the other hand, the gospel itself does not provide ready-made solutions for the social, political, economic, and cultural problems of contemporary Asia. As the Bishops' Institute for Social Action put it in 1975, "The need has been felt to analyze critically and technically the problems we are faced with. We cannot jump from our faith experience to the concrete decisions of social action without due technical investigations and due account of the ideologies under whose influence we are living."[57] As guide for this process of discernment and interpretation, the FABC has developed a four-step method called the pastoral cycle.

The first step, *exposure-immersion*, exposes the theologians to and immerses them in the concrete situation of the poor with whom and for whom they work: "Exposure is like a doctor's visit for diagnosis; immersion is like the visit of a genuine friend entering into the dialogue-of-life. Exposure-Immersion . . . follows the basic principle of the Incarnation."[58] The purpose of this first step is to provide the theologians with an experiential knowledge of and concrete solidarity with their suffering people. This is the perspective in which the theological labor will be carried out, not from some abstract doctrinal principles.

The second step is *social analysis*. The objects to be investigated include the social, economic, political, cultural, and religious systems in society as well as the signs of the times, the events of history, and the needs and aspirations of the people. Indeed, without this technical analysis, the FABC's international congress on mission in 1979 in Manila pointed out, "the naivete of all too many Christians regarding the structural causes of poverty and injustice often leads them to the adoption of ineffective measures in their attempts to promote justice

---

[56] FABC, *Methodology*, 38. The text adduces two celebrated statements of John Paul II. First, "the Spirit's presence and activity affect not only individuals but also society and history, peoples, cultures and religions" (*RM*, no. 28). And second, "every authentic prayer is prompted by the Holy Spirit, who is mysteriously present in every human heart" (*RM*, no. 29).

[57] *For All the Peoples of Asia,* 1:204.

[58] Ibid., 1:131. Exposure-immersion should not be seen merely as a temporary phase, though often it takes place in a short period of time. The FABC repeatedly insists that the church must share the lives and the poverty of the people to whom it proclaims the good news: "Quite clearly, then, there is a definite path along which the Spirit has been leading the discernment of the Asian Church: the Church of Asia must become the Church of the poor" (ibid., 1:145). This phase corresponds to praxis, which Latin American liberation theology insists is the methodological presupposition for doing theology.

and human rights."[59] The FABC does not specify which method of social analysis is to be employed. However, it warns of the dangers of "deception either by ideology or self-interest" and of incompleteness.[60]

This brings us to the third step, *contemplation*, or as the FABC puts it, "integration of social analysis with the religio-cultural reality, discerning not only its negative and enslaving aspects but also its positive, prophetic aspects that can inspire genuine spirituality."[61] Contemplation is needed in order to discover God's active presence in the society and preferential love for the poor. This contemplative dimension brings theologians into a sympathetic and respectful dialogue with Asia's great religions and the religiosity of the poor. Through this double dialogue the authentic values of the gospel—such as "simplicity of life, genuine openness and generous sharing, community consciousness and family loyalty"[62]—are discovered and appreciated.

The fourth step is *pastoral planning,* which seeks to complete the first three steps by formulating practical and realistic policies, strategies, and plans of action in favor of integral human development. As these policies, strategies, and plans of action are implemented, they are continuously submitted to evaluation by a renewal of the first three steps of the pastoral cycle. Thus the ultimate test of the validity of theological insights is their ability to generate concrete actions in favor of justice and liberation.[63]

Doing theology in Asia, then, is much more than an academic enterprise. Of course, theology always is *intellectus fidei*—understanding of the faith—no matter where it is done. However, the starting point of Asian theologies is neither the Bible nor Christian tradition from which conclusions are drawn by means of deductive logic and then applied to particular situations and circumstances. Rather, Asian theologians are implicated from the outset in the socio-political, economic, cultural, and religious conditions of their suffering and oppressed

---

[59] Ibid., 1:145. Indeed, almost all documents issued by the FABC and its various institutes begin with a careful analysis of the social, political, economic, cultural, and religious condition of Asia or parts of Asia as appropriate.

[60] Ibid., 1:231. Implicitly, the FABC considers Marxist social analysis, which was favored by early Latin American liberation theology, insufficient for the Asian situation. The FABC's fifth plenary assembly says: "Social analysis [must] be integrated with cultural analysis, and both subjected to faith-discernment" (see ibid., 1:285).

[61] Ibid., 1:231.

[62] Ibid., 1:232. Aloysius Pieris calls this step "introspection." He argues that "a 'liberation-theopraxis' in Asia that uses only the Marxist tools of *social analysis* will remain un-Asian and ineffective until it integrates the psychological tools of *introspection* which our sages have discovered" (*An Asian Theology of Liberation*, 80).

[63] See *For All the Peoples of Asia,* 1:232. There is a parallel between the FABC's pastoral cycle and the method of Latin American liberation theology. Clodovis Boff describes the method of liberation theology as composed of three mediations: socio-analytic mediation (= social analysis), hermeneutic mediation (= contemplation), and practical mediation (= pastoral planning). These three mediations are preceded and accompanied by praxis in favor of justice and liberation (= exposure-immersion). See Clodovis Boff, *Theology and Praxis: Epistemological Foundations*, trans. Robert R. Barr (Maryknoll, N.Y.: Orbis Books, 1987).

people, with whom they must stand in effective solidarity. It is from the perspective of this praxis that scripture and tradition are read and interpreted.

Toward an Asian Hermeneutics

For Asian theologies, scripture and tradition will, of course, continue to function as normative resources with their profession of faith in Jesus as the incarnated Word of God and savior of humanity. As the Office of Theological Concerns states unequivocally: "The first and most important resource for the interpretation of the Bible is the Christocentric faith that accepts Jesus Christ as the eternal Word of God who became incarnate to save the human race."[64]

Granted this fundamental profession of faith, the task of biblical hermeneutics still remains a complex one. In line with the historical-critical method, the Office of Theological Concerns affirms the primacy of the "literal sense," that is, "the meaning of a text in its original context, which is recovered through a critical, historic-literary study."[65] However, Asian theologians reject the hegemony of the historical-critical method that has dominated Western exegesis. Instead, they propose a multi-pronged hermeneutics in light of the multicultural and multi-religious context of Asia. For them the primary task of biblical hermeneutics is to make the word of God concrete in the contemporary context for the people of today, and not simply to retrieve the literal meaning of the text. In other words, the interpreter must not only discover the world *behind* the text but also appropriate the words *in* and *in front of* the text for personal and societal transformation that is the culminating moment of the hermeneutical enterprise as a whole.[66]

To achieve this goal, Asian theologians insist that all biblical interpretation must be contextual. Interpreters must be cognizant not only of the context of the text but also of their own context, that is, their social location as well as their gender, class, and race biases, and the socio-political and religio-cultural context in which the Bible is being proclaimed. Neither the text nor the interpretation of the text is ever objective, if by objective one means ideologically unbiased. The text is written by the "historical winners," who do not simply tell *the* story but *their* story, and the interpreter must be aware of the interplay among knowledge, power, and interests to identify the distortions and dysfunctions in the text and possibilities of transformation. As a consequence, in approaching the text interpreters must keep in mind the following questions: "Who inscribes what for the interest of whom and at the expense of which group or sector of

---

[64] FABC, *Methodology*, 40.

[65] Ibid., 41. The document carefully distinguishes this literal meaning from the fundamentalist or literalist sense, which it categorically rejects.

[66] For a helpful explanation of this threefold hermeneutics, see Sandra Schneiders, *The Revelatory Text: Interpreting the New Testament as Sacred Scripture*, 2d ed. (Collegeville, Minn.: Liturgical Press, 1999).

society?" "Who stands to gain as a result of the formation of the canon and who is being discriminated against?"[67]

Given the presence of the teeming masses of the poor, the vitality of diverse religions, and the richness of many cultures on their continent, Asian theologians take the perspectives of their poor, their religions, and their cultures as the lens or focus in reading the Bible. The uppermost questions in their mind are: How can the message of the Bible become good news for those who are poor, oppressed, and marginalized? How can it be understood by the followers of other religions? How can it be enriched by Asian cultural expressions? Methodologically, Asian biblical hermeneutics takes at least three directions: retrieval of the hermeneutical tradition of the Eastern churches, multicultural and multifaith hermeneutics, and people-based hermeneutics.

Hermeneutics of the Eastern (Syriac) Tradition

The three theological traditions of Christianity, namely, Syriac, Greek, and Latin, are all represented in Asia. Unfortunately, the Syriac tradition, which is indebted to such theologians as Aphraates, Ephrem, Jacob of Serugh, and Babai the Great, has often been forgotten and suppressed, even in Asia, where it has its historical roots. In India, this tradition is preserved by the Saint Thomas Christians, despite the fact that there has been an attempt at Latinizing them, particularly with the Synod of Diamper in 1599. Currently remaining in communion with the Roman church are the Syro-Malabar and Syro-Malankara churches, the latter rejoining the Catholic church in 1930.

With regard to the Syriac tradition, the Office of Theological Concerns says: "The Syriac theological tradition is a legacy that enriches the whole Church. In particular it has to be given a very important place in the restoration/reform of the ecclesial life of the St. Thomas Christians in India today. This, in turn, will be a valuable contribution to the Church in Asia and to Asian theology."[68] Such a contribution will enrich Asian theologies, especially because the Syriac tradition privileges typological exegesis, emphasizes the centrality of liturgy and doxology, accords priority to mysticism and apophaticism, highlights the special role of the Holy Spirit, and favors the use of icons, symbols, paradoxes, and poetry in theological expressions. These are all methodological approaches that accord well with the Asian way of thinking.[69]

---

[67] Archie C. C. Lee, "Refiguring Religious Pluralism in the Bible," in *Plurality, Power and Mission: Intercontinental Theological Explorations on the Role of Religion in the New Millennium*, ed. Philip L. Wickeri, Janice K. Wickeri, and Damayanthi M. A. Niles (London: The Council for World Mission, 2000), 222.

[68] FABC, *Methodology*, 19.

[69] For a brief exposition on Eastern, and more specifically Syriac theological and church tradition, see ibid., 11-19. Pope John Paul II urges respect and promotion of the traditions of the Catholic Eastern Churches in Asia: "The situation of the *Catholic Eastern Churches*,

Multicultural and Multi-faith Hermeneutics

The second important hermeneutical approach of Asian theologies is what has been called multi-faith or multi-religious or cross-cultural or cross-textual or comparative or contextual reading. This approach includes four distinct but interrelated elements. First, in general, as the Office of Theological Concerns puts it, "Asian interpreters of the Bible, both at the scholarly and the popular levels, search for the meaning of biblical texts: (1) in relation to Asian worldviews and cultures which are cosmic, Spirit-oriented, family and community-oriented; and (2) in relation to Asian situations in the socio-economic, political and religious fields."[70] Second, because most countries of Asia have been devastated by a long history of Western colonialism and imperialism, a reading of the Bible in relation to their socio-economic and political situations inevitably leads to a postcolonial hermeneutics. Third, this approach requires a knowledge of how other religions interpret their own sacred scriptures: "If Christians wish to understand and dialogue with peoples of other faiths, it is important they understand how they have interpreted their text down the ages."[71] Learning how the adherents of other religions interpret their sacred texts enriches the hermeneutical strategies that Christians have traditionally deployed. Fourth, this approach places the sacred texts of Christianity side by side with those of other religions and allows them to throw light on one another, challenge, complement and even correct one another.[72] A brief word on each of these four elements is in order.

The first hermeneutical aspect is simply part of the effort of Asian Christians to become a truly local church, that is, a church not only *in* but *of* Asia. The final statement of the FABC's seventh plenary assembly in 2000 on the basis of the report of Archbishop Orlando Quevedo, general secretary, summarizes the eight features that form the vision of a renewed Asian Christianity: a church of the poor and the young; a truly inculturated and indigenous church; a church of deep interiority and prayer; a church as a communion of communities of authentic participation and co-responsibility; a church committed to integral evangelization; a church with an empowered laity; a church engaged in the struggle for human rights and in the service of life; and a church practicing the triple

---

principally of the Middle East and India, merits special attention. From Apostolic times they have been the custodians of a precious spiritual, liturgical and theological heritage. Their traditions and rites, born of a deep inculturation of the faith in the soil of many Asian countries, deserve the greatest respect. With the Synod Fathers, I call upon everyone to recognize the legitimate customs and the legitimate freedom of these Churches in disciplinary and liturgical matters, as stipulated by the Code of Canons of the Eastern Churches" (*EA,* no. 27).

[70] FABC, *Methodology,* 41-42.

[71] Ibid., 39-40.

[72] For a helpful introduction to third-world hermeneutics, see R. S. Sugirtharajah, ed., *Voices from the Margin: Interpreting the Bible in the Third World* (Maryknoll, N.Y.: Orbis Books, 1991).

dialogue with other faiths, the poor, and with the cultures.[73] Interpreting the Bible in relation to the Asian context is the first and most important step toward implementing this vision of church.

Second, such a biblical interpretation is by necessity a postcolonial hermeneutics. As R. S. Sugirtharajah has amply demonstrated in the Indian context,

> historical-critical methods were not only colonial in the sense that they displaced the norms and practices of our indigenous reading methods, but in that they were used to justify the superiority of the Christian texts and to undermine the sacred writings of others, thus creating a division between us and our neighbors. Such materials function as masks for exploitation and abet an involuntary cultural assimilation.[74]

In contrast, a postcolonial scriptural reading is marked, according to Sugirtharajah, by five features: (1) it looks for appositional or protest voices in the text by bringing marginal elements to the front and, in the process, subverts the traditional meaning; (2) it will not romanticize or idealize the poor; (3) it will not blame the victims but will direct the attention to the social structures and institutions that spawn victimhood; (4) it places the sacred texts together and reads them within an intertextual continuum, embodying a multiplicity of perspectives; and (5) it will address the question of how people can take pride and affirm their own language, ethnicity, culture, and religion within the multilingual, multiracial, multicultural and multireligious societies.[75]

Third, a postcolonial hermeneutics must be enriched by the ways in which the followers of other religions have interpreted their own sacred writings. Concretely, there must be an effort in Asia to learn how Hindus, Buddhists, Muslims, Confucians, and Taoists read their own sacred scriptures.[76] In familiarizing themselves with these interpretative methods, Asian theologians may learn that not only are there striking parallels between these methods and the traditional Christian approach to the Bible, but also that these methods are more in tune with the Asian world views and modes of knowing and speaking than the Western ones and therefore can enrich Christian hermeneutics. Thus, for example, Christian theologians can learn from classical Vedanta's teaching on the three steps in the process of moving from the desire to know Brahman to the liberating experience of Brahman in the perfect integration *(samadhi)* of the self *(atman)* and Absolute Reality, that is, hearing *(sravana)*, reflecting *(manana)*,

---

[73] See FABC, *A Renewed Church in Asia: A Mission of Love and Service*, 3-4. The text of Archbishop Quevedo is available in *A Renewed Church in Asia: Pastoral Directions for a New Decade*. FABC Papers, no. 95 (Hong Kong: FABC, 2000), 12-16.

[74] R. S. Sugirtharajah, *Asian Biblical Hermeneutics and Postcolonialism: Contesting the Interpretations* (Maryknoll, N.Y.: Orbis Books, 1998), 127.

[75] See ibid., 20-24.

[76] For a helpful overview of these five hermeneutical methods, see FABC, *Methodology*, 43-84.

and meditating *(nididhyasana)*, each containing in itself various acts of inter-pretation. From Buddhism, Christians will learn the necessity of "taking ref-uge" in the "Three Jewels," that is, the Buddha, the *dharma* (his teaching), and the *sangha* (the community) and its four rules of interpretation.[77] In relation to Islam, Asian theologies can benefit from the Sunnite emphasis on exegesis through the traditions *(hadith)*, from the Shi'ite stress on allegorical interpreta-tion *(tawil)*, and from the Sufi preference for mystical interpretation.[78] Confu-cianism teaches Christian interpreters the necessity of linking knowledge with action and the use of images, stories, parables and dialogues as ways to convey truths. Finally, from Taoism Asian theologians learn the mode of apophatic thinking appropriate to dealing with the eternal and nameless Tao, the "mystery upon mystery."

Last, because of the overwhelming presence of non-Christian soteriologies in Asia, Asian theologians also practice an interfaith or multi-faith hermeneu-tics. They abandon the earlier apologetical approach of using the Bible as a yardstick to judge the sacred texts of other religions. Rather, they read the Bible in light of the other sacred texts and vice versa for mutual cross-fertilization.[79] The purpose of such reading is not to prove that the Christian Bible and the sacred scriptures of other religions are mutually compatible, to find linguistic and theological parallels between them for some missiological intent, but to enlarge our understanding of both, to promote cross-cultural and cross-religious

---

[77] The four rules are "the doctrine *(dharma)* is the refuge and not the person; the mean-ing *(artha)* is the refuge and not the letter; the sutra of precise meaning *(niartha)* is the refuge, not the sutra the meaning of which requires interpretation *(neyartha)*; direct knowledge *(jnana)* is the refuge and not discursive consciousness *(vijnana)*" (see ibid., 55-56).

[78] *Methodology* highlights the following three Islamic hermeneutical principles: "i. that the meaning should be sought from within the Qur'an, and never should a passage be interpreted in such a manner that it may be at discrepancy with any other passage; ii. no attempt should be made to establish a principle to establish on the strength of alle-gorical passages, or of words liable to different meanings; iii. when a law or principle is laid down in clear words, any statement carrying a doubtful significance, or a statement apparently opposed to the law so laid down, must be interpreted subject to the principle articulated. Similarly, that which is particular must be read in connection with and sub-ject to more general statements" (ibid., 63).

[79] For examples of interfaith hermeneutics, see the brilliant essays of Samuel Rayan, "Reconceiving Theology in the Asian Context," in *Doing Theology in a Divided World*, ed.Virginia Fabella and Sergio Torres (Maryknoll, N.Y.: Orbis Books, 1985), 134-39 and "Wrestling in the Night," in *The Future of Liberation Theology: Essays in Honor of Gustavo Gutiérrez*, ed. Marc H. Ellis and Otto Maduro (Maryknoll, N.Y.: Orbis Books, 1989), 450-69; Peter K. H. Lee, "Re-reading Ecclesiastes in the Light of Su Tung-p'o's Poetry," *Ching Feng* 30/4 (1987), 214-36; idem, "Ta-T'ung and the Kingdom of God," *Ching Feng* 31/4 (1988), 225-44; idem, "Two Stories of Loyalty," *Ching Feng* 32/1 (1989), 24-40; Choan-Seng Song, *Tell Us Our Names: Story Theology from an Asian Perspective* (Maryknoll, N.Y.: Orbis Books, 1984). See also the essays in the fourth part of Sugirtharajah, *Voices from the Margin*, 299-394; and idem, *Frontiers in Asian Theol-ogy*, 65-137.

dialogue, to achieve a "wider intertextuality"[80] To carry out this exercise successfully, what is needed is a "dialogical imagination." Kwok Pui-lan explains the implications of this dialogical model:

> A dialogical model takes into consideration not only the written text but also oral discussion of the text in different social dialects. It invites more dialogical partners by shifting the emphasis from one scripture (the Bible) to many scriptures, from responding to one religious narrative to many possible narratives. It shifts from a single-axis framework of analysis to multiaxial interpretation, taking into serious consideration the issues of race, class, gender, culture, and history. It emphasizes the democratizing of the interpretative process, calling attention to the construction of meanings by marginalized people, to the opening up of interpretive space for other voices, and to the creation of a more inclusive and just community.[81]

Thus Kwok Pui-lan suggests that the Bible be seen not as a fixed and sacred canon giving rise to one normative interpretation but as a "talking book"—the juxtaposition of *talking* with *book* highlighting the rich connections between the written and the oral in many traditional cultures. The image of the Bible as a talking book puts the emphasis not on the text but on the community that talks about it; not on the written but the oral transmission of the text; not on the fixed but the evolving meaning of the text; not on one canonical voice but many voices, often suppressed and marginalized, in the text; not on the authoritarian decision about the truth of the text but on the open, honest, and respectful conversation about what is true.[82]

People-Based Hermeneutics

The image of the Bible as a talking book brings us to the third track of Asian interpretive method, namely, people-based hermeneutics. In Asia the biblical interpreters are not only professionally trained scholars, whose work is of course important for the community, but also the ordinary believers themselves, especially as they gather in basic ecclesial communities for Bible study and worship. Furthermore, people-based hermeneutics makes extensive use of popular myths, stories, fables, dance, and art to interpret biblical stories. The

---

[80] George M. Soares-Prabhu, "Two Mission Commands: An Interpretation of Matthew 18: 16-20 in the Light of a Buddhist Text," *Biblical Interpretation* 2/3 (1994), 282. See also Archie Lee, "Biblical Interpretation in Asian Perspective," *Asia Journal of Theology* 7/1 (1993), 35-39.

[81] Kwok Pui-lan, *Discovering the Bible in Non-Biblical World* (Maryknoll, N.Y.: Orbis Books, 1995), 36.

[82] See ibid., 42.

most prominent advocate and practitioner of this hermeneutics is Choan-Seng Song, a Taiwanese Presbyterian.[83]

The most celebrated example of this story-based hermeneutics is Song's *The Tears of Lady Meng*, in which he develops a powerful political liberation theology from the story of a woman (Meng Chiang) whose husband was buried alive in the wall that Emperor Ch'in Shih was building. Lady Meng went in search of her husband at the wall and her tears made the wall collapse. The emperor ordered her to be brought to him and, struck by her beauty, asked her to be his wife. Lady Meng agreed, but only on condition that a forty-day festival be held in her husband's honor; that the emperor and all the court officials be present at his funeral; and that a forty-nine-foot high terrace be built on the bank of the river. When everything was ready, Lady Meng climbed on the terrace, cursed the emperor in a loud voice for his wickedness, and then jumped into the river. The emperor ordered his soldiers to cut up her body into little pieces and grind her bones to powder. But then the little pieces turned into little silver fish, in which the soul of faithful Meng Chiang lives forever.[84]

Will an Asian theology constructed with Asian resources and along the hermeneutical approach indicated above be different from a Euro-American theology? a black theology? a Hispanic/Latino theology? an African theology? a Latin American theology?[85] The question is perhaps otiose, since de facto Asian theologians have already produced a theology that is recognizably distinctive and different. This is obvious to anyone familiar with the works of Choan-Seng Song, Archie C. C. Lee, Kwok Pui-lan, Jung Young Lee, Chung Hyun Kyung, Kosuke Koyama, Kazoh Kitamori, Aloysius Pieris, Tissa Balasuriya, Rasiah S. Sugirtharajah, Michael Amaladoss, Felix Wilfred, M. M. Thomas, Stanley Samartha, José M. de Mesa, and numerous other men and women theologians associated with the FABC, the Christian Conference of Asia, and EATWOT (to mention only those whose writings are available in English).[86]

---

[83] The following are Song's most important works: *Third-Eye Theology*, rev. ed. (Maryknoll, N.Y.: Orbis Books, 1990); *The Compassionate God* (London: SCM Press, 1982); *Tell Us Our Names: Story Theology from an Asian Perspective* (Maryknoll, N.Y.: Orbis Books, 1984); *Theology from the Womb of Asia* (Maryknoll, N.Y.: Orbis Books, 1986); *Jesus, the Crucified People* (New York: Crossroad, 1990); *Jesus and the Reign of God* (Minneapolis: Fortress Press, 1993); *Jesus in the Power of the Spirit* (Minneapolis: Fortress Press, 1994); *The Tears of Lady Meng: A Parable of People's Political Theology* (Maryknoll, N.Y.: Orbis Books, 1982); and *The Believing Heart: An Invitation to Story Theology* (Minneapolis: Fortress Press, 1999).

[84] See Song, *The Tears of Lady Meng*.

[85] For a discussion of black, Hispanic, and Asian theologies in the United States, see Peter C. Phan, "Contemporary Theology and Inculturation in the United States," in *The Multicultural Church: A New Landscape in U.S. Theologies*, ed. William Cenkner (New York: Paulist Press, 1995), 109-30, 176-92.

[86] A useful introduction to many of these theologians is available in Sugirtharajah, *Frontiers in Asian Christian Theology*.

THEOLOGICAL EDUCATION FOR THE MULTICULTURAL
AND MULTI-RELIGIOUS CONTEXT

No doubt the widespread situation of cultural and religious pluralism demands a new approach to the theological education and formation of future church ministers. In fact, concrete steps have already been taken by many seminaries and theological institutes to meet the challenges of cultural and religious pluralism.[87]

I have written elsewhere of the implications of multiculturalism for theological education in seminaries and universities, with respect to students, professors, curriculum, and institutional organization.[88] I have insisted on the necessity of recruiting a critical mass of Asian students; adding some Asians to the faculty and staff; offering some appropriate courses on Asian languages, history, and culture; blending liturgical and cultural celebrations; attending to popular devotions and religiosity; combining inculturation with social justice; and fostering a spirituality that cultivates appreciation for otherness, empathy, and imagination.

Rather than repeating my remarks about and my concrete suggestions for a theological education that takes into account identity claims, I would like to stress here the fact that, if Walbert Bühlmann's prognostication is correct, in the near future there will be more Catholics in South America than in Europe and more Catholics in the southern hemisphere than in the northern.[89] Another fact deserving our reflection is that Christians, after two thousand years of history and three hundred years of mission, still form but the tiniest part of the Asian population. These two facts should disabuse us of the notion that Euro-American churches and their theologies, with their economic and ecclesiastical power, should be regarded as the paradigms for a universal ecclesiology and theological education.

As people engaged in theological education in a privileged world, we have the duty to promote the kind of theological reflection that fosters, within the catholic unity of the church, the four "selfs" of the local churches: self-governing, self-support, self-propagation, and self-theologizing.

---

[87] See Katarina Schuth, *Seminaries, Theologates, and the Future of Church Ministry: An Analysis of Trends and Transitions* (Collegeville, Minn.: Liturgical Press, 1999).

[88] See my articles "Aspects of Vietnamese Culture and Roman Catholicism: Background Information for Educators of Vietnamese Seminarians," *Seminaries in Dialogue News* 23 (1991), 2-8; "Preparation for Multicultural Ministry," *Seminary News* 30/1 (1991), 15-23; "The Seminary Theologian in Service to a Multicultural Society," *Seminary News* 32/1 (1993), 31-42; "Multiculturalism, Church, and University," *Religious Education* 90/1 (1994), 8-29; and "Theological Research and Scholarship as a Service to Faith," *Theological Education* 32/1 (1995), 31-41; and "Asian Identity, Theology, and Theological Education," in *L'Universalité catholique face à la diversité humaine*, ed. Lucien Vachon (Montréal: Médiapaul, 1998), 291-303, 328-30.

[89] See W. Bühlmann, *Weltkirche: Neue Dimensionen, Modell für das Jahr 2001* (Graz: Styria, 1984).

Let us not repeat for our students the experience that Chung Hyun Kyung suffered:

> My Third World awareness led me to question the colonialism and neoco-
> lonialism in theology. Throughout my formal theological education in
> Korea, I was taught all about the European theologies of Schleiermacher,
> Barth, Tillich, Bultmann, Moltmann, and Pannenberg, the so-called theo-
> logical giants of the nineteenth and twentieth centuries. I was not taught
> anything about Korean people and their theological reflections on Korea's
> history and culture. My learning in the university, therefore, did not help
> me to discern the activity of God in my people's everyday struggle in
> Korea.[90]

To Chung's list of theological giants, Catholics can add Augustine, Thomas, Congar, Rahner, Schillebeeckx, von Balthasar, and many others. But the devas-tating effects are the same: the loss of self-identity and much worse, the eclipse of God in the joys and sufferings of Asian peoples.

---

[90] Chung, *Struggle to Be the Sun Again*, 3.

11

Reception of Vatican II in Asia

HISTORICAL AND THEOLOGICAL ANALYSIS

The Second Vatican Council has been characterized as the most significant event of the twentieth century, both in secular and ecclesiastical history. Given the extensive reforms it has spawned in the Roman Catholic Church worldwide and its ramifications for ecumenical unity and the society at large, the description seems by no means overblown.

While Vatican II's impact on the Western churches is clearly discernible and has been subjected to frequent evaluations,[1] whether and to what extent the council has influenced the churches in other parts of the world has not been extensively documented. The purpose of this chapter is to determine and evaluate Vatican II's impact on the churches of Asia.[2] Such an evaluation is extremely complex, not only because the field of enquiry is so vast and theological

---

[1] The literature, especially theological, is immense. On the official level, Pope John Paul II convoked an Extraordinary Synod of Bishops on the twentieth anniversary of the closing of the council (24 November to 8 December 1985) to take stock of the conciliar reforms. Though not official, Josef Ratzinger's assessment of Vatican II in *The Ratzinger Report* (San Francisco: Ignatius Press, 1985), an interview with Vittorio Messori, is influential, given his position as prefect of the Congregation of the Doctrine of the Faith. Among theological evaluations the most comprehensive is the massive three-volume work edited by René Latourelle, *Vatican II: Assessment and Perspectives. Twenty-five Years After (1962-1987)*, published simultaneously in several European languages. The English edition was brought out by Paulist Press in 1988. An earlier and helpful assessment of Vatican II is Giuseppe Alberigo, Jean-Pierre Jossua, and Joseph Komonchak, eds., *The Reception of Vatican II*, also published in several languages. The English translation, by Matthew J. O'Connell (The Catholic University Press of America, 1987), is hereafter cited as *Reception*. Other helpful general works include Alberic Stacpoole, ed., *Vatican II Revisited by Those Who Were There* (Minneapolis, Minn.: Winston Press, 1986); F. X. Kaufmann and A. Zingerle, eds., *Vatikanum II und Modernisiering: Historische, theolologische und soziologische Perspektiven* (Paderborn: Schöning, 1996); and David Tracy, with Hans Küng and Johann B. Metz, eds., *Toward Vatican III: The Work That Needs to Be Done* (New York: The Seabury Press, 1978).

[2] By Asian churches here is meant primarily the Roman Catholic churches of the Indian subcontinent and of the Far East (excluding the churches of the Near and Middle East and of Central Asia). These churches (and others) form part of the FABC.

bibliography scarce, but also because in many countries empirical data on the churches' activities are practically impossible to obtain.[3] Furthermore, the expression *Vatican II* is itself highly ambiguous, and, of course, unless there is a consensus on what is meant by *Vatican II,* an evaluation of its impact on the churches of Asia lacks a clear focus.[4]

With these limitations in mind, I begin with a brief overview of Vatican II and the current situation of Asian Catholic churches. I next examine the various areas of church life in Asia in which the council has exercised a significant influence, with reference to the achievements of the FABC. I end by offering a theological evaluation of the council's impact by examining one of the most important events in the life of the Asian churches, namely, the special assembly of the Synod of Bishops for Asia.[5]

VATICAN II AND THE ASIAN CHURCHES

Announced by Pope John XXIII to the consternation and thinly veiled opposition of his advisers on 25 January 1959 and formally convoked on 25 December 1961, the Second Vatican Council opened on 11 October 1962. Suspended by Pope John's death on 3 June 1963 and continued by Pope Paul VI, the council concluded on 8 December 1965. The council issued sixteen documents of various levels of authority (four constitutions, nine decrees, and three declarations).[6] Of these documents, it is generally agreed that, dogmatically speaking, the most important is the dogmatic constitution on the church *(Lumen gentium)*; in terms of immediate impact on church life, the constitution on the liturgy *(Sacrosanctum concilium)* is the most significant; and in terms of the influence on the society at large, the pastoral constitution on the church in the modern world *(Gaudium et spes)* is the most influential. In addition, for Asia, given its multi-religious context and the church's minority status, the decree on the church's missionary activity *(Ad gentes)* and the declaration on the relationship of the church to non-Christian religions *(Nostra aetate)* are of particular relevance.

To form a correct assessment of Vatican II, it is important to recall that Vatican II was intended by Pope John XXIII to be a "pastoral" council.[7] Instead of being

---

[3] This is particularly true of churches under the communist regime, such as mainland China, North Korea, and Vietnam.

[4] It will be suggested below that *Vatican II* should be taken in a comprehensive sense.

[5] This chapter is by design predominantly bibliographical. It is intended to be a modest contribution to the history of the post–Vatican II Catholic church in Asia, which remains largely unwritten.

[6] For English translations of Vatican II documents, see Austin Flannery, ed., *Vatican Council II*, new rev. ed. (Collegeville, Minn.: Liturgical Press, 1975); or Walter Abbott, ed., *The Documents of Vatican II* (New York: Guild Press, 1966),

[7] Giuseppe Alberigo has usefully warned against a misunderstanding of the "pastoral" character of Vatican II, taking it to mean excluding or minimizing the importance of doctrines. See *Reception*, 16 n. 53. Alberigo explains: "By using this adjective, then, he [John XXIII] was giving Vatican II an ecclesial scope that was not solely dogmatic or solely disciplinary but all-embracing" (ibid. 17).

"a discussion of one article or another of the fundamental doctrine of the Church," the council was directed to make "a step forward toward a doctrinal penetration and a formation of consciousness in faithful and perfect conformity to the authentic doctrine."[8] The question to ask when assessing Vatican II's impact on the Asian churches is therefore not whether in the post-conciliar period they have produced new doctrines but whether they have achieved a deeper understanding of the Christian faith and formed a keener consciousness of their Christian identity and mission in conformity with their faith.[9]

Another factor to be kept in mind is that Vatican II itself could not implement its own reform programs and therefore called for the establishment of various post-conciliar commissions (for example, the Concilium for the Implementation of the Constitution on the Liturgy) and secretariats (such as the secretariats for the promotion of Christian unity, for non-Christian religions, and for nonbelievers) to devise concrete ways and measures to carry out the church reform instituted by the council. It is reasonable, then, that in assessing the impact of Vatican II, attention should not be limited to the event of the conciliar meeting itself nor to its sixteen documents but must link them to the official post-conciliar documents (numerous liturgical books, the new Code of Canon Law, the *Catechism of the Catholic Church*, etc.), and institutions, indeed, to the entire pontificates of Paul VI and John Paul II.

Vatican II was the first ecumenical council that the Asian bishops took part in, though many of them were not Asian-born but expatriate missionaries. Nor did their voices carry much weight, since Vatican II—though the first general council truly represented by the *oikoumene* and hence ushering in the "world church"[10]—was still very much a European affair, dominated by European prelates and the preoccupations of the Western churches. This lack of influence was due to the fact that the number of Asian bishops was relatively small and that many Asian churches were still in mission lands. This minority status of Christianity in Asia, except in the Philippines, with all its disadvantages, must be taken into account when we note that Vatican II has not achieved the impact on the Asian churches that it could have.

It would be useful, then, before we embark upon a study of the reception of Vatican II by the Asian churches, to take a brief look at their current situation. In Asia, Catholics (105.2 million in 1997) represented only 2.9 percent of the nearly 3.5 billion Asians. Moreover, well over 50 percent of all Asian Catholics are found in one country—the Philippines. Thus, if one excludes the Philippines, Asia is only about 1 percent Catholic. Despite its extreme minority status, the Catholic church in Asia continues to grow. In 1988 there were 84.3

---

[8] Pope John XXIII's opening speech to the council.

[9] On this point see the many works of John F. Kobler, in particular *Vatican II, Theophany and the Phenomenon of Man: The Council's Pastoral Servant Leader Theology for the Third Millennium* (New York: Peter Lang, 1991).

[10] This is Karl Rahner's famous interpretation of Vatican II (see Karl Rahner, "Towards a Fundamental Theological Interpretation of Vatican II," *Theological Studies* 40 [1979], 716-27).

million Catholics. By 1997 they had reached 105.2 million. It is also interesting to note that most of the Asian clergy and religious are indigenous. In 1997 Asia had 617 bishops (out of 4,420 bishops in the world) and 32,291 priests (17,789 diocesan and 14,502 religious). Two-thirds of all religious priests are Asian; the vast majority of religious sisters (88 percent) are also Asian.[11] This numerical minority, however, and other political, economic, and religious factors have impeded a full implementation of Vatican II. On the other hand, these situations have also shaped the particular ways in which the Asian churches responded to Vatican II's call for reform.

THE RECEPTION OF VATICAN II IN ASIA

The first way in which the Asian churches received the Second Vatican Council was to translate its sixteen Latin documents into their own languages. While this task was somewhat easy for countries where English is by and large the second language (for example, the Philippines and India), it posed considerable challenges to churches in countries where even a basic Christian vocabulary was not yet available, let alone highly technical theological and canonical terms, and where experts in both theology and the local languages were in short supply. In these cases most often the translation of the conciliar documents was equivalent to an appropriation and inculturation of the theological orientations of the council itself. Hence, the translations were themselves major theological achievements of the Asian churches.[12]

---

[11] For resources on statistics of the Asian churches, consult *Catholic Almanac* (Our Sunday Visitor, Inc.), *Statistical Yearbook of the Church* (Vatican Press), and "Annual Statistical Table on Global Mission," in the first number of each volume of *International Bulletin of Missionary Research*.

For statistics on Catholics in individual countries belonging to the FABC, the following data are given, with the name of the country, its estimated population in millions for the year 2000, and the percentage of Catholics: Bangladesh (145.8/0.27 percent); Bhutan (1.8/0.02 percent); Burma/Myanmar (48.8/1.3 percent); Cambodia (10.3/0.02 percent); China (1,239.5/0.5 percent); Hong Kong (6.9/4.7 percent); India (990/1.72 percent); Indonesia (202/2.58 percent); Japan (127.7/0.36 percent); North Korea (22.6/ ?); South Korea (47.2/6.7 percent); Laos (6.2/0.9 percent); Macao (0.5/5 percent); Malaysia (22/3 percent); Mongolia (2.5/? percent); Nepal (23/0.05 percent); Pakistan (142.6/ 0.8 percent); Philippines (74.8/81 percent); Singapore (3.1/6.5 percent); Sri Lanka (20.8/ 8 percent); Taiwan (22.1/1.4 percent); Thailand (61.6/0.4 percent); Vietnam (78.2/6.1 percent). I am grateful to Rev. Dr. James H. Kroeger, M.M., for information on these statistics.

[12] The following translations, besides English, are available: Chinese: *Chiao hui hsien chang: fu shih* (T'ai-chung: Kuang ch'i ch'u pan che, 1966) [Taiwanese] (early translation); *Fan-ti-kang ti erh chieh ta kung hui I wen hsien* (T'ai pei: Chung-kuo chu chiao t'uan mi shu ch'u ch'u pan: T'ien chu chiao chiao wu hsieh chin ch'u pan she, 1979) [revised translation]. Korean: *Che-ch'a Pat'ik'an Konguihoe munhon: honjang, kyoryong, sononmun* (Seoul T'ukpyolsi: Han'guk Ch'onjugyo Chungang Hyobuihoe, 1969). Bahasa Indonesia: *Dokumen Konsili Vatikan II* (Jakarta: Dokpen KWI dan Obor, 1993). Vietnamese: *Thanh Cong Dong Chung Vaticano II*, 2 vols. (Da Lat: Phan Khoa Than Hoc Giao Hoang Hoc Vien Thanh Pio X, 1972). There are also Japanese and Thai translations.

Second, it is universally agreed that the most immediate and visible impact of Vatican II was its liturgical reforms, not only with its encouragement of the use of vernaculars in liturgical celebrations but also thanks to a slew of post-conciliar new liturgical books (missal, liturgy of the hour, ritual, and pontifical) composed by the Consilium for the Implementation of the Constitution on the Liturgy established by Pope Paul VI in 1964. The goal of the reforms is to promote a "full, conscious, and active participation in liturgical celebrations" (*SC*, no. 14). Once again, the task of translating these liturgical books was a daunting one, but there is no doubt that with the use of vernaculars and the new rites, the faithful in Asia were enabled to achieve a full, conscious, and active participation in the liturgical celebrations that had not been possible before the council.

Third, the reception of Vatican II's liturgical reforms in Asia, however, went far beyond the translation of the liturgical books composed by the Roman authorities into vernaculars. It included also an explicit effort of liturgical inculturation by bringing elements of the local cultures into sacramental and liturgical celebrations. This inculturation occurs at many levels. On a more superficial level, it includes the use of local music and songs, vestments, gestures, rituals, sacred objects, architecture.[13] On a deeper level, it involves the compo-

---

[13] In India, the person most responsible for the process of liturgical reform was no doubt Duraisamy Simon Amalorpavadass. Only a representative bibliography on liturgical adaptation in Asia since Vatican II can be given here. See Michael Amaladoss, "Musique et rite en Inde," *La Maison-Dieu* 108 (1971), 138-42; "Adaptation in Liturgy and the Problem of Meaning," in *God's Word among Men*, ed. G. Gispert-Sauch (Delhi: Vidyajyoti, 1973), 305-14; idem, "Liturgy and Creativity: Fourth All-India Liturgical Meeting," *CM* 38 (1974), 124-33; idem, "Liturgical Adaptation in the Light of History," *WW* 8 (1975), 381-91; idem, "Liturgical Renewal and Ecclesiastical Law," *WW* 10 (1977), 249-60; idem, "The Liturgy: Twenty Years after Vatican II," *VJTR* 47 (1983), 231-39; idem, "Relaunching the Indian Liturgy: Some Reflections on Our Experiment," *VJTR* 49 (1985), 446-55; idem, "Ritualità, teologia, cultura. Una reflessione sull'inculturazione nella liturgia," *La Civiltà Cattolica* 4276 (1986), 440-54; Duraisamy Simon Amalorpavadass, "Liturgy and Catechetics in India Today," *TAN* 6/4 (1969), 378-88; idem, *Towards Indigenization in the Liturgy* (Bangalore: National Biblical, Catechetical and Liturgical Centre/St. Paul Press, 1971); Duraisamy Simon Amalorpavadass, ed., *Post-Vatican Liturgical Renewal in India at All Levels*, vols. 2-4 (Bangalore: National Biblical, Catechetical and Liturgical Centre, 1972, 1976, 1977); Jos De Cuyper, "First All-India Liturgical Meeting," *CM* 32 (1968), 221-24; idem, "The Future of the Liturgy in India," *CM* 33 (1969), 525-37; Jacques Dupuis, "Second All-India Liturgical Meeting," *CM* 33 (1969), 219-23; idem, "Christ and the Holy Spirit in Liturgical Worship," *CM* 35 (1971), 190-98; idem, "Planning the Liturgy of Tomorrow (Third All-India Liturgical Meeting)," *CM* 36 (1972), 93-105; Tissa Balasuriya, "Renewal of the Liturgy in Asia," *CM* 32 (1968), 53-64, 121-29; idem, "Renewal of the Liturgy in Asia," *TAN* 5/2 (1968), 175-99; idem, *The Eucharist and Human Liberation* (Maryknoll, N.Y.: Orbis Books, 1979); Eduardo P. Hontiveros, "Composing Music for an Asian Local Church," *EAPR* 19 (1982), 38-47; Anscar J. Chupungco, *Liturgical Renewal in the Philippines: Maryhill Liturgical Consultations* (Quezon City, Philippines: Maryhill School of Theology, 1980); idem, *Towards a Filipino Liturgy* (Quezon City, Philippines: Maryhill School of Theology, 1976); idem, "A Filipino Attempt at Liturgical Inculturation," *Ephemerides Liturgicae* 91 (1977), 370-76; idem, "A Filipino Adaptation of the Liturgical Language," in *Eulogia Miscellanea Liturgica in Onore di P. Burkhard*

sition of new sacramental rituals for significant events in a person's life, such as marriage and funerals.[14] It sometimes includes the use of sacred writings in addition to the Christian scriptures.[15] In some countries sacred rituals such as the cult of ancestors are incorporated into the liturgy.[16] Because of their academic resources and favorable political conditions, two countries have made significant contributions to the reception of Vatican II's liturgical reform in general: India and the Philippines.[17]

Fourth, liturgical inculturation is only an aspect of the larger enterprise that Vatican II has spawned in Asia, perhaps more extensively than anywhere else

Neunheuser, O.S.B. (Roma: Editrice Anselmiana, 1979), 45-55; idem, *Liturgical Renewal in the Philippines* (Quezon City, Philippines: Maryhill Theological School, 1980); idem, "Liturgical Inculturation," *EAPR* 30 (1993), 108-19; Subhash Anand, "The Inculturation of the Eucharistic Liturgy," *VJTR* 57 (1993), 269-93.

[14] See Anton Pain Ratu, "A Proposed Marriage Rite for Dawanese Catholics," *TAN* 11 (1974), 3-21, 99-119; Peter Knecht, "Funerary Rites and the Concept of Ancestors in Japan: A Challenge to the Christian Churches?" in R. Hardawiryana et al., eds., *Building the Church in Pluricultural Asia*. Inculturation, Working Papers on Living Faith and Cultures, vol. 7 (Rome: Centre "Cultures and Religions"—Pontifical Gregorian University, 1986), 121-44; T. Pereira, *Towards an Indian Christian Funeral Rite* (Bangalore: National Biblical, Catechetical and Liturgical Centre, 1980); R. Serrano, "Toward a Cultural Adaptation of the Rite of Marriage," S.T.D. dissertation, Pontifical Liturgical Institute of San Anselmo, Rome, 1987; Thomas Cherukat, "Christian Sacraments and Hindu Samskaras: A Theological Analysis of Baptism and Confirmation Compared to the Hindu Initiation Rite of Upanayana Samskara in the Context of Inculturation and Interreligious Dialogue in India," Ph.D. dissertation, University of Vienna, Austria, 1991.

[15] See Michael Amaladoss, "Textes hindous dans la prière chrétienne," *Christus* 67 (1970), 424-32; idem, "Text and Context: The Place of Non-Biblical Readings in the Liturgy," in Duraisamy Simon Amalorpavadass, ed., *Research Seminar on Non-Biblical Scriptures* (Bangalore: National Biblical, Catechetical and Liturgical Centre, 1974), 210-21; idem, "Non-Biblical Scriptures in Christian Life and Worship," *VJTR* 39 (1975), 194-209; G. Gispert-Sauch, "Sacred Scriptures in Indian Religions," *VJTR* 39 (1975), 217-22; Virginia K. Kennerley, "The Use of Indigenous Sacred Literature and Theological Concept in Christian Eucharistic Liturgy in India," *Studia Liturgica* 19 (1989), 143-61.

[16] See the documents of the Vietnamese bishops on the veneration of ancestors and heroes (14 June 1965 and 14 November 1974). The Vietnamese text of the former declaration is printed in *Sacerdos* (Saigon) 43 (1965), 489-92; its French translation is found in *Documentation Catholique* 63 (1966), cols. 467-70.

[17] For an assessment of India, see Louis Maliekal, "Liturgical Inculturation in India: Problems and Prospects of Experimentation,"*Jeevadhara* 18 (1988), 279-92; Antony Nariculam, "The Liturgical Crisis in the Syro-Malabar Church," *Jeevadhara* 18 (1988), 293-302; J. Saldanha, "Liturgical Adaptation in India: 1963-1974," *VJTR* 40 (1976), 20-31; Paul Puthanangady, "Inculturation of the Liturgy in India since Vatican II," in *Liturgy: A Creative Tradition,* ed. Mary Collins and David Power, *Concilium,* vol. 162 (New York: Seabury Press, 1983), 71-77; idem, "Liturgical Inculturation in India," *Jeevadhara* 23 (1993), 193-207; Jose Matthew Kakkallil, "Liturgical Inculturation in India," *Questions Liturgiques* 77 (1996), 109-16. For an assessment of the Philippines, see, besides the works of Chupungco, Paul William Diener, "The Philippines and Vatican II: The Impact of an Ecumenical Council," Ph.D. dissertation, Temple University, 1972; and Julio X. Labayen, "Vatican II in Asia and the Philippines," *Ecumenical Review* 37/3 (1985), 275-82.

in the Catholic world. Whereas the Catholic church in Latin America has been more concerned with the socio-economic oppression of the poor and marginalized, and hence more focused on *liberation,* Asian Christians, while also concerned with the issues of justice, have been more engaged the *inculturation* of the Christian faith. Of course, these two aspects—liberation and inculturation—must not be understood as two competing and unrelated tasks. Indeed, it is a fundamental axiom of Asian theologians and the FABC that they cannot and must not be separated from each other. Liberation without inculturation suffers from a truncated anthropology that sees humans simply as economic beings, while inculturation without liberation becomes an elitist, antiquarian quest irrelevant to people's lives.[18]

In terms of the reception of Vatican II, it may be said that while Latin American liberation theology gives special importance to numbers 63-76 of the *Pastoral Constitution on the Church in the Modern World,* the Asian churches, living as they do in the midst of ancient, rich, and diverse cultures, focus their attention far more closely on numbers 54-62.[19] From the existing literature, there is no doubt that inculturation has occupied the lion's share of the attention of Asian theologians. This is true particularly of India[20] and the

---

[18] This thesis has been powerfully asserted by Aloysius Pieris. See his *An Asian Theology of Liberation* (Maryknoll, NY: Orbis Books, 1988).

[19] Numbers 63-72 speak of economic and social life and numbers 73-76 of the political community; numbers 54-62 speak of cultural situations today and some more urgent duties of Christians in regard to culture.

[20] The bibliography is immense. For India, see G. Gispert-Sauch, "Towards an Indian Theology," *CM* 33 (1969), 547-51; idem, "Towards an Indian Theology," *CM* 35 (1971), 262-64; Samuel Ryan, "An Indian Christology: A Discussion of Method," *Jeevadhara* 1/3 (1971), 212-27; idem, "Inculturation and People's Struggles," *IMR* 19/1 (1997), 33-45; Michael Amaladoss, "Inculturation: Theological Perspectives," *Jeevadhara* 6 (1976), 293-302; idem, "Theologizing in India Today," *VJTR* 43 (1979), 213-25; idem, "Inculturation and the Tasks of Mission," *EAPR* 17/2 (1980), 117-25; idem, "Inculturation in India," *EAPR* 18 (1981), 320-30; idem, "L'Église en Inde: Vingt ans après Vatican II," in *Le Retour des certitudes,* ed. Paul Ladrière and René Luneau (Paris: Centurion, 1987), 13-33; idem, *Becoming Indian: The Process of Inculturation* (Rome: Center for Indian and International Studies, 1992); idem, "Inculturation in India: Historical Perspectives and Questions," *Yearbook of Contextual Theologies 1994* (Aachen: Missio, 1994), 42-58; idem, "The Gospel, Community and Culture: Inculturation in Tamil Nadu (India) Today," *Zeitschrift für Missionswissenschaft und Religionswissenschaft* 80 (1996), 179-89; idem, *Beyond Inculturation: Can the Many Be One?* (Delhi, India: Indian Society for Promoting Christian Knowledge, 1998); Duraisamy Simon Amalorpavadass, "Theological Reflections on Inculturation," *Studia Liturgica* 20/1 (1990), 36-54, 116-36; Sebastian Elavathingal, *Inculturation and Christian Art: An Indian Perspective* (Rome: Urbaniana University Press, 1990); Josef Neuner, "Indisierung oder Hinduisierung der Kirche? Problem der Inkulturation in Indien," *Die Katholischen Missionen* 106 (1987), 189-95; Joseph Prasad Pinto, *Inculturation through Basic Communities: An Indian Perspective* (Bangalore: Asian Trading Corporation, 1985); Arul M. Varaprasadam, "Inculturation: The Crucial Challenges in the Indian Situation," in *Building the Church in Pluricultural Asia,* ed. R. Hardawiryana et al. (Rome: Centre "Cultures and Religions"—Pontifical Gregorian

Philippines.[21] However, churches in other countries have not neglected this aspect of Christian mission: Japan,[22] Indonesia,[23] Korea,[24] Malaysia,[25] Pakistan,[26] Sri Lanka,[27]

University, 1986), 39-62; Subhash Anand, "Inculturation in India: Yesterday, Today and Tomorrow," *IMR* 19/1 (1997), 19-45; Kurien Kunnupuram, "Inculturation and Ecclesiology," *IMR* 19/1 (1997), 46-55; Kurien Kunnupuram and Lorenzo Fernando, eds., *Quest for an Indian Church: An Exploration of the Possibilities Opened Up by Vatican II* (Anand, Gujarat, India: Gujarat Sahitya Prakash, 1993); Gavin D'Costa, "Inculturation, India and Other Religions: Some Methodological Reflections," *Studia Missionalia* 44 (1995), 121-47; Felix Wilfred, *From the Dusty Soil: Contextual Reinterpretation of Christianity* (Madras: University of Madras, 1995); idem, "Interkulturelle Begegnung statt Inkulturation: Prolegomena zum Verstehen von Begegnungen zwischen Kultur und christlichem Evangelium im Kontext Indiens/Asiens," *Jahrbuch Mission 1995* (Hamburg: Missionshilfe Verlag, 1995), 114-33.

[21] See Leonardo Mercado, *Elements of Filipino Theology* (Tacloban City: Divine Word University Publications, 1974); idem, *Inculturation and Filipino Theology* (Manila: Divine Word Publication, 1992); idem, *Christ in the Philippines* (Tacloban, Philippines: Divine Word University, 1982); Carlos Abesamis, "Doing Theological Reflection in a Philippine Context," in *The Emergent Gospel: Theology from the Underside of History*, ed. Sergio Torres and Virginia Fabella (Maryknoll, N.Y.: Orbis Books, 1978), 112-23; Ed Garcia, *The Filipino Quest* (Quezon City: Claretian Publications, 1988); A. B. Lambino, "Toward an Inculturated Theology in the Philippines," *South East Asian Journal of Theology* 20 (1979): 35-38; Ladislav Nemet, "Inculturation in the Philippines: A Theological Study of the Question of Inculturation in the Documents of CBCP and Selected Filipino Theologians in the Light of Vatican II and the Documents of the FABC." S.T.D. dissertation, Pontifical Gregorian University, 1994. Perhaps the most impressive fruit of the theological inculturation by the Filipino Church is the *Catechism for Filipino Catholics* (Manila: Word and Life Publications, 1997), produced by the Catholic Bishops' Conference of the Philippines. It has the distinction of being the first national catechism composed under the guidance of the *Catechism of the Catholic Church* and approved by Rome.

[22] See A. Takehiro Kunii, "Inculturation in Japan," *EAPR* 18 (1981), 337-42; Joseph Sasaski, "God's Word in Japanese Culture and Tradition," *EAPR* 17 (1980), 51-60; T. F. Tagaki, "Inculturation and Adaptation in Japan before and after Vatican II," *Catholic Historical Review* 79/2 (1993), 246-67.

[23] See Hubertus J. W. M. Boelaars, "*Indonesianisasi*: Het omvormingsproces van de Katholieke Kerk in Indonesie tot de Indonesische Katholieke Kerk," Ph.D. dissertation. Katholieke Universiteit Brabant (Netherlands), 1991; J. B. Banawiratma and Tom Jacobs, "Doing Theology with Local Resources: An Indonesian Experiment," *EAPR* 26 (1989), 51-72.

[24] See Luke Jong-Hyeok Sim, "A Theological Evaluation of *Minjung* Theology from the Perspective of Inculturation in Christianity," *EAPR* 29 (1992), 406-26; Philip You-Chul Kim, "Inculturation in the Process of Evangelization: With Reference to the Catholic Church in Korea." S.T.D. dissertation, Pontificia Universitas Lateranensis, 1996.

[25] See Jonathan Yun-ka Tan, "Toward a Theology of '*Muhibbah*' as the Basis for Cross-Cultural Liturgical Inculturation in the Malaysian Catholic Church." MA thesis, Graduate Theological Union, Berkeley, California, 1997.

[26] See Anonymous, "Inculturation in the Light of Islam in Pakistan," *Pastoral Notes* 4 (1980), 114-24.

[27] See K. Lawrence, "Sri Lanka: Some Aspects of Inculturation," *EAPR* 18 (1981), 344-46; Aloysius Pieris, "Inculturation as a Missionary/Evangelical Presence in a Religiously Plural Society: Two Examples from Sri Lanka," *EAPR* 32 (1995), 81-86.

Taiwan,[28] Thailand,[29] and Vietnam.[30] In light of these efforts at inculturation, it is clear that by implementing Vatican II's teaching, the Asian churches have decisively moved away from the dominant model of mission as the *plantatio ecclesiae* of the pre–Vatican II era.

A fifth aspect of the Asian churches, intimately intertwined with their efforts at liberation and inculturation, is their commitment to interreligious dialogue, and this, again, as a response to Vatican II. Among the council's documents, the *Declaration on the Relation of the Church to Non-Christian Religions (Nostra aetate)*, though brief and of lesser ecclesiastical weight, has exercised a profound influence on the Asian churches, since it is they (and not the Western churches) that have to rub shoulders daily with followers of other religions. Dialogue with other religions has become a constitutive dimension of the church's evangelizing mission. This dialogue has assumed different forms: dialogue of life (common living as good neighbors), dialogue of action (collaboration for development and liberation), dialogue of theological exchange (understanding of different religious heritages), and dialogue of religious experience (sharing of spiritual riches) (see *DP*, no. 42). These activities are being carried out on a daily basis by the Asian churches throughout Asia, whenever social, political, and religious circumstances permit.[31]

---

[28] See Antonio S, Samson, ed., *Towards Indigenization of Religious Forms: Proceedings of the 1986 Workshop* (Manila: Association of Christian Universities and Colleges in Asia, 1986).This work contains essays on inculturation in Hong Kong, Indonesia, Japan, Korea, the Philippines, Taiwan, and Thailand.

[29] See Saad Chaiwan, "A Study of Christian Mission in Thailand," *EAPR* 2/1 (1984), 62-74.

[30] See Peter C. Phan, "The Christ of Asia: An Essay on Jesus as the Eldest Son and Ancestor," *Studia Missionalia* 45 (1996), 25-55; idem, "Jesus as the Eldest Brother and Ancestor? A Vietnamese Portrait," *The Living Light* 33/1 (1996), 35-44; idem, "Doing Theology in the Context of Mission: Lessons from Alexandre de Rhodes," *Gregorianum* 81/4 (2000), 723-49 (see Chapter 9 herein).

[31] A representative bibliography is given here. Asandas D. Balchand, "The Salvific Value of Non-Christian Religions according to Asian Christian Theologians' Writings in Asian-Published Theological Journals, 1965-1970," *TAN* 10 (1973), 10-37, 115-52; Parmananda Divarkar, "Ecumenical Dialogue with Muslims," *Clergy Monthly Supplement* 8 (1967), 177-81; A. D'Souza, "Evangelization and Dialogue with Muslims," *CM* 38 (1974), 456-61; Mariasusai Dhavamony, ed., *Evangelization, Dialogue and Development: Selected Papers of the International Theological Conference, Nagpur (India), 1971* (Rome: Editrice Università Gregoriana, 1972); Josef Neuner, "The Place of World Religions in Theology," *CM* 32 (1968), 102-15; Michael Amaladoss, *Faith, Culture and Inter-Religious Dialogue* (New Delhi: Indian Social Institute, 1985); idem, "The Pluralism of Religions and the Significance of Christ," *VJTR* 53 (1989), 401-20; idem, *Walking Together: The Practice of Inter-Religious Dialogue* (Anand, Gujarat, India: Gujarat Sahitya Prakash, 1992); idem, "The One and the Many: Reality and Manifestation," *Indian Theological Studies* 29 (1992), 305-28; idem, "Dialogue interreligieux et inculturation du christianisme: Perspectives indiennes," *Revue de l'Institut Catholique de Paris* 51 (1994), 9-19; idem, "Inter-Religious Dialogue: A View from Asia," *Landas* 8 (1994), 208-18; Zacharias Paranilam, *Christian Openness to the World Religions: Catholic Approach to the World Religions according to* Nostra Aetate *of Vatican II with*

Sixth, another salient characteristic of the post–Vatican II Asian churches is their engagement in the work of social development and liberation. Even before the council they had been known for their work in education, health care, and social services. However, in the past these activities, especially those in the field of education, were often carried out for the benefit of Catholics or as a means for proselytization. In the light of Vatican II, and under the influence of Latin American liberation theology, they are now seen as an integral part of the proclamation of the good news, for and by the poor.[32] In recent times Asian theologians have frequently and vigorously underscored the intrinsic unity of the three activities of the church's mission: inculturation, interreligious dialogue, and liberation.[33]

A seventh significant development in the Asian churches as the result of Vatican II is the commitment to and work for ecumenical unity. Church division, which was the heritage of historical circumstances in the West and was imported into Asia by denominational missionaries, is perceived as a hindrance to the mission of the church.[34] Whereas the Protestant churches had long been engaged in organizing various church unions (for example, the Tranquebar and Tambaran Conferences), the Catholic church took the work of ecumenical dialogue seriously only after Vatican II.[35] Nevertheless, it must be said that in the

---

a Special Reference to Hinduism (Kerala, India: Pontifical Institute Publications, 1988); J. Kuttianimattathil, *Practice and Theology of Interreligious Dialogue: A Critical Study of the Indian Christian Attempts Since Vatican II* (Bangalore, India: Kristu Jyoti College, 1995); Sebastian Painadath, "Theological Perspectives of FABC on Interreligious Dialogue," *Jeevadhara* 27 (1997), 272-88; George M. Soares-Prabhu, "The Indian Church Challenged by Pluralism and Dialogue," *SEDOS Bulletin* 26 (1994), 171-82; Felix Wilfred, "Some Tentative Reflections on the Language of Christian Uniqueness: An Indian Perspective," *Bulletin* 85/86, no. 1 (1994), 40-57.

[32] On how the theme of social justice has been taken further by the post-conciliar church, see Gustavo Gutiérrez, "The Church and the Poor: A Latin American Perspective," in *Reception*, 171-93. Gutiérrez describes the reception of Vatican II by the Latin American church as follows: "The Latin American Church . . . has made its own the insights of John XXIII vis-à-vis the Church of the poor, and it has tried to interpret the great themes of the Council in light of this insight. . . . There is no question, however, of a simple, mechanical application of Vatican II. Rather, the Latin American Church is endeavoring in a profoundly mature way to be faithful, with the Council, to the Lord of history and to a church that is beginning to become truly universal, as Karl Rahner has said" (193). The same thing should be said about the Asian churches.

[33] See James H. Kroeger, *Human Promotion as an Integral Dimension of the Church's Mission of Evangelization: A Philippine Experience and Perspective Since Vatican II—1965-1984* (Rome: Pontifical Gregorian University, 1986); Sung-Hae Kim, "Liberation and Inculturation: Two Streams of Doing Theology with Asian Resources," *EAPR* 24/4 (1987), 379-91; Peter C. Phan, "Human Development and Evangelization: The First to the Sixth Plenary Assembly of the Federation of Asian Bishops' Conferences," *Studia Missionalia* 47 (1998), 205-27.

[34] For a survey of the ecumenical movement in Asia, see "Ecumenical Movement," in *A Dictionary of Asian Christianity*, ed. Scott Sunquist (Grand Rapids, Mich.: Eerdmans, 2001), 258-65.

[35] See Masatoshi Doi, "Vatican II and Ecumenism," *Japan Christian Quarterly* 33 (Summer 1967), 177-81; E. R. Hambye, "All-India Seminar on Ecumenism," *Clergy Monthly* 35 (1971), 84-86; Prudent De Letter, "Ecumenical Developments after the Council," *Clergy Monthly* 31 (1967), 23-29.

Catholic churches of Asia, ecumenical dialogue has taken second place, with the primary emphasis given to interreligious dialogue. Happily, in recent years collaboration between the FABC and the Christian Conference of Asia (CCA) has been taking place. In 1994 the two bodies founded the Asian Movement for Christian Unity (AMCU). So far the movement has had three meetings, the first (1996) with the theme "Theology of Ecumenism"; the second (1998) with the theme "Ecumenical Formation as Churches of Asia Move towards the Next Millennium"; and the third (2001) with the theme "Giving Shape to a New Ecumenical Vision of Asia."[36]

An eighth noteworthy recent development in the Asian churches is the founding of several missionary societies. This phenomenon can be regarded as a reception of Vatican II's emphasis on mission *ad gentes* as the task of the whole church, including the so-called mission territories.[37] Currently there are six *ad gentes* missionary societies: The Mission Society of the Philippines, The Missionary Society of St. Thomas the Apostle (India), Catholic Foreign Mission Society of Korea, Missionary Society of Heralds of Good News (India), Missionary Society of Thailand, and Lorenzo Ruiz Mission Society (the Philippines).[38]

Thus far we have discussed the various areas in which the churches of Asia have responded to the challenges of Vatican II. However important these activities may be, they could not have been successfully carried out without the guidance and encouragement of the FABC, whose establishment was certainly a landmark in the history of Christianity in Asia.[39] During the meeting of 180 Asian bishops in Manila in November 1970, on the occasion of the visit of Pope Paul VI, initial steps were taken for the organization of the FABC. These were completed in Hong Kong on 24-25 August 1972, when the statutes of the FABC were accepted, confirmed, and submitted to the Holy See for approval. This approval, granted on 16 November of the same year, marked the official establishment of the FABC. In a sense, the FABC is both the concrete result of the reception of Vatican II and its effective instrument of implementation.[40]

---

[36] See Asian Movement for Christian Unity III, *Giving Shape to a New Ecumenical Vision*. FABC Papers, no. 99 (Hong Kong: FABC, 2001).

[37] "The Church on earth is by its very nature missionary" (*AG*, no. 2). See also *RM.*

[38] For information on these societies, see James Kroeger, *Asia-Church in Mission: Exploring Ad Gentes Mission Initiatives of the Local Churches in Asia in the Vatican II Era* (Quezon City, Philippines: Claretian Publications, 1999).

[39] For the documents of the FABC and its various institutes, see Gaudencio Rosales and C. G. Arévalo, eds., *For All the Peoples of Asia: Federation of Asian Bishops' Conferences. Documents from 1970 to 1991*, vol. 1 (Maryknoll, N.Y.: Orbis Books; Quezon City: Claretian Publications, 1992); Franz-Josef Eilers, ed., *For All the Peoples of Asia: Federation of Asian Bishops' Conferences. Documents from 1992 to 1996*, vol. 2 (Quezon City: Claretian Publications, 1997); and Franz-Josef Eilers, ed., *For All the Peoples of Asia: Federation of Asian Bishops' Conferences. Documents from 1997 to 2002*, vol. 3 (Quezon City: Claretian Publications, 2002).

[40] For a brief history and evaluation of the FABC, see Felix Wilfrid, "The Federation of Asian Bishops' Conferences (FABC): Orientations, Challenges and Impact," in *For All the Peoples of Asia*, 1:xxiii-xxx. The current members of the FABC are fourteen episcopal conferences as full members (Bangladesh, Taiwan, India, Indonesia, Japan,

Structurally, the FABC has no president, only a general secretary, whose task is to execute the policies and decisions of the FABC with the assistance of a central secretariat. The highest body of the federation is the plenary assembly, convened ordinarily once every four years (seven times so far), in which the presidents of each conference and its delegates participate. The direction of the FABC is carried out by the central committee, which is made up of the presidents of the member conferences and a standing committee of elected members. To assist the operations of the federation, there are six offices for various aspects of Christian life, each with several episcopal members: evangelization, social communication, laity, human development, education and student chaplaincy, and ecumenical and interreligious affairs. Finally, there is also the theological advisory commission.[41]

There is no doubt that the FABC, through its plenary assemblies and offices, has made an immense contribution to the life of the Asian churches. Its third plenary assembly offered the following assessment of its work:

— the creation of bonds of mutual knowledge and understanding, of friendship and solidarity, involving
— a sharing of thought, of prayer, theological and pastoral orientations, even of some material and personnel resources;
— joint study and reflection, leading to a greater community of vision, discernment, decisions, responses to common or similar situations and challenges.[42]

It is to be noted that the grand vision of both Vatican II and the FABC for the church has not always been enfleshed in concrete actions and programs. This failure has not been due to a lack of goodwill, much less to open opposition to the council, as in the West, for instance, in the case of Archbishop Marcel Lefebvre and various ultraconservative groups.[43] Rather, it is to be attributed to various factors, most of which are beyond the control of the Asian churches, such as hostile governments (for example, in China and Vietnam) and the lack of resources. As Felix Wilfred puts it, "The resources at the disposal of the bishops in Asia are so limited that they feel helpless in implementing the grand vision of the FABC."[44] And we may add, the vision of Vatican II as well.[45]

South Korea, Laos-Cambodia, Malaysia-Singapore-Brunei, Myanmar [Burma], Pakistan, the Philippines, Sri Lanka, Thailand, and Vietnam) and ten associate members (Hong Kong, Kazakhstan, Kyrgyzstan, Macao, Mongolia, Nepal, Siberia, Tajikistan, Turkmenistan, and Uzbekistan).

[41] For an organizational chart of the FABC, see *For All the Peoples of Asia,* 2:314.

[42] Ibid., 1:54.

[43] On opposition to Vatican II, see Daniele Menozzi, "Opposition to the Council (1966-84)," in *Reception,* 325-48.

[44] *For All the Peoples of Asia,* 1:xxx.

[45] One of the themes of Vatican II that has not been sufficiently received in Asia is ecumenism. The focus has been more on interreligious dialogue than on ecumenical dialogue.

THE ASIAN SYNOD: THE ASIAN CHURCHES REACHING MATURITY

What the Asian bishops did not or could not do at the Second Vatican Council, their successors did splendidly during the Special Assembly of the Synod of Bishops for Asia. Convened by Pope John Paul II as part of the celebration of the Jubilee Year 2000, the Asian synod met in Rome, 19 April-13 May 1998. The theme chosen by the pope for it was "Jesus Christ the Savior and His Mission of Love and Service in Asia: 'That They May Have Life, and Have It Abundantly' (John 10:10)."

In preparation for the synod, the general secretariat of the Synod of Bishops sent out to all the bishops of Asia an outline of the themes to be discussed (the *Lineamenta*), and solicited their comments and suggestions.[46] On the basis of these, the secretariat prepared an *Instrumentum laboris* presenting the issues to be discussed by the synod. This working document was later summarized in a text called the *Relatio ante disceptationem*. The synod began with 191 eight-minute "interventions" by synod participants. A summary of these interventions, called the *Relatio post disceptationem*, together with a list of questions, was used as the basis for group discussions. At the end of these discussions fifty-nine "propositions," expressing the consensus of the synod participants, were compiled and voted upon. They were then submitted to the pope for his use in writing the post-synodal apostolic exhortation. On 6 November 1999 John Paul II promulgated *Ecclesia in Asia* in New Delhi, India, in which the pope said he wished "to share with the church in Asia and throughout the world the fruits of the special assembly" (*EA,*, no. 4).

In terms of theology the Asian synod did not introduce anything beyond what had been said by the various plenary assemblies and documents of the FABC. What was new was not what the Asian bishops said but *that* they said it and *how* and *where* they said it. In front of the pope and the Roman curia, with surprising boldness and candor, humbly but forcefully, the Asian bishops affirmed that the churches of Asia not only learn from but also have something to

---

[46] Criticisms of the *Lineamenta* were sharp, some of which came from episcopal conferences, in particular the Japanese bishops. For other evaluations see, for instance, Chrys McVey, "The Asian Synod: What Is at Stake," *EAPR* 35/1 (1998), 143-46; Michael Amaladoss, "Expectations from the Synod for Asia," *VJTR* 62 (1998), 144-151; G. Gisbert-Sauch, "The *Lineamenta* for the Asian Synod: Presentation and Comment," *VJTR* 61 (1997), 8-17; Paul Puthanangady, "*Lineamenta* for the Asian Synod," *Jeevadhara* 27/160 (1997), 231-48: Kuncheria Pathil, "*Lineamenta* for the Asian Synod: Some Observations and Comments," *Jeedvadhara* 27/160 (1997), 249-259; J. Constantine Manalel, "The Jesus Movement and the Asian Renaissance: Some Random Reflections for the Asian Synod," *Jeevadhara* 27 (1997), 133-53; Francisco Claver, "Personal Thoughts on the Asian Synod," *EAPR* 35/2 (1998), 241-248; S. Arokiasamy, "Synod for Asia: An Ecclesial Event of Communion and Shared Witness of Faith," *VJTR* 62/9 (1998), 666-75; Gali Bali, "Asian Synod and Concerns of the Local Church," *Jeevadhara* 27 (1998), 297-330; John Mansford Prior, "A Tale of Two Synods: Observations on the Special Assembly for Asia," *VJTR* 62 (1998), 654-65; and Luis Antonio Tagle, "The Synod for Asia as Event," *EAPR* 35/3-4 (1998), 366-78.

teach the church of Rome as well as the universal church, precisely from their experiences as churches not simply *in* but *of* Asia. What was being proposed was not a new doctrine but a new way of being church, namely, being truly *Asian* churches through the triple dialogue with the Asian poor, Asian cultures, and Asian religions. In the 191 interventions on the floor and in the small-group discussions, again and again it was affirmed that it is imperative that the church in Asia be truly Asian, otherwise it will have no future. Appeal was frequently made to Vatican II's ecclesiology, expressed in the *Dogmatic Constitution on the Church,* that the church is a *koinonia,* a "communion of communities." There-fore, it was pointed out, the mode of operation in the church must be character-ized by affective and effective collegiality.[47]

Furthermore, this new way of being church in Asia demands a new ecclesiology. This is a theme repeatedly emphasized by the FABC, especially in its third and fifth plenary assemblies in Bangkok (1982) and in Bandung, Indonesia (1990). This ecclesiology de-centers the church in the sense that it makes the center of the Christian life not the church but the reign of God. The mission of Christians in Asia is not to expand the church and its institutional structures *(plantatio ecclesiae)* in order to enlarge the sphere of influence for the church over society but rather to be a transparent sign and effective instru-ment of the saving presence of the reign of God, the reign of justice, peace and love, of which the church is a seed.

The significance of the Asian synod lies, then, not so much in what its Asian participants said as in signifying that the churches of Asia have reached matu-rity. They have arrived at this stage because, in appropriating the teaching of Vatican II, they have set out consciously to put into practice what they call the Asian Integral Pastoral Approach (ASIPA) toward a new way of being church in Asia.[48] The goal of this approach is to develop "genuine Christian communi-ties in Asia—Asian in their way of thinking, praying, communicating their own Christ-experience to others."[49] Or, to put it in terms of Pope John XXIII's vision for Vatican II, quoted above, the task is to achieve "a step forward toward a doctrinal penetration and a formation of consciousness in faithful and perfect conformity to the authentic doctrine," but always in truly and authentically Asian terms.

With the Asian synod in Rome the Asian churches have made a full circle. It was from the Second Vatican Council held in Rome that they had learned how to be church, "receiving" and appropriating the council's ecclesiology and the various reforms coming out of it. At the Asian synod, the Asian churches re-turned to Rome and showed how well they have "received" Vatican II and as a result had something to teach the church of Rome and the church universal.

---

[47] It has been noted that among the themes of Vatican II that have been insufficiently received, collegiality stands out (see Lukas Vischer, "The Reception of the Debate on Collegiality," in *Reception,* 233-48).

[48] See *For All the Peoples of Asia,* 2:107-11, 137-39.

[49] Ibid., 1:70.

Index